Give Them Roots, Then Let Them Fly:

Understanding Attachment Therapy

D1240801

THE ATTACHMENT CENTER

AT EVERGREEN

The Attachment Center at Evergreen, Inc.
© 1995

Most of the anecdotal material in this book is true to life and included
with the permission of the persons involved. Some illustrations are com-
posites of real situations and any resemblance to people living or dead is
coincidental. In an effort to preserve anonymity, case examples sometimes are compilations of actual cases and do not include racial or cultural identifiers. In the absence of a genderless third-person pronoun,
we have used the masculine and feminine forms throughout the book to
avoid awkward constructions and to facilitate readability. We hope our
reader understands these unenviable constraints and will understand.

NOTE: CHAPTER 2 AND CHAPTER 6 ARE:
Reproduced in part with permission from: Levy, Terry M. and Orlans,
M., Intensive short-term therapy with attachment-disordered children,
Innovations in Clinical Practice: A Source Book (Vol. 14) by L.
VandeCreek, S. Knapp, and T. L. Jackson (Eds.), Sarasota, FL:
Professional Resource Press, Copyright 1995 by the Professional
Resource Exchange, Inc., P.O. Box 15560, Sarasota, FL 34277-1560.

The Attachment Center at Evergreen, Inc.
Carole A. McKelvey, Editor
    Give Them Roots, Then Let Them Fly: Understanding
    Attachment Therapy/
    Includes bibliographical references
    ISBN # (softcover) 0-9649851-0-1
    1. Attachment Therapy, Theory—United States
    2. Holding Therapy—United States
    Library of Congress Catalog Card Number 95-95371

Printed in the USA by

Morris
PUBLISHING

3212 E. Hwy 30
Kearney, NE 68847
800-650-7888

DEDICATION:

*This book is dedicated to the thousands
of attachment disordered children and their parents
And to the professionals who are working so hard
to make a difference in their lives.*

Table of Contents

PART THREE:
THE IMPLICATIONS OF ATTACHMENT THERAPY

APPENDIXES & BIBLIOGRAPHY

BIBLIOGRAPHY

Acknowledgement of Contributors

Throughout this book, the editor and contributors will give the reader a clear picture of exactly what attachment disorder looks like, feels like, presents like, is like. These views are based on clinical observations, anecdotal materials, and the solid research cited and in subsequent chapters.

Those affiliated with the Attachment Center at Evergreen, Inc., know all too well that attachment disorder truly does exist and is a major mental illness affecting thousands of children throughout the world. It is a mental illness that is, unfortunately, growing expedientially day by day because of the abuses to children through dysfunctional families; war; institutionalization and the "invisible" institution of the American foster care system.

It is our declared mission to help these children. To help them overcome their early histories of abuse and neglect and to see that they make the human connections so vital to be able to live a full and happy life. It is also our mission to do this work in the most caring, loving, safe environment possible.

Within these pages the reader will gain insight into attachment disorders, will learn about the proven system of treatment at the Attachment Center, and about therapeutic parenting. The reader will hear the words of wise experts in the field, and about how we must develop a community approach — a community awareness — of the dangers of attachment disorder.

Nowhere in the literature can be found the combination of experts writing together which we present in this book. Among the extremely distinguished contributors to this book you will find (in alphabetical order):

• Dianne Allred, community relations manager at the Attachment Center, — for years her voice was often the first one desperate parents heard when they called the Center seeking help in what they felt was a hopeless situation. Dianne brings her expertise to the areas of Public Relations, Marketing and Fundraising as well as being the parent of an Attachment Disordered child.

• Lloyd Boggs, LCSW — and clinical consultant with the Attachment Center. Lloyd Boggs has a national reputation as a caring, committed and extremely professional clinician in the field of attachment disorder.

• Dr. John Alston, psychiatrist and consultant to the Attachment Center at Evergreen, Inc., whose guidance has helped countless children. He is extremely knowledgeable in the field of Attachment Therapy, diagnostics and the use of psychotropic medication.

• Dr. Foster Cline, a pioneer in the attachment disorder field. Dr. Cline is one of the original founders of the Youth Behavior Program, the predecessor of the Attachment Center. Today he writes and lectures from his ranch in Idaho. His latest book is: <u>Conscienceless Acts and Societal Mayhem</u>, by Love and Logic Press, Inc., Golden, Colorado.

• Neil Feinberg, LCSW — Clinical consultant with the Attachment Center whose wisdom and knowledge have contributed to the attachment therapy field for many years. Neil Feinberg is known for his series of tapes, "Conducting a Two-Week Intensive: Attachment Therapy and Theory" and the book <u>Becoming Your Own Parent: A Journey of Self Discovery</u>.

• Deborah Hage, Professional Therapeutic Foster Parent — Deborah Hage and her husband, Paul, have served as therapeutic foster parents with the Attachment Center for many years; they are the parents of eleven children most of them adopted with severe emotional needs. Her article, "Therapeutic Parenting" is included in Dr. Foster Cline's book, <u>Hope for High Risk and Rage Filled Children.</u>

• Forrest Lien, ACSW, Program Manager, Clinical Training and Assessment Specialist at the Attachment Center at Evergreen. Forrest is new to the Attachment Center staff in 1995, but brings with him impressive credentials. For a number of years he has worked at the prestigious Casey Family Program in Tucson, Arizona. He brings the expertise gained at Casey to The Attachment Center at Evergreen, Inc.

• Terry Levy, PhD, clinical consultant with The Attachment Center and with Evergreen Consultants. Terry Levy is an authority in the attachment field, and the past president of the national organization, ATTACh. He is the author of numerous articles on attachment, including a contribution to the professional publication, <u>Innovations in Clinical Practice: A Source Book</u> (Vol. 14).

• Carole A. McKelvey, M.A., editor and counselor. McKelvey is the co-author of two published books: <u>High Risk: Children Without a Conscience</u> and <u>Adoption Crisis: The Truth About Adoption and Foster Care</u>. Her upcoming book, to be released in 1996 by Pocket Books of New York, is: Out of the Frying Pan: International Adoption. She is a former member of the Board of Directors of the Attachment Center at Evergreen and a practicing counselor.

• Margaret Meineke, MSW, and Paula Cyd Seigel, MSW — both talented therapists with the Attachment Center at Evergreen. It is their excellent follow-up that soothes the way for the reintegration of children back into their homes after long-term placement and two week intensives at the Center.

• Diane Meyer, LCSW. — Program Manager, Clinical Services, of The Attachment Center at Evergreen, Inc. Diane Meyer's contributions to the attachment field are well known. She has been serving the Attachment Center, coordinating therapy with attachment disordered children for more than two years.

• Michael Orlans, M.A. — a valued clinical consultant at The Attachment Center at Evergreen, Inc., and of Evergreen Consultants, and a national lecturer and writer. With Terry Levy, Michael Orlans is the author of Interventions in Clinical Practice: A Source Book (Vol. 14).

• Paula Pickle, LCSW, ACSW — Executive Director of The Attachment Center at Evergreen, Inc. Under Paula Pickle's capable leadership the Center is being guided into the next century of service to attachment disordered children. She comes to this commitment as a talented therapist, nationally recognized speaker, and the parent of attachment disordered children.

• Elizabeth Randolph, RN, PhD — nationally known researcher, statistician, speaker and attachment therapist. Her book, Children Who Shock and Surprise, is a respected work in the attachment field.

• Susan A. Taylor — who works in the practice of Lloyd Boggs in Ft. Collins, Colorado, assisting him in his unique community approach to working with attachment disordered children.

• Connell Watkins, MSW — past director of The Attachment Center at Evergreen, Inc., and Director of Connell Watkins and Associates, a private therapy consortium in Evergreen, Colorado. Connell Watkins is a national speaker and therapist who is a leader in the field of child therapy.

The Attachment Center at Evergreen, Inc., is proud to highlight the writings and wisdom of this very distinguished group of contributors to Give them Roots, Then Let them Fly: Understanding Attachment Therapy.

In this book, our mission is to inform — to tell the world that attachment disorder does exist and that it is the terrible outcome of a childhood gone wrong. It also does not have to be a life sentence. Children with attachment disorder are being helped daily through the efforts of individuals such as the contributors to this book and others around the United States. Their's is good and vital work.

Foreword

Understanding the Essentials: Bonding/Attachment Theory
By Dr. Foster Cline

Nearly thirty years ago, in the early 70s, The Attachment Center at Evergreen had its beginning in The Youth Behavior Program.

At that time, in a then fairly new concept, Tim Faust and other founding therapists took children with identified problems into the wilds of Colorado. Wilderness experiences in the early 70s were being directed for youth all across the United States. Few, however, directly targeted moderately to severely disturbed youth and identified the experience as therapeutic with the therapist accompanying the youth on the trips. In those days there were no challenge courses and no one outside of the armed services had heard of aerial obstacle courses. We found that difficult teens and disturbed younger children somehow were quickly able to relate in a healthy, new and tighter therapeutic alliance with their therapists after they had dangled from a rope, feared being swept down a river, or reached a mountain top that they had previously felt would be impossible to climb.

In those days, we did not conceptualize the Bonding Cycle with the precision that it is now taught and understood. We only knew that something special happened after these problem city youth were encouraged (euphemism) or pushed and cajoled (more accurate) into a situation where they achieved after definitely feeling unsure of themselves. In the beginning of these experiences, most were confounded, confused, and downright scared in an unknown surrounding far away from peers, booze and bravado. When challenged to excel in a far different environment than their urban underpinnings something marvelous often happened.

Although we were not fully theoretically clear in those days, we did know that somehow the mix of downright fright, or at least solid concern, followed by achievement, pride, gratification and relief produced a therapeutic alliance that was far tighter more quickly than what we could generally obtain in the office using good traditional techniques.

We might have even characterized it as a bonding experience. In the 70s, we did recognize that, strangely, following the experience, the youth identified with, emulated and wanted to be like the youth leader.

At the same time (in the early to mid 70s), an old therapist -- a walking amalgam of wisdom, therapeutic genious, boisterous humor, and dogmatic positions wrapped in a cantankerous personality -- came to Evergreen, Colorado, to teach and consult on very difficult youth. This controversial figure, Robert Zaslow, and his team of graduate students taught all across the nation. He sometimes left both acrimony and adulation in his wake, and even without few published writings, his influence was vast.

Zaslow taught about Bonding with a capital **B**. He also taught that it was necessary to disturb the disturbed. He clarified that Bonding and Attachment were far different that the growth of love or the building of an alliance in the more traditional therapeutic sense. He was an unabashedly directive therapist in a therapeutic universe that mainly preached non-directiveness, reflective listening, and the slow process and analysis of transference and countertransference.

As such, he took extremely disturbed youth, forced eye contact in a holding position, and carried out family therapy in a circle around the prone youth while the mother or father held the youth's head. He taught parents to be confrontive, and straight with themselves and the child they held. He coaxed parents to bond with their child. With his controversial techniques he achieved dramatic results.

That was then.

Now is now. In the mid-1990s America has become a much more protective, victim-oriented and regulated environment. And the directive techniques that encourage rapid attachment and bonding have, for a number of reasons, fallen on difficult times or been revised and changed as a reaction to the times.

Attachment therapy in the 1990s was undergoing a tremendous evolution, changing from the directive procedure it started from into a technique drawing from numerous disciplines.

Before exploring those reasons here, let us first look with some precision at the Bonding Theory upon which all Attachment Therapy is based:

> Bonding Theory is based on both observations and clinical assumptions that evolve from clinical experience. The two basic empirical observations appear to be unarguable at this point. They are observations that everyone can validate with their

own inspection and commitment. These observations were first remarked upon by John Bowlby and his followers nearly half a century ago. These observations have not been seriously contested since Bowlby's time and are now incorporated officially as part of the American Psychological Association's Diagnostic and Statistical Manual, IV (DSM-IV) as Reactive Attachment Disorder:

1) The normal bonding process between child and mother takes place in infancy, mainly around feeding and physical contact in a flow that occurs as the mother and child interact around the child's distress.

2) Most severely disturbed individuals have had developmental problems occurring during the time of the bonding cycle, problems occurring early in life, generally around early parenting techniques or early life developmental disorders. Generally, alone or in combination, such individuals:

> a) Have had physical or mental developmental disorders such that the normal cycle of pain followed by gratification and relief could not be achieved.
>
> b) Have suffered early abuse and/or neglect
>
> c) Have, before birth, been bathed in alcohol or drugs to the extent that the normal early neurologic functioning is impaired.
>
> d) Have been moved from care taker to care taker early in life
>
> e) Have had the physical trauma of either surgery, pain or undiagnosed infantile illnesses, such that the normal bond cannot form -- such infants generally have problems recognizing or obtaining relief from their distress.

Bonding Theory is based upon the following four arguable clinical assumptions. These assumptions, at the foundation of Attachment Therapy are open to disagreement, but believed to be true by the vast majority of practicing therapists:

1) All true bonding has elements of trauma, pain, difficulty or uncertainty followed by gratification and/or relief.

All true bonding involves, in short, the successful completion of an ordeal. Bonding, then, is a process that is different than the growth of love, esteem, respect and sense in that it is usually visualized. Bonding experiences take place in normal infancy; in the armed services; in the use of challenge courses; to survivors following a catastrophe, to cult members; in interrogation and indoctrination routines; in brainwashing situations and in reparenting and certain attachment therapy routines.

Bonding routines can be seen throughout the <u>Bible</u>; in <u>Mein Kamph</u>; and in many other situations. In fact, bonding routines are everywhere, from the shores of Normandy, to college campuses where Greeks involve plebs in hell week.

Thus, it may be seen that bonding routines can be used for good or for evil purposes. It depends on who is in control, the motives and the outcome.

2) The lack of completion of the normal bonding cycle results in predictable symptoms: They include but are not limited to:

> a) The inability to show Gratification, Basic Trust, Love, Attachment and normal affection to parental figures.
>
> b) The internalization of rage and anger that leads to childhood cruelty to animals and other children, lack of self respect and severe control problems.
>
> c) Other first year of life developmental problems such as hoarding and gorging on food, an inability to show remorse, and a general lack of conscience.

3) That if the normal bonding cycle has not been completed at a developmentally appropriate time, during infancy, then it must be repaired in a corrective emotional experience.

4) That this corrective emotional experience, when used in therapy, is the purposeful use of a bonding cycle with the therapist, parents or other significant others and that the bonding routines will generally involve, in one way or another, an ordeal followed by feelings of relief, achievement or gratification.

But there are problems in the therapeutic use of purposeful use of therapeutic bonding routines. Therapists have always been best at rescuing people, and providing nurturing, sometimes insight, and even, infrequently, confrontation when individuals are upset. However, the helping community looks with some suspicion on the encouragement of upset, or the purposeful provocation of painful emotions in order to provide the client with opportunity to work through those emotions in a corrective emotional experience.

Freud taught that the negative transference and neurotic feelings would, in and of themselves, eventually appear if the therapist took a non-directive course and eventually the client would work through these feelings. Of course, psychoanalysis took a long time. And it was based on the assumption that the individual wanted to change.

Nevertheless, even decades ago, a few therapists often braved the doubt, if not outright scorn of the professional majority by encouraging the pushing of patients into primary angry, anguished, and painful feelings to facilitate their working through these emotions. Such were the early writings of Jacqui Schiff in All My Children; Janov in The Primal Scream; Helen Waite in Valiant Companions; Daniel Casriel in A Scream Away from Happiness and Milton Erickson in Jay Haley's Uncommon Therapy.

In the 70s, outside the therapeutic mainstream, Reality Attack Groups and other high intensity groups used in-your-face confrontation to bond patients into a family of ex-drug abusers at Synacore, Sydrinar and on Delancy Street.

More modern versions of high confrontation have been attempted in the boot camps for youth and other programs attempting to bond youth into a more healthy group identification and a healthier way of life. Regardless of the effectiveness of such groups, they all tended to remain, as may Attachment Therapy itself, just outside the mainstream of therapeutic methods.

There are a number of reasons, for this, but perhaps the most prominent reason for mainstream suspiciousness and rejection is the fact that these methods do carry inherent risks. These risks can always be minimized, but they can never be completely vanquished. And over the last 30 years, I have seen many outstanding treatment centers closed or hassled by well-meaning outsiders because their techniques were perceived as dangerous, too harsh or robbed individuals of their individual rights. There are six reasons why any bonding technique, regardless of its safeguards, nurturing environment and appropriateness is open to such charges:

> 1.) The individuals who need the therapy often have been victimized previously in their lives.
> 2.) Character-disturbed individuals may not see themselves as having problems. They are filled with denial, and are unlikely to establish the necessary therapeutic contract in a traditional manner. At any age, they must be cajoled, or strongly encouraged to engage in therapy by an outside force -- either parents in the case of children, or by court motivation in the case of adults or by the requirements of the organization in the case of the armed services.
> 3.) Many traditional therapists believe the symptoms engendered by abuse or dysfunctional childhoods should be respected. That is, if a woman has trouble with men, she should see a female therapist to work through her problem; if an abused child has trouble with touch, then touch should take place cautiously, if at all; if a child has been sexually abused,

then he or she should not be held by an adult of the same sex as the abuser; etc.

4.) Such individuals easily feel victimized and claim victimization in situations where others would not feel victimized.

5.) The therapy needed to establish the bond does always involve an ordeal in one form or another. The therapy, in cross section, without taking reasons and usual outcome into account could be seen as abusive.

6.) This is a litigious society where people are quick to sue over perceived abuse. Much of the legal system remuneration is based on finding pain and suffering. If the job of therapy is truly to disturb the disturbed, and if bonding therapy is more disturbing than the usual therapy, then litigation is always possible, if not likely.

Aside from the inherent problems that bonding and attachment therapy face, there are, in addition, five commonly expressed concerns about aspects of the various bonding therapies as they are used in Attachment work. These include:

1) It is built upon the belief that the end justifies the means.
2) It is dangerous work.
3) It doesn't always work.
4) There is no proof positive it works at all.
5) The therapy merely recreates the traumatic abuse cycle that caused the problems in the first place. It creates a trauma bond.
These thoughtful concerns must be briefly addressed.
* It is built upon the belief that the end justifies the means:
Although the world of psychology and mainstream psychology has trouble with the end justifying the means, most of medicine and all of surgery expresses this axiom. Attachment therapists do not equivocate here.
As many, if not most, of the individuals treated with the therapy, will most likely lead non-productive lives and will continue to be a danger to themselves and others, the therapists feel the probable good outcome necessitates the method.
* It is dangerous work. This is true:
However, in general, the more effective any technology, the more dangerous it may be perceived. This is true of airplanes, digitalis, and bonding techniques. Nevertheless, the negative results that may be used to illustrate the dangers of using bonding techniques often does not hold up under close scrutiny. Whenever a therapy is unorthodox the therapy may be blamed

for producing results that were there in the first place and that
it was attempting to remedy.
* It doesn't always work:
True. And this is true of all the psychological therapies. There is
a problem however, that those treated with bonding techniques
have often been refractory to the more traditional techniques.
Usually the bonding techniques are not attempted as a first
approach. In dealing with a particularly difficult population,
some failure must be accepted.
* There is no proof it works:
Unfortunately, much of the dynamic therapies suffer from this
criticism. There is no proof positive that Gestalt Therapy, Family Therapy or Play Therapy are effective. This is because the
establishment of control groups is difficult and global results
are sometimes hard to quantify. However, all therapists using
bonding techniques were schooled and trained in good traditional techniques. No therapist I have encountered uses the
bonding techniques exclusively. Most wish they were not
needed at all. Other techniques are neither as demanding nor
as controversial. If the techniques were not overwhelmingly
successful, no therapist would have motivation for using them.
They provide no more remuneration, and are much more
likely, within the therapeutic community, to cause problems
for the therapist. Studies are now underway to quantify improvement. The remarkably positive results on long term follow-up of 47 children treated in Evergreen are given in my
book Hope for High Risk and Rage Filled Children. And the
work of therapist Liz Randolph, who writes in this book, notes
the successful outcome that can be reached in attachment
therapy. There are an increasing number of therapists who
have written of their first hand experiences with the bonding
techniques used for attachment therapy, and they give strong
testimony to its effectiveness. Most of the current proof, however, is anecdotal.

* The therapy merely recreates the traumatic abuse cycle that caused
the problems in the first place. It creates a trauma bond and abuse takes
place when a child is put through an ordeal to gratify the needs of an
adult, with painful outcome leaving residual problems to work through.
Therapeutic bonding situations:
Put one through an ordeal to help the person face their own impedi-
ments to growth with a positive outcome, alleviating the residual problems
previously present. There is no doubt that in cross section, not taking the

motivation or outcome into account, that the method could appear abusive, for it generally does provide an ordeal of one type or another.

If an ordeal is considered trauma then it is present in almost all bonding situations. All bonding could then be considered a trauma bonding whether the bonding be in infancy, in the service, in a boot camp or in reparenting and attachment techniques. Perhaps it is better to clarify that trauma bonding per se occurs when one is unable to work through the negative outcome of a cycle designed to meet the perpetrator's needs, in a situation in which the victim was unable to cope.

Bonding, on the other hand, encourages the development of coping skills in a safe environment that revisits the negative or traumatized feelings and confronts the individual's inability to express loving emotions.

Many traditional therapists believe strongly in respecting a person's neurosis. For instance: An abused child should not be held if the child has problems with being held -- particularly by a person of the same sex as the perpetrator.

If a woman has trouble with men, then that should be respected and she should work through her feelings with a female therapist.

A child who has been emotionally bruised should never be treated with a loud voice, etc.

Attachment therapists feel that therapists who object because of the above reasons have tragically confused respecting the person with respecting their neurosis.

Attachment therapists believe that the corrective emotional experience involves the re-experience of the traumatic situation with a different and loving outcome.

Moreover, attachment oriented therapists feel by not confronting the problem and holding the abused child, the abuse is validated and locked in. For instance, when a person who has been sexually abused is never hugged -- because of the sexual overtones it may raise, then that person is doomed to forever feel that physical contact means sex.

This book could be characterized, depending upon the reader's belief system, as being filled with writings that are the cutting edge of therapeutic technique. It should be of some enlightenment to realize that the cutting edge of any field, prior to its eventual acceptance, has always been characterized as on the fringe.

But the hundreds of children and adults who have been helped by this therapy, or who are going to be helped by it, appreciate these authors straightforward candor and explicit sharing of their techniques so that everyone can better understand this controversial work.

--Foster W. Cline, M.D.
April 27, 1995

References:

Bascom, Barbara & McKelvey, Carole (1996) Through The Golden Door: A Guide to International Adoption, Pocket Books, New York: NY.

Cline, Foster (1992) Hope for High Risk and Rage Filled Children, EG Publications, Evergreen, CO.

Cline, Foster (1979) The Series, What Should We Do With this Child? EG Publications, Evergreen, CO. (the "Red Book", "Green Book", "Yellow Book", "Blue Book")

Keck, Greg & Kupecky, Regina (1995) Adopting the Hurt Child: Hope for Families with Special-Needs Kids, Pinon Press, Colorado Springs, CO.

Magid, Ken & McKelvey, Carole (1988) High Risk: Children Without a Conscience, Bantam Books, New York: NY.

Mansfield, Linda & Waldmann, Christopher (1994) Don't Touch My Heart: Healing the Pain of an Unattached Child, Pinon Press, Colorado Springs, CO.

McKelvey, Carole & Stevens, JoEllen (1994) Adoption Crisis: The Truth Behind Adoption and Foster Care, Fulcrum Publishers, Golden, CO.

Randolph Elizabeth, (1994) Children Who Shock and Surprise: A Guide to Attachment Disorders, RFR Publications, 8655 Water Rd., Catati, CA. 94931

Welch, Martha (1988) Holding Time, Simon & Schuster, New York: NY.

PART ONE

🌱🌱🌱

Understanding
the
Attachment
Theory

**Give Them Roots,
Then Let Them Fly**

Introduction

By Carole A. McKelvey, M.A.
& By Elizabeth Randolph, RN, PHD

"There are two lasting bequests we can
give our children,
one is roots
the other is wings."

Author unknown

They have been called "children without a conscience" (Magid & McKelvey, 1988); "rage filled children" (Cline, 1990); and "troubled transplants" (Delaney, 1993).

Generally, they are referred to as being "attachment disordered". They are children who experienced serious abuse, neglect, physical pain, and/or repeated separations from their birth mother. Their response to these early life experiences is to be angry, resentful, hurtful, hostile, argumentative, oppositional, and blaming of others.

They have sometimes been called "psycopaths" or "sociopaths," because of their seeming lack of conscience for the sometimes heinous acts they inflict on others. They may be diagnosed with conduct disorder, or oppositional defiant disorder, among other diagnoses.

We have many names for these children, but just what do all those names mean in the real world? The terms "psychopath" and "sociopath" are often used interchangeably to refer to people who have pathological social skills presumed to result from inadequate parenting and conscience development in early childhood (Harrington, 1972). These pathological social skills can mean these people are:

- usually superficially charming with a grandiose sense of self-worth.
- in need of stimulation in their lives and they may invent dangerous activities to meet this need.
- excellent liars, who lie almost constantly, conning and manipulating others to get what they want.
- unable to feel much of anything deeply, lacking remorse or guilt for their actions.
- impulsive, lacking control over their behavior and feelings.
- often sexually promiscuous.

Generally, they have a parasitic lifestyle, living off of and taking advantage of others. They have a history of behavior problems as children (and are not considered to be psychopaths if they lack a childhood history of behavior problems). They are also irresponsible, lacking the ability to make and keep long-term plans, as they live for the moment. They never take responsibility for their actions, leaving behind them a trail of broken relationships. They engage in a wide variety of criminal activities; they are given many different labels.

Conduct disorder refers to children who have little empathy or concern for the feelings and well-being of others (APA, 1994). They are aggressive to other people and to animals, destroy the property of others, lie, steal, and ignore the rules of society.

Oppositional defiant children, on the other hand, are negativistic, hostile, defiant, throw temper tantrums, argue, deliberately annoy others, are easily annoyed by others, and are angry, resentful, spiteful, and vindictive.

Attachment disordered children are described as lacking the ability to give and receive affection, being cruel to other people and animals, being self-destructive, being phony, having problems with eating (hoarding, stealing, and gorging on food), having problems with their speech, a lack of long-term friends, abnormalities in eye contact, marked need for control of others, preoccupations with fire, blood and gore, superficial attractiveness and friendliness with strangers, learning disabilities, and a peculiar type of lying that flies in the face of reality (Cline, 1979). In addition, their parents typically appear overly angry and hostile, because they are so fed up with the child's behavior.

In Give Them Roots and Then Let Them Fly, the reader will find information that helps them differentiate between the three labels. And, the most complete analysis of attachment disorder and the issues revolving around this disorder published to date.

It can easily be seen from the above discussion that there are many similarities between attachment disordered children and psychopaths, conduct disordered children, and children with oppositional defiant disorder. How, then, can we tell the difference between a child who has an attachment disorder, one who is a psychopath, or one who has either conduct disorder, oppositional defiant disorder, or both?

While there is a considerable amount of research in the area of attach- / ment, there is virtually no research in the area of attachment disorders.√ A number of studies on attachment have explored the effects of abuse, neglect, maternal depression, prematurity, and physical illness on the child's ability to attach. These studies use Ainsworth's (1978) strange situation (where a child is left with a stranger after playing with his mother for five to ten minutes, and then his behavior is evaluated after being reunited with his mother) to assess types of attachment. In Ainsworth's initial research, she defined three classifications of attachment:

1. secure,
2. insecure avoidant,
3. and insecure ambivalent.

Virtually all studies that have been conducted using the strange situation with normal children find that 65 percent to 70 percent of normal children are securely attached to their mothers; 15 percent to 20 percent are insecure avoidant; and 10 percent to 15 percent are insecure ambivalent (Lamb, 1987).

It is known that long-term follow-up studies of attachment classifications indicate that about 70 percent of children in all three categories above continue to show the category of attachment that they had as one-year-olds, even when they are six years old (Main & Cassidy, 1978).

For the 30 percent of children whose attachment behavior changed as they grew older, most experienced family distress/disruption during the intervening years. Children with insecure, ambivalent attachment showed the greatest consistency in their attachment behavior over time, while some formerly secure children became insecure avoidant, and some formerly insecure avoidant children became securely attached.

Several studies have examined behavior in three- to six-year-olds with different attachment classifications to determine if any behavior patterns (or behavior problems) were consistent with certain types of attachment. For example, Fagot and Kavanagh (1990) examined the behavior of insecure avoidant and securely attached children and found that there were no differences in the frequency of problem behaviors between these two groups, nor was any particular behavior pattern characteristic of insecure avoidant children.

Several similar studies have found similar results. In fact, Lewis, Feiring, McGuffog, and Jaskir (1984) found that birth order and whether or not the child was planned were more related to whether or not the child had behavior problems than was the child's attachment classification.

While early research into attachment focused primarily on healthy, middle class families, by the 1980's researchers began to investigate the effects of abuse, neglect, and lower income status on attachment. Perhaps the most interesting finding of the studies on maltreated infants was that many of these infants did not fit into one of Ainsworth's three categories. Instead, they showed a mixture of behaviors characteristic of all three categories (Crittenden, 1985). Eventually researchers developed a fourth category of attachment behavior, referred to as either unclassified, disorganized, or mixed avoidant/ambivalent attachment. These children were noted to be highly resistant (even when they were seeking contact with their mothers), persistently cranky, aggressive, and engaged in unusual or stereotypical behaviors (rocking on the floor, heads cocked off to one side, huddling in a ball on the floor). The more severely abused/neglected the child was, the more severe these behaviors were.

The behavior of five- to twelve-year-olds with a history of abuse for both the children and their mothers by a male adult was studied by Shaw and Emery (1987) to determine if there were specific types of behavior characteristic of these high-risk children. They found that maternal depression had the highest correlation with behavior problems in these children, and that, the greater the stress the child had experienced, the greater the likelihood that child would have behavior problems. However, this study did not examine the relationship between attachment and behavior in abused and stressed children, so it is not known whether or not such a relationship exists.

A second area of interest to this discussion is that of research using the Exner Comprehensive System for administering and scoring the Rorschach, particularly as it relates to children with conduct disorders. Such research, however, is limited primarily to two studies.

However, as can be seen in this review of previous research, no studies have actually examined the attachment classifications of children with various psychiatric diagnoses to determine whether or not there are differences in their social relatedness and the types of behavior (and behavior problems) they exhibit.

To explore the issues brought up in the literature review discussed above, a study was conducted by researcher Randolph to present the Children's Behavior Questionnaire as a means of assessing behavior problems known to be present in attachment disordered children. It was also hoped to be able to compare the results of that test with the frequency of human, human movement, texture, and cooperative human movement responses to the Rorschach cards.

One hundred forty-five children between ages 6 and 16, who had been referred to a clinic for treatment of a variety of psychological problems, were the subjects for this study. All children had a minimum IQ of 90, and were free of major neurological and physical problems. Subjects were divided into four groups:

1. Children with severe behavior problems consistent with attachment disorder (ADS; N=63), and with a history of severe abuse/neglect;
2. Children with severe behavior problems not consistent with attachment disorder (DBD; N=28), and without a history of abuse/neglect;
3. Children who met the diagnostic criteria for major depression (DEP; N=34) who had no history of abuse/neglect; and
4. Children with no apparent problems and who had never been referred for therapy (NORM; N=20).

All children completed the Rorschach inkblot test using the Exner method, and the parent bringing them for the evaluation (usually the mother) completed the Child Behavior Questionnaire (see Appendix II). Rorschach results were scored by an examiner blind as to the diagnosis of each child. The CBQ was scored by this researcher using the scoring guidelines for that test. This is the first examination of its kind in the literature. These results were interesting, indeed:

- The results of the study clearly show strong support for the usefulness of the CBQ in assessing attachment disorders.
- The results show that it is a reliable instrument that has excellent differential validity in separating out children with attachment disorders from children who have conduct disorders, or depression, or who have no disorder.
- The results also clearly demonstrate that there are considerable differences between conduct disorder and attachment disorder. This finding was true with the results of the Rorschach, as well as the CBQ.

The results of this study are consistent with the findings of Weber, Meloy, and Gacono (1992), who found that 71 percent of their conduct disordered group failed to make any texture response. Thirty-three percent of their conduct disordered group failed to make a human response, which is similar to the 27 percent of attachment disordered subjects in this study, but is considerably greater than the 4 percent of conduct disordered subjects in this study. It is likely that this difference is due to the fact the Weber et al. group was more severely disturbed than the group used in this study. Their group consisted of subjects in an inpatient facility, while the subjects in this study were all in outpatient therapy.

Further study of the issues considered in this research is necessary, particularly in terms of obtaining larger groups of conduct disordered, depressed, and normal subjects.

In addition, a comparison group of more severely disturbed conduct disordered subjects would be useful to determine whether or not the CBQ distinguishes as well with this population as it does with moderate conduct disorders.

Also of use would be a study of the predictive validity of the CBQ in terms of the outcome for children who score at different levels on the CBQ. Do children who have higher scores on the CBQ have more serious problems with criminal activities as adults, or are the traits measured by the CBQ unrelated to adult criminal activities?

These findings also support the findings of a previous study by this researcher (Randolph, 1995) which found that attachment disordered children differ from conduct disordered and depressed children on a number of Rorschach variables. It provides strong support for the theory that attachment disorder is a separate entity from conduct disorder or psychopathic behavior.

In Give Them Roots and Then Let Them Fly, the reader will find more analysis and information about attachment disorder and the issues surrounding the disorder. This is vital information that should help all struggling with the issues of childhood attachment disorder, professional and parent alike. It is the children whom those working with attachment disorder want to help so desperately. Children who are suffering.

There is an old proverb:

> *"If you can make a difference for but one child,*
> *you can make a difference for the world."*

-- *Carole A. McKelvey, editor*

REFERENCES:

Ainsworth, M.D., Blehar, M.C., Waters, E., and Wall, S. (1978) Patterns of Attachment. Hillsdale, N.J.: Erlbaum.

Cline, F.W. (1979). Understanding and Treating the Severely Disturbed Child. Evergreen, CO: EC Publications.

Cline, F.W. (1992). Hope for High Risk and Rage Filled Children, Evergreen, CO: EC Publications.

Crittenden, P.M. (1985). "Maltreated infants; Vulnerability and resilience." Journal of Child Psychology and Psychiatry, 26(1), 85-96.

Delaney, R.J. and Kunstal, F.R. (1993). Troubled Transplants. University of Southern Maine.

Exner, J.E. (1990). The Rorschach: A Comprehensive System. (Vol. 2, 3rd ed.). New York: John Wiley & Sons.

Fagot, B.I. and Kavanagh, K. (1990). The prediction of antisocial behavior from avoidant attachment classification. Child Development. 61, 864-873.

Greco, C.M. and Cornell, D.G. (1992). Rorschach object investigation of attachment and anxiety in antisocial personality disorder. The Journal of Nervous and Mental Disease, 179(9), 546-552.

Gacono, C.B., Meloy, J.R., and Heaven, T.R. (1990). A Rorschach investigation of narcissism and hysteria in antisocial personality. Journal of Personality Assessment, 55(1&2), 270-279.

Goldfarb, W (1942). Infant rearing and problem behavior. American Journal of Orthopsychiatry, 249-265.

Goldfarb, W (1943). The effects of early institutional care on adolescent personality. Child Development, 14(4), 213-223.

Greco, C.M. and Cornell, D.G. (1992). Rorschach object relations of adolescents who committed homicide. Journal of Personality Assessment, 59(3), 574-583.

Lowery, L.G. (1940). Personality distortion and early institutional care. American Journal of Orthopsychiatry, (3), 245-265.

Tizard, B. and Hodges, J. (1978). The effect of early institutional rearing on the development of eight-year-old children. Journal of Child Psychology and Psychiatry, 19, 99-118.

Tizard, B. and Rees, J. (1975). The effect of early institutional rearing on the behavior problems and affectional relationships of four-year-old children. Journal of Child Psychology and Psychiatry, 16, 61-73.

Weber, C.A., Meloy, J.R., and Gacono, C.B. (1992). A Rorschach study of attachment and anxiety in inpatient conduct-disordered and dysthymic adolescents. Journal of Personality Assessment, 58(1), 16-26.

1

An Overview

By Carole A. McKelvey, M.A.
John Alston, M.D.

Why "give them roots and then let them fly"? This motto has been the operating code of the Attachment Center at Evergreen (ACE) for more than 20 years. Simply, it means the therapists and professionals and parents who make up the team at the unique Attachment Center, are dedicated to meeting the therapeutic needs of severely disturbed children who are attachment-disordered. These are children who have no *roots* (they have not made healthy attachments with a caring primary care giver); our goal is to see that they get an anchor in the stormy sea of life and then, to let them soar to the heights of which they are capable.

Thus: Give them Roots, And Then let them Fly.

The goal of this treatment is to be able to reintegrate then healthy children back into their placing families so they can give them the foundation they need to go out into the world feeling safe and secure and able to test their own wings.

The Attachment Center at Evergreen (ACE) does this by making use of a variety of treatment modalities. The central treatment for children coming into the Center, however, is called Attachment Therapy. Attachment Therapy is known by many different titles, including: Holding Therapy, DEAP therapy, Intrusive Therapy, Confrontive Therapy, Bonding Therapy, Z Therapy, Dynamic Attachment Therapy and Rage Reduction Therapy. Each of these therapies have something in common and some things not in common. All of these therapies are on the "cutting edge" and at times have been or are considered to be controversial.

The purpose of this volume, written by contributors highly respected in the therapeutic community and whom are involved with severely disturbed children on a daily basis, is to explain and enlighten the public -- professionals and lay -- regarding the therapy that is often the last chance for children so severely disturbed that their next stop could be an institution, if this therapy is unable to help them.

These are children so severely abused, neglected and traumatized that traditional talk therapies generally do not work with them -- children who may become sociopaths as they grow and children whom society may grow to fear as adults.

Children like Angie:

ANGIE TRENBERTH

Her name is Angie, as in Angel. This curly-headed petite blonde cutie, however, was an Angel from hell. When Gail and Kevin Trenberth first laid eyes on baby Angie, she was an 8-month-old infant with wispy blonde hair. As Illinois foster parents, they were called by social services on the spur of the moment to see if the couple could take in baby Angie and her 2-year-old sister, for temporary foster care.

The children's babysitters had called police. They had warned the girls' parents that they would do so, if the little ones showed up one more time battered and bruised. The birth parents, the sitters said, had obviously mistreated their little girls. And, when it happened again, that fateful day, the sitters did as they promised, calling the police to report child abuse.

It was after social services fetched the girls that a frantic search was on for a home to place them. At the time the Trenberths were getting ready for a trip with their own 4-year-old daughter, Annika. They were planning to travel to Kevin Trenberth's home turf in New Zealand. "But we agreed to take them for a short time," Gail says. "We had the two girls for only about three weeks and then they had to be placed with someone else while we were gone." It was three months after the family had returned to Illinois that they were reunited with Angie, now a crawling, curly-haired almost one-year-old. They were not asked to care again for the older sister. This baby, however, crawled into their hearts, despite warnings that she had suffered early severe abuse, including sexual abuse. The Trenberths plunged into the relationship. "We were foster parents for two years and had a chance to see she had problems. But we thought we could help her." Gail says. "We never dreamed how bad it would get, how badly scarred she was."

So scarred was this child of abuse that as she grew she was unable to get emotionally close to anyone. She acted out all the time and was very demonstrative sexually. At ages 4 and 5, in fact, this beautiful child turned the family into virtual hermits, because they could not take her out in public or invite friends to their home. Angie would go up to guests and grab them in their private parts. She would put her hand down women's blouses. She'd try to masturbate on anyone's leg.

"She was totally out of control. We didn't know then what we do now. That Angie was an unattached child. We didn't know how to get her the right treatment and we felt helpless. But we couldn't give up on this child."

The Trenberths, like many adoptive parents of very troubled children, went ahead with the adoption in the face of all this anger and craziness. "We just felt if we loved her enough and gave her a stable environment that she would get well," Gail says.

This mother was wrong.

As she grew older and it was time to go to school, Angie's actions were intractable. It only took three days for her to be expelled from kindergarten for disruptive behavior. When their local school district could not provide a classroom setting that could handle the child, the couple was forced to looked elsewhere. They finally turned to a religious residential treatment center for Angie. All the time they were getting no financial support from the adoption agency in Illinois and only a small amount from Colorado social service organizations. Insurance was of little help, so the couple faced mounting psychiatric bills for Angie.

Still, they wouldn't give up. The only alternative was to relinquish Angie, to see her spend her childhood in a series of foster homes or in an institution. They wouldn't allow this. "I don't know how to explain this," says Gail. "But she was my baby. I had bonded with her and I wasn't about to give up." After a year at the residential treatment center, the Trenberths saw no positive change in Angie. "In fact, she was much worse," Gail said.

It was then that their love would meet its greatest test. On a field trip from the home, Angie bragged to other children about alleged sexual abuse from her adoptive father. The allegations were reported to authorities by the treatment center. This childish braggadocio was Angie's way of getting the limelight, the attention. It backfired miserably for the Trenberths, who were brought before authorities and grilled about the accusations, which Gail calls "totally unbelievable." The accusations devastated the couple. It didn't take long for the determination that the accusations had no credibility and the Trenberths were declared completely innocent. The accusations and veiled threat that the couple might lose this child, that they'd invested so much time and energy in, almost cost Gail her sanity. She was so hysterical about the situation her doctor prescribed tranquilizers and nearly had to hospitalize her for a nervous breakdown.

"To this day," Gail says, "I suffer from medical problems caused by the stress of that time." For months this mother could not sleep a full night. "I would get up and wander around the house, baking bread, washing floors. Sometimes I would go for drives in the middle of the night. I just couldn't sleep."

Finally, the family found help. A Boulder psychologist referred them to the Attachment Center at Evergreen. "I called and talked to Connell Watkins, then the director, about Angie," Gail says. "As we talked, all of a sudden a light bulb went off in my head. She described attachment disorder symptoms to me. And I thought, 'She's describing my house, my child.' All of a sudden I knew what was wrong with Angie. "And for the first time I had hope she might be able to be helped." The Trenberths removed Angie from the residential treatment home as soon as possible. They obtained two-thirds financing from other sources and could finally afford the sort of treatment Angie needed. As she turned 7 years old Angie began to receive attachment therapy.

Angie was placed in an ACE therapeutic foster family; she would attend for two years. The Trenberths then took a "healing vacation" to New Zealand. As the distance between Angie and Gail increased, this mother could finally get some sleep.

"When we returned we didn't know what to expect, but they included us in the therapy sessions and Angie was a changed child. We couldn't believe it. Friends who had known her before have said, 'It is Angie's body, but there is another child in there.' We were ecstatic, but scared.

When it came time to assimilate her back in our family I was terrified.

"I was so afraid I'd never be able to love and trust her again. I had been raised to feel that love and trust come together. But I wasn't sure I could ever trust her." Watkins soothed Gail by telling her:

"You know, love is always there, but trust must be earned."

Angie is now in her teens and she is a joy for Gail and Kevin Trenberth and her older sister, Annika. "Oh, she still has a few small problems," Gail acknowledges, "but what child doesn't? But she is well, she is cured."

*As for the trust? Sometimes Gail still doesn't have it totally. Most of the time, however, her little angel comes through for her. "Do you know what she did the other day?" Gail asks, her eyes sparkling. "We were chatting while I cooked dinner. She said, 'Mom, do you know what I want to be when I grow up?' I thought, oh she's changed her mind again on a profession, and I didn't think too much about it, so I asked her 'What?'," Gail said. Angie turned to her mother and said, "I want to be just like you." Tears well up in this mother's eyes as she remembers the moment. Gail stammers and says, "You know, no unattached child could ever say that. They **never** want to be like their mothers, because their mothers are the ones they're so angry at. I couldn't believe she said that. I didn't know what to say, because I was all choked up. It's so wonderful."[1]*

Angie Trenberth is one of the lucky ones. She is a damaged, adopted child who found a family who could love her, despite the problems, and work through the hard times. Even children from very adverse conditions can do beautifully and rise to the top, as Angie is doing. She is doing so well because her parents, Gail and Kevin were willing to take on a special needs child with attachment disorders. And she is doing so well because she found the Attachment Center and the attachment and holding therapy (AHT) used there.

ACE and other therapists working with this population of severely disturbed children recognize the severity of their condition and are dedi-

---

[1] McKelvey, Stevens, <u>Adoption Crisis: The Truth Behind Adoption and Foster Care</u>, Fulcrum Books, Golden, CO. (1994)

cated to helping save children others have deemed "unsalvageable". These
are children to whom ACE means the end of the road.

* * * * * * * * * *

Defining The Problem
Dr. John Alston

The common history, symptoms and diagnoses of the children accepted
into specialized foster care and treatment within the Attachment Center
at Evergreen's program is a story of children who possess deplorable and
tragic histories. Children such as Angie, mentioned above.

Because of these histories, these are children who come to the Center
highly resistant, aggressive and with sociopathic symptoms. Many of these
children fit into several categories of diagnostic labels (as described in the
DSM-IV)[2], such as:

- Oppositional Defiant Disorder
- Reactive Attachment Disorder, and
- Post-Traumatic Stress Disorder, and others.
- Bipolar Disorder
- Attention Deficit Disorder
- Fetal Alcohol Effects/Fetal Alcohol Syndrome

At The Attachment Center at Evergreen these children enter a specialized foster care-treatment program that is, in many ways, unique, in
my opinion. All of these children have severe behavioral difficulties due,
regrettably, to a remarkably uniform history involving severe emotional,
physical and sexual abuse. The only exception are a few children who
have become emotionally distanced as a result of continuing profound
medical disorders -- often these children come to ACE after having stayed
with one or another or both birth parents.

At least 90 to 95 percent of our children are adopted following relinquishment by the birth parents. This relinquishment often has occurred
because the system has taken the children away because of persistent and
sustained severe abuse and/or neglect to the children within the first 18

---

[2] Diagnostic and Statistical Manual of Mental Disorders, Fourth Edition,
American Psychiatric Association, pp. 116

months to two years of life. Most of these children have been in several foster homes prior to their current adoptive placement or have been in several potential adoptive homes that have disrupted because of continuing behavioral disturbances on the part of the children.

It is not at all uncommon, indeed it is typical, for the overwhelming majority of the children in the Attachment Center program to have had five, ten or more transient experiences within foster homes; sometimes foster home placements have been highly abusive experiences. Nor is it unusual for the average child in our program to have been through at least a couple prospective adoptive situations, which have aborted also because of uncontrollable behavior on these children's part.

While I hate to make an absolute stereotype of our children, there is likely far more uniformity in the consistency of the typical child that we treat. We certainly appreciate the separate and unique characteristics of each child in our program. However, we cannot discount that the children referred to us arrive in Evergreen because we are known for our experience and expertise in treating severe behavioral and emotional disorders which occurred as a result of severe abuse and neglect within the first years of life.

Most, if not all, of the biological parents of these severely abused children would, themselves, be considered severely anti-social. This commonly has occurred because these parents themselves experienced severe abuse and neglect in their early childhood. A few of the parents would be diagnosed psychotic, but most would be considered severely anti-social, with little or no regard for their children's welfare.

Because the birth parents were anti-social, they often alienated their own families, so family support systems for these children were generally nonexistent, inconsistent or inadequate. None of these parents wanted to be pregnant with these children. As a result, it is very common that the parents had their own self-centered priorities. This often translated to the reality that neglect and abuse began for the children, often within the first days to early weeks of life. This meant these children's likely intrauterine, perinatal and postnatal experiences were all ones in which any child would have felt deprived. Even though most of the children in our program had infrequent contact with medical personnel, several had been diagnosed as Failure To Thrive infants during early childhood.

There is documentation that many -- if not most -- of the children seen at ACE had spent multiple hours or days as young children with their physical needs being completely ignored. This means being neither fed nor given touch or any contact with the world whatsoever. It is no wonder that literally all of our children have a perception -- based in reality -- that the world is a cruel and hostile place, and the only way to survive is to turn primitive anxieties into resistance and control over the environment, at least to the extent that an infant or toddler can manage. Most of these children had contact with a care giver that was barely able to sustain the child's physical needs. These children were minimally looked at, talked to, held or even touched.

The Attachment Center at Evergreen is never the first referral for these children. All of these children have been managed by Social Service Departments and referred to individual and family therapy, commonly for years, with no benefits. It has been our consistent experience, with the abuse and neglect histories of these children, that traditional psychotherapies have been not only useless, but in many ways contraindicated. This is because traditional therapy is so child focused, that they actually reinforce the adaptive controllingness that is at the core of these children's pathologies. In other words, these children -- being the excellent observers that they are -- routinely tell psychotherapists what they want to hear, which tends to align the therapist with the child. This often alienates the children from usually well meaning foster or adoptive parents. I use the world "contraindicated" in the sense that the child's experience with these traditional psychotherapies is such that their effective anti-social mechanisms of controlling behaviors is reinforced.

One fortunate evolution with the Attachment Center, perhaps a reflection throughout the country, is that we appear to be getting younger children referred to us during recent years. It is my experience, from the late 1972's to at least mid-1980's, that the average age of a child accepted into the program was from perhaps 10 to 16. Several admissions of children five to six years old have also been handled, but our experience is that few children over age 12 are accepted into foster care (and into this treatment center). The average ages of entry now typically are 7 to 9. Because of this, the psychopathologies of these younger children are much less entrenched than those in the teen-age years. This fact improves overall long term prognosis.

Systematically, all of the children admitted to the Attachment Center program are severely characterologically disturbed. While there are broad, substantial individual nuances unique to each child in the program, there are also broad symptom complexes within which literally every one of these children fits. Based on these children's common experiences of abuse and neglect in the early stages of their life, they experience:

- themselves as worthless people and,
- the world as an unsafe place within which to live.

All of these children have to become excellent observers of the world around them in such a way that they are able to mimic social relations but have an inability to either give or receive genuine affection (they are phoney). While this may sound extreme, any affection that is shown by these children (at the time of their admission), represents a manipulation or an attempt to control on their part. Knowing this sounds hard-hearted or extreme, this is a genuine, factual description of the children's lack of trust either in themselves as lovable, dependent people or in the world as never having adequately, consistently met their needs.

All of these children exhibit substantial self-defeating, even self-destructive behavior. Several of these children exhibit self-mutilating behavior. All of these children exhibit substantial cruelty to others, most particularly to other children who are equally or more helpless than themselves. A number of these children's cruelty is of such a dimension that they have literally tortured and killed a number of household pets before coming to the Attachment Center.

There is a somewhat unique insincerity and phoniness about these children in their effort to control others around them. Being the excellent observers that they are, they match their style of response to people around them so that, until someone learns to know them in greater depth, they initially come across as highly believable; it is only later that one learns that much of what they say that has anything to do with closeness or intimacy turns out to be fabricated. This phoniness, lying, and insincerity tends to be ingrained at a very early age, as if their genuine perceptions are distorted. In the intensity of treatment, however, it becomes clear that such attempts to be so controlling are conscious, deliberate, purposeful and intentional acts.

Given all of these children's food issues -- in almost all cases, deprivation of food -- it is not surprising that the overwhelming majority of these children have substantial difficulties with stealing food, hoarding food, gorging upon food and, at other times, the commonly utilized self-defeating mechanisms of self-starvation.

All of these children have marked control problems with authority figures. None of these children could be considered compliant or agreeable children. Most of them are overtly defiant and oppositional and if that is unsuccessful, become passively procrastinative, obstinate, and forgetful. All of these children have strong tendencies to either openly resist or to dawdle and/or do lousy jobs at following directions authorities set for them.

It is this compensatory over-control of their environment that is universally shared by all of the children. This is often the issue at the very heart of their initial referral to the program. If they cannot control in one way, they will control in another. All of these children are unable to sustain eye contact. Still others will use abnormalities of speech (such as, talking extremely slowly, exceedingly fast, very loud, or talking almost inaudibly) as control mechanisms.

Given their severe difficulties with both self esteem and the lack of emotional connectedness to other people, these children routinely have enormous difficulties relating to anyone for a prolonged period of time. (For example, they do not sustain bonds of friendship.)

While the overwhelming majority of these children are superficially engaging, even charming, none of these children are able to sustain any meaningful, intimate relationships. True intimacy requires trust and dependence. These children have learned that being trusting and dependent sets them up for abuse. As such, their survival instincts are ones in which they would rather survive and be in control, than to place themselves in any vulnerable or dependent position that leaves them susceptible to a history of abuse and abandonment.

Diagnostically, all of the ACE children fit DSM-III-R and DSM-IV criterion for Oppositional Defiant Disorder. All of these children fit the diagnosed criterion in both DSM-III-R and DSM-IV for Reactive Attachment Disorder of Infancy or Early Childhood. All of the children would generally fit several characteristics of Post-Traumatic Stress Disorder.

Because of the concomitant, overriding attachment disturbances, their Post-Traumatic Stress Disorder symptoms take the form of avoidance of placing themselves in overwhelming or traumatizing situations, as opposed to their openness to reexperiencing any traumatic events.

Approximately 40 percent of the children in the program have coexistent diagnoses of Attention Deficit Hyperactive Disorder (ADHD) or Bi-Polar Disorder. There are also presently three children in this program with a diagnosis of Tourett's Syndrome.

John Alston, M.D.

* * * * * * * * * *

Reactive Attachment Disorder

Children with attachment disorders are said in the DSM-IV to be suffering from Reactive Attachment Disorder. To be diagnosed with Reactive Attachment Disorder, a child must have these diagnostic criteria for 313.89 Reactive Attachment Disorder of Infancy or Early Childhood:

A. Markedly disturbed and developmentally inappropriate social relatedness in most contexts, beginning before age 5 years, as evidenced by either (1) or (2):

(1) persistent failure to initiate or respond in a developmentally appropriate fashion to most social interactions, as manifest by excessively inhibited, hypervigilant, or highly ambivalent and contradictory responses (e.g., the child may respond to caregivers with a mixture of approach, avoidance, and resistance to comforting, or may exhibit frozen watchfulness)

(2) diffuse attachments as manifest by indiscriminate sociability with marked inability to exhibit appropriate selective attachments (e.g., excessive familiarity with relative strangers or lack of selectivity in choice of attachment figures)

B. the disturbance in Criterion A is not accounted for solely by developmental delay (as in Mental Retardation) and does not meet criteria for a Pervasive Developmental Disorder.

C. Pathogenic care as evidenced by at least one of the following:

(1) persistent disregard of the child's basic emotional needs for comfort, stimulation, and affection.

(2) persistent disregard of the child's basic physical needs

(3) repeated changes of primary caregiver that prevent formation of stable attachments (e.g., frequent changes in foster care)

D. There is presumption that the care in Criterion C is responsible for the disturbed behavior in Criterion A (e.g., the disturbances in Criterion A began following the pathogenic care in Criterion C).

Specific type:

Inhibited Type: if Criterion A1 predominates in the clinical presentation.

Disinhibited Type: if Criterion A2 predominates in the clinical presentation.

Preview

Throughout this book, readers will gain insight into Reactive Attachment Disorder and the work of the Attachment Center with the children described above. These are children with severe psychopathologies who come to Evergreen, because of the commitment of the adults who are now in their lives.

Now, it is the task of the fine therapists, the staff, the parents and the consultants at The Attachment Center at Evergreen, to try to restore their childhood, while their youth remains. That is what this book is about. Below, a preview of what you will discover:

Chapter Two: Attachment Theory and Assessment

The scope of the problem of attachment disorder in the United States is enormous. More than 600,00 babies were born to teen-age mothers in 1991. From 1979 to 1991, 50,000 children were killed by guns. Fifteen million children lived in poverty in 1992.

Each year, three million children are reported abused or neglected.[1] Four hundred thousand children per year are exposed to drug or alcohol abuse prior to birth.[2]

Looking at these statistics, it is easy to see why there is an increased interest in attachment-related theory, research and therapy, coinciding with the complexities and problems of modern society. To understand the nature of attachment and its impact on children and families, this discussion will have the following objectives:
- Review basic attachment theory and research;
- Describe the relationship between various attachment patterns and psychosocial development;
- Define the behavioral, emotional, cognitive and interpersonal symptoms of attachment disorder, and
- Delineate the rationale, goals and methods of a specific therapeutic approach to attachment-disordered children, adolescents and families.

Chapter Three: Insight into Attachment

Attachment is the foundation of our ability to love, feel compassion, and empathy. It is how we sustain nurturing, form long term relationships with other humans and with our world.

In this chapter, attachment is defined as a result of a bonding process that occurs between human beings. It is the basis for our ability to form attachment on the most basic levels; where our ability to form attachment is imprinted and mapped out during the in-utero experience and the first two years of life.

To understand how a child becomes attachment-disordered it is important to look at the child's first few years. The first two years of life are critical to a child. The most important things a child must have during those formative years to grow up healthy of body and mind are: love, touch, lactose(milk), movement and eye contact from a consistent caregiver (mother or father).

Chapter Four: Does Attachment Disorder Exist?

Child therapists have long known that children who experience early abuse and neglect have difficulty adjusting in both later childhood and adulthood. In 1940 Lowrey noted that children who had been raised in institutions for the first three years of their lives "undergo an isolation type of experience with resulting isolation type of personality, characterized by unsocial behavior, hostile aggression, lack of patterns for giving and receiving affection, inability to understand and accept limitations; delays in development; egocentricity is marked; and, they do not recognize the individuality and needs of others". In addition, Goldfarb (1942) notes that "case workers have for a long time noted the hyperactivity, destructiveness and aggressiveness which seemed to be especially characteristic of foster children whose babyhood had been spent in institutions"

Chapter Five: Life in the Trenches/Placing Parents

Placing parents often find ACE through word of mouth or through a network. The first contact with The Attachment Center is often through telephone discussions. An intake procedure walks parents through the process that is required to bring a child into the ACE therapeutic family.

Often placing parents (usually adoptive or foster) bringing children to the Attachment Center are in crisis themselves. Living with an extremely disturbed child who is manipulative, unloving and uncaring and who cannot give back the love the parents have been pouring into the child can create a diagnostic condition called Post Traumatic Stress Disorder. Many of the parents coming for help at the Center are suffering from this malady.

It is because of these dynamics that the Center approaches an attachment disordered child's treatment in the context of the family situation. This is a family that requires "healing", not just a child.

Chapter Six: The Therapeutic Team

One of the things that makes the attachment center's approach different from other like agencies is the therapeutic treatment team that surrounds each and every child with love and support. Key to this team approach and the element that distinguishes ACE, is the participation of highly-trained therapeutic foster families. These foster families are at the very heart of the ACE program. The treatment plan includes the child (and sometimes the placing family) living in the home of a therapeutic family.

Each of ACE's therapeutic foster families has been trained over the years in therapeutic parenting that reinforces the therapy the child is receiving on a regular basis. And, each therapeutic family participates in that therapy by providing opportunities for the children in their home that facilitate bonding and attachment.

In addition to the **primary therapist** and **therapeutic family**, each child's treatment team may include a **secondary therapist, psychiatrist, placing parents** (or agency representative), **home-town therapist, and the program manager**. This group works as a team to accomplish the goals established in the treatment plan.

Chapter Seven: Two Week Intensives

Many of the children referred to or brought to The Attachment Center at Evergreen, Inc., for treatment initially undergo what is called a Two Week Intensive program of therapy referred to above.

In this therapeutic approach, the child, parents, and, when appropriate, other family members (e.g., siblings) participate in thirty hours of therapy over a two week period (three hours per day for ten consecutive working days). This therapy format was originally developed to provide treatment to children and families in need of services unavailable in their own geographic locale. These families traveled to Evergreen from every region of the United States, as well as abroad, to receive specialized treatment for attachment disorders. Soon it was realized that this short-term format provided an array of clinical advantages for these typically highly resistant, controlling, non-trusting children. The consistency and intensity of daily therapeutic contact created a context in which defenses were reduced, motivation increased, and a trusting therapeutic relationship was established. All of this occurs within a framework of nurturing support for both the child and the family.

Chapter Eight: Long Term Treatment

Reciprocity, acceptance and empathy provide the guidelines for the ongoing treatment of attachment disordered children. Whatever techniques and interventions are being utilized therapeutically, the therapist must focus on the learning of reciprocity, responsibility, and empathy in working with this severely disturbed client population.

Reciprocity is essentially the Golden Rule "Do onto others as you would have others do onto you." In a very real, albeit negative manner, this is exactly what an attachment disordered child is doing in organizing his relationship to the rest of the world. He is doing to others what has been done to him. He is rejecting, destroying, abusing and lying. His internalized model for how the world works and how he must operate in order to get his needs met is essentially based on "negative reciprocity."

He needs, however, to learn "positive reciprocity" if the psychological damage is to be healed. Only by learning "positive reciprocity" does the attachment disordered child mature beyond the infantile narcissism in which so many are behaviorally and emotionally stuck. Initially, this positive reciprocity needs to be learned within the context of the mother-child relationship and then expanded or generalized to other family members and then to peer relations.

Chapter Nine: Therapeutic Parenting (Part I)

The theory behind therapeutic parenting as practiced by ACE and its families revolves around one primary theme:

- to enable parents to be able to continue working with their child on their life and,
- still take good care of themselves.

By taking good care of themselves and placing the units of concern for wellness on the child, parents are able to maintain their loving relationship with the child and help with the healing process.

Writing about the parenting of emotionally and behavioral problematic children is not so much to teach parents how to mold their children into responsible and cooperative human beings, as it is to enable them to have the tools, desire and energy to stay their children's parents over the long haul.

It is more valuable to find ways to make the relationship work within the constraints of already developed personalities than the aim of changing the other person into someone more easily loved.

Chapter Ten: Therapeutic Parenting (Part II)

These are the foundations of the techniques developed by therapeutic parents at the Attachment Center. The question is not:

- "How do we make our children more lovable?"
- Rather it is, "How do we love unlovable children?"

The essence of therapeutic parenting is to learn how to love children who have learned in the past that love hurts, who are afraid of love and who actively seek to rebuff love. How to do this is the meat of the therapeutic parenting that occurs at and is taught at The Attachment Center at Evergreen.

Chapter Eleven: Reintegration

Reintegration is the extensive process that assists an ACE graduate and his/her family handle the difficult transition involved with the child returning home. This is a transition not to be taken lightly. No child who comes to ACE in such a severely disturbed place can easily be just "sent home."

It is in the reintegration process that ACE employs family preservation techniques to make sure the transition is a safe and secure one for both family and child. A year-long reintegration and follow-up period helps the family to adjust to changes and continue to develop healthier relationships patterns. All members of the therapeutic team continue to work together to accomplish the treatment plan they have established. Consultation, support, respite care, visits, are all part of the reintegration plan.

Chapter Twelve: Developing a community approach

Developing a community approach to healing severely disturbed children has global implications for society. As we have mentioned throughout this book and in the forward by Dr. Foster Cline, the children who eventually find their way to ACE for treatment are very severely disturbed. Those outside the ACE family often have no idea how very disturbed an attachment disordered child can become and very little idea of how such a child can be helped. ACE is often the very last effort an adoptive or foster parent or birth parent will make before institutionalization of a child.

It is the Attachment Center's belief that without the specialized treatment found in Evergreen, many of these children would grow up filled with hatred. Early abuse and neglect will render them unable to love throughout their lives and will cause them to turn away from society. These children are sometimes doomed to becoming adult sociopaths.

It is by establishing alliances with the caring community that ACE is able to continue its work with these severely disturbed children. Among those who help ACE accomplish its work are: Social Service agencies, the legal system, the medical community, parents and their networks, and other caring professionals and non-professionals in Colorado and around the country.

The Prologue

The implications for American society of thousands of children growing up with attachment disorder are staggering. Each day, in America, the situation is getting worse. Children are being born now, this minute, who are destined to be abused and neglected to the extent they will never trust anyone. Never trust anyone, that is, unless they get help. The earlier in their life they are diagnosed, the easier it is to help them regain their childhood.

Some attachment disordered children will grow up to kill others and end up in prison, others will go through life as con artists, living a parasitic lifestyle. Not one of these children will be able to have a secure, loving relationship with anyone. None of them will contribute to the community good of society; they will be parasites and predators.

This is the face of attachment disorder in this country. It isn't an easy face to look into. It is the disaster that the Attachment Center at Evergreen and everyone else committed to working with such children are attempting to avert.

If a society does not take care of its children when they are small, that society may learn to fear those children when they are adults. The small expense of saving these children now will be more than offset by the savings of a reduced prison population. The implications for society are staggering. As Dr. Foster Cline has said:

> The hundreds of children and adults who have been helped
> by this therapy appreciate these authors straightforward
> candor and explicit sharing of their techniques so that every-
> one can better understand this controversial work.

In the chapters that follow, the reader will discover the intricacies of a therapy that has a proven track record of helping children who are destined to have few or no connections as adults. Through the words and expertise of those contributing to this volume, the reader will find out how this unique therapy based on loving, connecting and protecting children is the answer to the paradox of attachment disorder that plagues our cities, streets and world.

The Attachment Center at Evergreen invites you to read and learn.

Editor's Note: All proceeds from this book have been designated by the Board of Directors of the Attachment Center to go to The Attachment Center at Evergreen, Inc., Scholarship Fund, which provides scholarships to the ACE program for children whose families would otherwise be unable to afford this vital therapy. Almost daily the Attachment Center staff becomes aware of a family needing Center services, but whom are unable to access the treatment for financial reasons. It is the mission of ACE to "Give Them Roots and Then Let Them Fly".

2

Attachment Theory And Assessment

Terry M. Levy, PHD.
Michael Orlans, M.A.

*"Life can only be understood backwards,
but it must be lived forwards."*

Kierkegaard

Attachment theory shares similar roots to family systems theory; they both represent a parading shift, a change in the way of conceptualizing the human condition. Rather than studying only the individual, viewing people as separate and isolated, the focus is on the context in which the person lives and develops -- the relationship. Attachment theory focuses on the most basic and primary of relationships, the infant-mother bond, and on the ways in which this bond serves as a foundation for further growth and development. Robert Karen writes, "The struggle to understand the infant-mother bond ranks as one of the greatest quests of modern psychology, one that touches us deeply because it holds so many clues as to how we become who we are" (Karen, 1994, page 1).

Attachment-related issues are especially relevent in today's society. Professionals from the fields of mental health, child protective services, medicine, judicial systems, and law enforcement struggle with difficult and complex questions that affect the lives of children, families, and society. What input do infants need so that they can learn to perceive the world in a positive way, develop a sense of their own value and worth, become capable of developing healthy relationships, and manage stress and adversity effectively? How can we create a foster care system that best serves the needs of children? How do we prepare adoptive parents to deal with a child's traumatic past? What is the most appropriate time and procedure for social service agencies and courts to separate a child from abusive or neglectful parents, and, what is the most effective intervention to heal the emotional damage? How can we intervene to identify high-risk families and encourage positive change before severe damage occurs to the child? How do we manage the realities of modern family life (day care, poverty, violence, teen pregnancy, single-parent and blended families) and the influences on parent-child bonds (Karen, 1994)?

The scope of the problem in the United States is enormous. More than 600,00 babies were born to teenage mothers in 1991. From 1979 to 1991, 50,000 children were killed by guns. Fifteen million children lived in poverty in 1992. Each year, three million children are reported abused or neglected (Children's Defense Fund, 1994). From 1982 to 1992 there was a 68 percent increase in the number of children in foster care. A 1988 study found that 48 percent of these children had between two and five different placements in the preceding three years. In 1993, half a million children were waiting to be adopted, and more than 50 percent were considered high-risk due to abuse, neglect, or disruption (series of short-term foster placements). This year (1995) almost one million children will be in out-of-home placements, with 550,000 in an overburdened foster care system and others in mental health or juvenile justice facilities. Four hundred thousand children per year are exposed to drug or alcohol prior to birth (McKelvey and Stevens, 1994). Cline (1994) writes, "Our society is producing a generation of severly disturbed children who lack conscience...these children grow up unattached --- incapable of caring about themselves and others, unable to distinguish right from wrong, unable to form loving relationships, unable to accept responsibility" (page 10).

There appears to be an increased interest in attachment-related theory, research and therapy, coinciding with the aforementioned complexities and problems of modern society. In order to understand the nature of attachment and its impact on children and families, this discussion has the following objectives:

(1) Review basic attachment theory and research;

(2) Describe the relationship between various attachment patterns and psychosocial development;

(3) Define the behavioral, emotional, cognitive and interpersonal symptoms of attachment disorder, and

(4) Delineate the rationale, goals and methods of a specific therapeutic approach to attachment-disorder with children, adolescents and families.

ATTACHMENT: BASIC CONCEPTS AND RESEARCH

The contributions of John Bowlby (1951, 1958, 1969, 1973, 1980, 1988) serve as the foundation for attachment theory and the development of basic attachment concepts. Bowlby submitted a report to the World Health Organization in 1951 entitled "Maternal Care and Mental Health" in which he reviewed the evidence regarding inadequate maternal care and its negative effects on personality development.

He emphasized two points: (1) The infant's need to attach (bond) to the parent is as basic as the need for food, and (2) Separation from or loss of the parent can produce damage to the developing child (Bowlby, 1951, 1958). Bowlby was influenced by ethologists whose studies in non-human species emphasized the instinctive nature of attachment. Lorenz (1965) described the strong bonds to a mother that developed, without maternal feeding, in certain bird species. Harlow (1958), in his now famous study, found that Rhesus monkey infants preferred a soft terry-cloth "mother" that lacked food to a wire-mesh one that provided food. Bowlby concluded that there is a biological basis for attachment behavior, it is separate from other instincts, and that this serves a survival value by keeping the mother and infant closely connected. Anxiety over separation keeps the infant available to the mother for protection as the offspring and attachment-figure (usually the mother) develop a reciprocal relationship (Hinde and Stevenson-Hinde, 1990).

Bowlby defined attachment as "an affectional tie with some other differentiated and preferred individual who is usually conceived as stronger and/or wiser" (1977a, p. 203). Bowlby proceeded to delineate the cognitive aspects of attachment between parent and child. The affectional bonds form the basis of internal representations of the relationship between self and others (working models) which serve as blueprints for all future relationships (Bowlby, 1973).

Based on: (a)the degree to which the infant can elicit these responses, the developing child forms a set of expectations and beliefs about self, others, and the environment. A positive working model develops when the caregiver is consistently accessible and responsive to the infant's signals and needs; the caregiver is perceived as a safe and secure base from which to explore the environment. A negative working model develops due to inconsistency, rejection, neglect or abuse; the caregiver is perceived as unsafe and unreliable (Lyddon, et al, 1993; Delaney and Kunstal, 1993).

The next stage in the development of attachment theory focused on the role of the primary caregiver in determining secure or insecure attachment. Mary Ainsworth and her colleagues (Ainsworth, Blehar, Waters, and Wall, 1978; Ainsworth and Wittig, 1969) identified three principal attachment styles which correlate with the behavior of the primary caregiver towards the infant: (1) secure, (2) anxious-avoidant, and (3) anxious-ambivalent. Using a technique called the Strange Situation, Ainsworth (1969) studied attachment during the infant's first year of life. Initially, mother-child interaction was observed in the home, focusing on the mother's attachment-behaviors towards the infant: feeding, smiling, eye contact, cuddling and response to crying. At twelve months of age the children were observed in a laboratory context in which they were exposed to separations from and reunions with their mothers. The securely-attached infants used the parent as a base for exploration, protesting and crying on separation, showed pleasure when the mother returned, were easy to console, and clearly preferred the parent to a stranger. These mothers had shown themselves to be available, sensitive to the needs and signals of the infant, and warmly responsive during the earlier observation period. The infants labeled as anxious-avoidant explored without using the parent as a secure base (independent), showed little protest when mother left, avoided contact when she returned, and did not discriminate between parent and stranger. These mothers were previously observed to be unresponsive and rejecting with their infants, lacking emotional warmth, expressiveness, and physical contact. Anxious-ambivalent infants did not explore the environment prior to separation, became severely agitated and anxious during separation, and simultaneously sought contact with and pulled away from the mother upon reunion. This pattern of attachment was promoted by the mother being inconsistent and unpredictable, available and responsive on some occasions but not others.

A fourth attachment style was identified by Main and Soloman (1990), referred to as disorganized-disoriented. These infants showed confusing and contradictory attachment behavior: expressed intense anger followed by a sudden dazed appearance; sought-out the parent, but with a stiff body; failed to seek out mother when frightened; attempted to leave with the stranger rather than remain with the parent; showed fear at the sight of the caregiver upon reunion. The mothers of these infants were found to be abusive and neglectful (Crittendon, 1985; Cicchetti and Carlson, 1989), severely depressed (Radke-Yarrow, et al, 1984), or had, themselves suffered physical and sexual abuse as children (Main and Hesse, 1990).

To summarize, attachment has its roots in an instinctual-based behavioral system that has survival significance. A homeostatic process regulates infant-parent proximity and interaction for purposes of safety and security. Attachment behaviors (crying, gazing, touching, seeking) are initiated when the infant is separated from the caregiver, apparently feeling fearful or anxious.

When reunited, the infant's behaviors changed in order to maintain the closeness (smiling, clinging), followed by exploration from a "secure base". As this cycle of attachment activation and deactivation repeats during the first year of life, the infant develops an attachment to the primary caregiver and internal working models, beliefs and expectations about the parent, the self, and the relationship. Secure, avoidant, ambivalent, and disorganized styles of attachment develop as a result of specific parental behavior, the reciprocal interactions between parent and infant, and the positive or negative working models which ensue.

Longitudinal and prospective studies show that patterns of attachment observed in the first year of life tend to persist into adolescence and adulthood. This is explained in two ways:

- Parental styles and behaviors towards the child typically do not change without intervention.
- Secondly, attachment styles tend to be self-perpetuating, forming an ongoing pattern (vicious circle) with caregivers and others (Bowlby, 1988).

A securely-attached child is happier, less demanding, and easier to parent than an anxiously-attached child. The child with ambivalent attachment may be clingy and demanding, while the avoidant child may reject the parent and be aggressive toward other children, thus provoking a negative parental response.

Sroufe (1983) found that attachment styles assessed at one year of age predict behavior three years later in pre-school. Securely-attached children are described by staff as cooperative, resourceful, and able to develop positive friendships. Children with anxious-avoidant attachment patterns are described as angry, isolated and attention-seeking. Anxious-ambivalent children are typically tense, impulsive, have a low frustration tolerance, and demonstrate helpless and passive behaviors. Other researchers found that attachment styles observed at twelve months are consistent with patterns of mother-child interaction at six years of age (Main and Cassidy, 1988; Wartner, 1986). Securely-attached six-year-olds relate to their parents in a relaxed, open and intimate manner. Anxious-ambivalent children are often hostile, fearful and sad, and seem superficially engaging and artificial. Children with anxious-avoidant patterns are isolated and distant, having little communication with their parents. The disorganized-disoriented children are oppositional and controlling, either reject or overprotect their parents, and experience parent-child communication which is fragmented and chaotic.

Further studies relate secure and insecure attachment styles to differences in behavior, personality and adjustment later in life. Children who experience prolonged separation from a primary caregiver manifest an array of psychosocial difficulties and respond to loss with a series of stages: initial lack of affect, followed by grief, sorrow and despair (Paterson and Moran, 1988). Securely attached children, as compared to insecure/anxious, are more resilient when under stress (Egelund and Sroufe, 1981a,

1981b), receive more positive responses from other children as they grow older (Jacobson and Wille, 1986), have better self-esteem, relate to others with more warmth and affection, and are less likely to display antisocial behavior (Grossman and Grossman, 1990). These children develop into adolescents and adults who have less anxiety (Feeney and Noller, 1990), demonstrate more empathy for others (Sroufe, et al., 1984), are more competent in social situations (Sroufe, 1983), and have more satisfying adult love relationships and friendships (Hendrick and Hendrick, 1989; Feeney and Noller, 1990). A significant correlation exists between attachment security, the quality of marital relationships, and the tendency toward rejection of the partner (Kobak and Hazan, 1991). Husbands with secure attachments have more positive interactions and fewer conflicts with their spouse than those with insecure attachments (Cohen, et al., 1992).

Attachment difficulties result from rejection, abuse, inconsistency and insensitivity to needs, as well as prolonged separation and disruption of the parent-child relationship. Later adoptions were found to result in more behavioral difficulties than earlier ones (MacDonald, 1985), consistent with the finding that disruptions promote poor attachment.

Similarly, multiple mothering during the infant's first six months correlates with antisocial behavior later (Cadoret and Cain, 1980), and prolonged separation from the mother during the first three years results in significant behavioral problems (MacDonald, 1985). DeJong (1992) found that adolescents and young adults who have a history of insecure attachments due to parental absence are more vulnerable to suicide.

Young adults who report feeling lonely also report a history of disrupted attachments (Hecht, 1984). A relationship between aggression, juvenile delinquency, sex offending, and poor attachment is suggested (Marshall, et al., 1993).

The inability to achieve intimacy, a consequence of poor attachment, results in the feeling of loneliness, which can lead to aggressive acting-out. Sex offenders report less intimacy and greater feelings of loneliness than others (Marshall, Seidman, and Check, 1991).

In summary, secure attachment occurs when the primary caregiver is available, responsive, and sensitive to the infant's needs in a consistent and affectionate way. These youngsters typically develop positive self-concepts, warm and caring relationships, and positive internal working models as they grow older.

Conversely, infants often develop insecure and anxious attachment as a consequence of loss (separation, disruption), abuse, or neglect. These children experience problems with self-esteem, develop negative working models, and have interpersonal difficulties.

ASSESSMENT

There are three major areas of assessment in reference to the therapy protocol described: child, parent (or primary caregivers), and family system. Prior to participation in therapy, parents are sent an initial information and assessment packet which they must complete, which includes: child symptom checklist, child's early history questionnaire, parent history questionnaire, family registration form, and a description of the treatment process. This serves as both an assessment and screening tool.

CHILD ASSESSMENT

Early History. Specific information regarding prenatal, perinatal and postnatal circumstances is critical to understanding the type of attachment that occurred and the nature of the disruption in the infant-mother bond. Historical data from self-reports and social service, medical, and legal records, is reviewed to obtain the following information: the emotional and physical condition of mother during pregnancy; wanted or unwanted pregnancy; drug and alcohol use before and after birth; post-partum depression; birth trauma; abuse (physical, sexual, emotional) and neglect during first several years: medical conditions (e.g., painful inner ear infections) and hospitalizations, and disruptions in the continuity of attachment (e.g., series of foster homes or other placements).

Current Signs and Symptoms. Symptoms of attachment-related disorder are grouped into four categories: disturbances of behavior, cognitive functioning, affectivity, and interpersonal functioning. Symptoms are determined on the basis of parents' reports (including symptom checklist), reports of others (teachers, social service caseworkers, prior or current therapists), and current clinical observations. [1]When we refer to children we are also referring to adolescents. [2]When we refer to parents we are also referring to the single parent.

Behavioral disturbances. Children with attachment disorders manifest a variety of antisocial and aggressive acting-out behaviors. They are often self-destructive, including self-mutilation (e.g., head banging, cutting or burning skin), suicidal gestures, and other self-defeating behaviors. They destroy the property of others, their own material possessions, or both. They are often impulsive and physically aggressive towards other children and adults. Aggression can be overt, such as acts of physical violence, or passive-aggressive, such as manipulative and surreptitious behaviors. Sadistic cruelty to animals, often secretive, is common. Stealing is typical, including theft outside and inside the home. Lying is of a pathological nature; they remain deceitful regardless of concrete evidence to the contrary. A preoccupation with fire, gore and blood sometimes occurs, and they tend to establish an affiliation with evil and the dark side of life. They can be ingenuous, devious and "phony", giving the appearance of sincerity but with ulterior and self-serving motives. For example, helping professionals often assume the child's seemingly cooperative responses are sincere, when in reality, the behavior is manipulative and controlling. Problems regarding food and eating-patterns are common, such as hoarding and gorging, and usually reflect control issues and power struggles. Children who have been sexually abused manifest inappropriate sexual behavior, attitudes and concerns, such as victimizing others, excessive masturbation and seductive manipulation. Sleep disturbances include recurrent nightmares, night terrors, and disturbed sleep patterns, including wandering at night. Enuresis and encopresis are typical manifestations of anger, aggression and control issues; these children may soil in closets, clothes and heating vents. Extreme defiant and oppositional behaviors include refusal to comply with authority, demanding and intrusive social styles, and persistent nonsense questions and incessant chatter.

Cognitive Functioning. A lack of cause-and-effect thinking is evident, failing to recognize and comprehend the relationship between actions and consequences. Thus, these children rarely take responsibility for their own choices and actions, and instead, blame others. Many of these youngsters, depending upon their level of disturbance, are lacking in moral development, feeling little or no remorse for their hurtful actions. Regarding cognitive style (i.e., working models), they perceive themselves as unwanted, worthless, impotent and "bad", perceive caretakers as unavailable, untrustworthy and threatening, and perceive the world as unsafe and hostile. They define themselves as helpless victims unable to impact their world, or conversely, as omnipotent, with a grandiose sense of self-importance as a defense against feeling helpless. Learning and language disorders are common and can occur as a result of neurological damage early in life (e.g., fetal alcohol syndrome, failure to thrive, physical abuse), or in conjunction with the matrix of psychosocial symptoms mentioned above.

Affectivity. The core emotions these children experience are intense levels of anger, fear, and pain. They frequently appear disheartened and depressed. Temper tantrums and rage reactions are common. They are emotionally labile with frequent and unpredictable mood changes. Due to years of avoidance and denial, they are not able to identify or express their emotions in clear and constructive ways. Unresolved loss is a basic emotional issue.

Interpersonal Behavior. Chronic non-compliance is manifested interpersonally as control battles, defiance of rules and authority, and inability to tolerate external limits. Thus, these youngsters create frequent conflict with caregivers, teachers, siblings and peers. They relate to others in a manipulative, controlling and exploitative fashion, lacking the ability to connect with genuine intimacy and affection. They lack trust in others, a direct result of unavailable, unreliable and hurtful caregivers in the early years, causing them to overcompensate in the direction of pseudo-independence. They are superficially engaging and charming, indiscriminately affectionate with strangers, and typically lack long-term meaningful relationships. Lack of eye contact is apparent when interaction is perceived as intimate, but they will maintain such contact for purposes of seduction or control. Typical social roles that they develop and maintain are victim (helpless, powerless) and/or victimizer (perpetrator, bully). Blaming others for their own mistakes and problems, and taking little or no responsibility for their actions and choices, further alienates and frustrates others.

Previous Testing and Diagnoses. Psychodiagnostic evaluations are reviewed as a part of the assessment procedure. These children typically have a long history of prior evaluation and treatment, with little or no positive results. Common diagnoses include: Reactive Attachment Disorder of Infancy or Early Childhood, Attention-Deficit/Hyperactivity Disorder, Oppositional Defiant Disorder, Conduct Disorder, Disruptive Behavior Disorder, Post Traumatic Stress Disorder, Depression, Learning and Communication disorders.

Medication. Children referred for treatment are typically using various psychotropic medications to modify mood, behavior and affect. In conjunction with a psychiatric consultation, we often recommend a reduction or termination of such medication, when appropriate. This allows the child to participate more completely and genuinely on behavioral and emotional levels. The need for medication is frequently reevaluated.

PARENT ASSESSMENT

The primary caregivers and custodians are foster or adoptive parents in most cases because the child was previously separated from the biological parents due to either abandonment or legal action by child protective services (abuse, neglect).

Children remaining with biological parents may also present with attachment disorders as a result of medical conditions (premature birth, prolonged hospitalization after birth), maternal depression, or other circumstances which cause a break in the infant-mother bond.

The parents' current psychosocial functioning, marital relationship, family-of-origin backgrounds, and own attachment histories, are assessed to determine their ability to provide for the special needs of the child. Parents complete family-of-origin questionnaires, psychodiagnostic evaluations, and clinical interviews.

FAMILY SYSTEMS ASSESSMENT

Three basic family systems principles provide the foundation for family assessment: context, circularity, and reciprocity. It is necessary to understand the individual within the context in which he or she functions. Rather than a traditional linear model, the family systems approach focuses on ongoing, circular interactions, in which each family member's behavior serves as both a response and trigger.

Reciprocity refers to the effect family members have on one another; reciprocal patterns of interactions maintain the system and symptoms. Thus, family assessment focuses primarily on identifying relationship patterns that cause and maintain dysfunction and stress.

Specific aspects of family functioning which are assessed include: roles, structure (boundaries, power and control, coalitions and alignments, subsystems), sibling patterns, resiliency, family-community interaction, destabilizing events (e.g., divorce, birth, death, loss of job), and developmental stages and pressures (Levy, 1983, 1984, 1987; Minuchin, 1974; Minuchin and Fishman, 1981).

Assessment is accomplished by clinical interview, review of prior records, and observation of dynamics and interaction during therapy sessions.

A CASE EXAMPLE: CHRIS

Chris is a twelve year old young man who came to Evergreen for treatment with his adoptive parents.

The following Attachment Symptoms checklist was filled out by his parents. Also included is a more comprehensive explanation of each of the specific symptoms.

ATTACHMENT SYMPTOMS

CHILD'S NAME:_____   DATE:_____

Please place a mark in the appropriate column for each symptom as it pertains to your child. On a separate sheet of paper, please give a brief description of your child's behavior regarding each of the symptoms checked as moderate or severe.

Symptoms	None	Moderate	Severe
1. Superficially engaging and "charming"		X	
2. Lack of eye contact on parental terms			X
3. Indiscriminately affectionate with strangers		X	
4. Not affectionate on parents' terms (not cuddly)			X
5. Destructive to self, others and material things (accident prone)			X
6. Cruel to animals		X	
7. Stealing			X
8. Lying about the obvious (crazy lying)			X
9. No impulse controls (frequently acts hyperactive)			X
10. Learning lags			X
11. Lack of cause and effect thinking			X
12. Lack of conscience			X
13. Abnormal eating patterns		X	
14. Poor peer relationships			X
15. Preoccupation with fire		X	
16. Persistent nonsense questions and incessant chatter			X
17. Inappropriately demanding and clingy		X	
18. Abnormal speech patterns		X	
19. Sexual acting out		X	

1. When Chris meets people on his terms (people to whom we didn't introduce him to) he is friendly and talkative. It is only after he gets to know someone does he let his hair down and start to act like "You can't make me do it."

2. Whenever his behavior is unacceptable and we tell him so down goes the head to avoid eye contact. We have to tell him to look at us to achieve contact.

3. When we first adopted him we would walk down the street and he would say hello to almost everyone walking down the street. But if we would meet someone he knew he would act shy when they said hello and "how are you?" to him. Even now when we have guests in the house he will go and hide around the corner or act very immature.

4. If we sit down next to him and try to put our arm around him when he was younger, he would try to get away. He would love to wrestle with me as long as he gave it to me but if I would hold onto his leg or arm for just a second he would scream. We still try to give the boys a goodnight kiss. Many times he hides his head under the covers. If you ask him about a kiss he says no.

5. When he walks or runs he many times falls down. He is always pushing or bumping into his brother if not restraining him, then will way, "It was an accident." He used to turn over furniture and make the pictures on the wall crooked when he was angry. He has drawn all over the bottom of the bunk bed (he sleeps on the bottom). When he is restricted in his room he slowly picks at the "bamboo" type shade. There is now about a five by five inch hole on one side.

6. Our dog was nine years old when we adopted Chris. She never nipped at anyone. A few days with Chris trying to restrain her and she nipped at him. Elizabeth's mother has dogs and one of them didn't like Chris much soon after we arrived for a visit. He just will not let them go where they want to. We have a new dog who is too big and spunky for Chris to restrain him but lately we have found the dog's bones hidden in strange places that a dog could not reach, i.e., on Chris' desk.

7. Chris was caught shoplifting about two years ago. At Easter he steals the candy out of other family members' baskets. He has gone through Elizabeth's purse many times taking some money and candy. He stole $20.00 from a friend's sister's bedroom. He has stolen two of my pocket knives. Allen locks up his coin collection, money and pocket knives. Elizabeth now hides her purse. At Easter the girls locked up their Easter baskets in their rooms.

8. Chris' lying is best exemplified by his, "I didn't take it." Allen found one of his knives under Chris' mattress. He left it there and called in Chris, again asking Chris about the whereabouts of the knife. Then Allen showed him the knife and said, "I know my other knife is in

here. You won't get out of here until I get it back." Chris denied he had it and even cried in protest. Twenty minutes later it was on the pillow on Allen's side of the bed. When Chris was asked where he hid the knife, he said, "I didn't hide it. I came into your room and found it between those books. Dad misplace it there." When he steals candy he comes downstairs with chocolate on his face and denies he has been eating candy. He also leaves the candy papers lying around.

9. I would not say he is hyperactive; however, he acts on his impulse and doesn't think of the consequences. When he wants to do something he wants it now, not a minute later. When asked to do certain chores he has a history of refusing right away and putting up a big fuss even though he knows he is going to have to do it anyway (we always follow through).

10. At the end of first grade he was already two or three months behind others. Our trying to help him at home made him go into a rage at times. He is now fifth grade and still struggles with school at times. Also we started him late and he could have been in sixth grade if we had started him at the "normal" time.

11. Absolutely. When playing chess his father can use the same moves to beat him time and time again (his school teacher runs the Chess Club and made the same observation). Presently he is staying out too late. If he stays out too late he is restricted the next day to the house. So the pattern lately is: Stays out late - restricted - stays out late - restricted, etc. He has never learned from past mistakes.

12. It seems he doesn't care who he hurts, even his brother. Chris will steal from him. In church he sits with the ugliest face on or squirming all around like a four year old but when he goes up for the children's sermon, he is a little angel. At times I've noted him giving someone the finger in church (his dad or is he trying to get me angry?)

13. He eats slowly or he gulps his food down. He picks at his meat (says he doesn't like any kind of fat, yet loads on the salami). He used to like spaghetti, then all of a sudden he would not eat the sauce. Now he is starting to eat the sauce again. The same with chicken - he used to like it now picks at it.

14. His best friends are kids three or four years younger than he is. When he plays with others, we have heard him bossing them, telling them how the game is to be played, as if he is the expert. In turn when things don't go his way he makes up new rules as to disallow this or that. In no time at all people get tired of his bossing and he has no friends. His teachers have always commented on his lack of friends. Last year's teacher said he picks the "worst" type of friends.

15. We have found a hidden pack of matches in his room. One year ago he was suspended from school for two days for being in the bathroom

trying to set a roll of toilet paper on fire. At Advent time he wasn't to be the one to light the Advent candles and blow them out. Allen has confronted him about burning paper in the basement wood stove. We have also noticed that his coat is singed a bit.

16. This usually happens after he is being punished. He can't watch TV so he decides to talk to Mom or Dad asking the silliest questions. When he was younger he would see me sawing wood and ask, "What are you doing?", then come back and ask the same question. He will see a picture in the paper and ask you what is going on. When he couldn't read, I would read him the caption but then he would say, "No, this and that happened." Once he gets started making a noise that bothers people he doesn't stop. For the first years after we adopted him, he would sit at the dinner table and go, "Please pass the, the, the." He usually wanted ketchup or some item he could easily say but acted as if he had forgotten what it was.

17. Demanding in the sense that when he wants to do something he usually asks for permission (I will give him credit for that) but if the answer is no, then he begins his pouting and talking back. He is worse with his sisters. He will call them, "Bitch," when they have to babysit him, even though he should know that there will be a restriction facing him when we get home. When we have company around he can become clingy. Going to the doctor he can be clingy or any new situations that come along.

18. He talked like a baby from the day we got him and this continued for years. He also had a hard time expressing himself and even joining in family conversations. He now joins in but at times what he says is not very logical or we are not sure where he is coming from. His speech is clear however.

19. When we first adopted him he touched his genitals continually. We told him if he wanted to do that he could do it in his room but not in front of us. After a while when he did it while watching TV, we felt he should have known the rules by then so we would send him off to his room. He went off yelling and screaming. At night time and morning he used to masturbate. Either he is not doing it anymore or he is more discreet now for we do not see him doing it and do not have to remind him to do it in private. More often than we liked it we found him laying on and rubbing himself on his brother when they took a bath together. Now he doesn't touch his genitals as he watches TV anymore but plays with his hair or sucks on his fingers.

RESOURCES

Ainsworth, M.D.S., & Wittig, B.A. (1969). Attachment and exploratory behavior of one-year-olds in a strange situation. In B.M. Foss (Ed.), *Determinants of Infant Behaviour*(Vol. 4). London: Methuen; New York: Barnes and Noble.

Ainsworth, M.D.S., Blehar, M.C., Waters, E., & Wall, S. (1978). *Patterns of Attachment:A Psychological Study of the Strange Situation*. Hillsdale, NJ: Erlbaum.

Bath, H. (1994). The physical restraint of children: Is it therapeutic. *American Journal of Orthopsychiatry*, 64, 40-49.

Biringen, Z. (1994). Attachment theory and research: Application to clinical practice, *American Journal of Orthopsychiatry*, 64, 404-420.

Bowlby, J. (1951). *Maternal Care and Mental Health*, Geneva: World Health Organization; London:Her Majesty's Stationery Office; New York: Columbia University Press. Abridged version: *Child Care and the Growth of Love* (2nd edition, 1965) Harmondsworth: Penguin.

Bowlby, J. (1958). The nature of the child's tie to his mother, *International Journal of Psycho-Analysis*, 39, 350-373.

Bowlby, J. (1969). *Attachment and Loss: Vol. 1. Attachment*. New York: Basic Books.

Bowlby, J. (1973). *Attachment and Loss: Vol. 2. Separation Anxiety and Anger*. New York: Basic Books.

Bowlby, J. (1977a). The making and breaking of affectional bonds: I. Aeitology and psychopathology in the light of attachment theory. *British Journal of Psychiatry*, 130, 201-210.

Bowlby, J. (1980). *Attachment and Loss: Vol. 3. Loss, Sadness, and Depression*. New York: Basic Books.

Bowlby, J. (1988), *A Secure Base*. New York: Basic Books.

Cadoret, R.J., & Cain, C. (1980). Sex differences in predictors of antisocial behavior in adoptees. *Archives of General Psychiatry*, 37, 1171-1175.

Children's Defense Fund, (1994). *The State of America's Children*. Washington, DC: Author.

Cicchetti, D., & Carlson, V. (1989). *Handbook of Child Maltreatment: Clinical and Theoretical Perspectives*(pp. 432-463), New York: Cambridge University Press.

Cline, F. (1992). *Hope For High Risk and Rage Filled Children: Reactive Attachment Disorder Theory and Instrusive Therapy*. Evergreen, Colorado: EC Publications.

Cline, F. (1995). *Conscienceless Acts: Societal Mayhem*. Golden Colorado: Love and Logic Press.

Cohn, D.A., Silver, D.H., Cowan, C.P., Cowan, P.A. & Pearson, J. (1992), Working models of childhood attachment and couple relationships. *Journal of Family Issues*, 13, 432-449.

Crittendon, P. (1985). Maltreated infants: Vulnerability and resilience, *Journal of Child Psychology and Psychiatry*, 26, 85-96.

De-John, M.L. (1992). Attachment, individualation, and risk of suicide in late adolescence. *Journal of Youth and Adolescence, 21, 357-373*.

Delaney, R.J. & Kunstal, R. (1993). *Troubled Transplants: Unconventional Strategies for Helping Disturbed Foster and Adoptive Children*. US: National Child Welfare Center, University of Southern Maine.

Egelund, B., & Sroufe, L.A. (1981a). Attachment and early maltreatment. *Child Development, 52, 44-52*.

Egelund, B., & Sroufe, L.A., (1981b). Developmental sequelae of maltreatment in infancy. In R. Rizley & D. Cicchetti (Eds.), *Developmental Perspectives on Child Maltreatment*(pp. 77-92). San Francisco: Jossey-Bass.

Feeney, J.A., & Noller, P. (1990). Attachment styles as a predictor of adult romantic relationships. *Journal of Personality and Social Psychology*, 58, 281-291.

Grossman, K.E., & Grossman, K. (1990). The wider concept of attachment in cross-cultural research. *Human Development*. 21, 31-47.

Harlow, H.F. (1958). The nature of love. *American Psychologist*, 13, 673-685.

Hecht, D.T. (1984). Loneliness and attachment patterns in young adults. *Journal of Clinical Psychology*, 40(1).

Hendrick, C., & Hendrick. S. (1989). Research on love: Does it measure up? *Journal of Personality and Social Psychology*, 56, 784-794.

Hinde, R. A., & Stevenson-Hinde, J. (1990) Attachment: Biological, cultural and individual disiderata. *Human Development*, 33, 62-72.

Jacobson, J. L., & Wille, D.E. (1986). The influence of attachment pattern on developmental changes in peer interaction from the toddler to the preschool period. *Child Development*, 57, 338-347.

Karen, R. (1994). *Becoming Attached*. New York: Warner Books.

Koback, R. & Hazan, C. (1991). Attachment in marriage: Effects of security and accuracy of working models. *Journal of Personality and Social Psychology*, 60, 861-869.

Levy, T. (1983). Practical issues and applications in family therapy. In P. Keller and L. Ritt (Eds.) *Innovations in Clinical Practice: A Source Book, (Vol. 2)*. Sarasota, FL: Professional Resource Exchange.

Levy, T. (1984). Brief family therapy: clinical assumptions and techniques. In P. Keller and L. Ritt (Eds.) *Innovations in Clinical Practice: A Source Book, (Vol. 3)*. Sarasota, FL: Professional Resource Exchange.

Levy, T. (1987), Brief family therapy; clinical assumptions and techniques. In P. Keller and L. Ritt (Eds.) *Innovations in Clinical Practice: A Source Book, (Vol. 6)*. Sarasota, FL: Professional Resource Exchange.

Lorenz, K. (1965). *The Evaluation and Modification of Behavior*. Chicago: University of Chicago Press.

Lyddon, W.J., Bradford, E. & Nelson, J.P. (1993) Assessing adolescent and adult attachment: A review of current self-report measures. *Journal of Counseling and Development*, 71, 390-395.

MacDonald, K. (1985). Early experience, relative plasticity and social development. *Developmental Review*, 5, 99-121.

Main, M., & Cassidy, J., (1988). Categories of response with the parent at age six: Predicted from infant attachment classifications and stable over a one-month period. *Developmental Psychology*, 24, 415-426.

Main, M., & Hesse, E. (1990). Lack of resolution of mourning in adulthood and its relationship to infant disorganization: Some speculations regarding casual mechanisms. In M. Greenberg, D. Cicchetti, & M. Cummings (Eds.), *Attachment in the Preschool Years: Theory, Research, and Intervention*(pp. 1610182). Chicago: University of Chicago Press.

Main, M. & Solomon, J. (1990). Procedures for identifying infants as disorganized/disoriented during the Ainsworth Strange Situation. In M. Greenberg, D. Cicchetti, & N. Cummings (Eds.), *Attachment in the Preschool Years: Theory, Research, and Intervention*(pp. 121-160), Chicago: University of Chicago Press.

Marshall, W.L., Seidman, B., & Check, J.V. (1991). *Intimacy and loneliness in sex offenders and nonoffender males*. Unpublished data.

Marshall, W.L., Hudson, S.M., & Hodkinson, S. (1993). The importance of attachment bonds in the development of juvenile sex offending. In H.E. Barbaree, W.L. Marshall, & S.M. Hudson (Eds.). *The Juvenile Sex Offender* (pp. 164-181). New York: Guilford Press.

McKelvey, C.A., & Stevens, JE. (1994). *Adoption Crisis*. Golden, Colorado: Fulcrum Publishing.

Minuchin, S. (1974). *Families and Family Therapy*. Cambridge: Harvard University Press.

Minuchin, S. & Fishman, C.H. (1981) *Family Therapy Techniques*. Cambridge: Harvard University Press.

Paterson, R.J., & Moran, G. (1988). Attachment theory, personality development, and psychotherapy. *Clinical Psychology Review*, 8, 611-636.

Radke-Yarrow, M. Cummings, E.M., Kuczynski, L., & Chapman, M. (1985). Patterns of attachment in two- and three-years-olds in normal families and families with parental depression, *Child Development*, 56, 884-893.

Sroufe, L.A. (1983). Infant-caregiver attachment and patterns of adaptation in preschool: The roots of maladaptation and competence. In M. Perlmutter (Ed.), *Minnesota Symposium on Child Psychology* (Vol. 16)(pp. 41-83). Hillsdale, NJ: Erlbaum.

Sroufe, L.A., Schork, E., Frosso, M., Lawroski, N., & LaFreniere, P. (1984). The role of affect in social competence. In C.E. Izard, J. Kagan, & R.B. Zajonc (Eds.). *Emotions, Cognitions, and Behavior* (pp. 289-319). Cambridge, England: Cambridge University Press.

Verny, T., and Kelly, J. (1981). *Secret Life of the Unborn Child.* New York: Dell.

Verrier, N., (1993) *Primal Wound.* Baltimore, MD: Gateway Press, Inc.

Wartner, U.G. (1986). *Attachment In Infancy and At Age Six, and Children's Self-concept: A Follow-up of a German Longitudinal Study,* Doctoral Dissertation. University of Virginia.

3

Insight Into Attachment

Connell Watkins, ACSW

ATTACHMENT.

You can't see it with your eyes. You can't feel it with your hands. It has no distinct sound or smell, and yet it is a fundamental part of our existence as human beings. Its existence or absence is experienced by us through all our senses: vision, smell, touch, sound, movement.

Attachment is the foundation of our ability to love, feel compassion, and empathy. It is how we sustain nurturing, form long term relationships with other humans and with our world.

Attachment is as real a factor in our lives as the ozone layer is in our environment. Like the ozone layer, we often minimize or forget it's importance until we experience the signs and symptoms of it not being there.

In this chapter, I define attachment as a result of a bonding process that occurs between human beings. It is the basis for our ability to form attachment on the most basic levels; where our ability to form attachment is imprinted and mapped out during the in-utero experience and the first two years of life.

This "basic programming" follows a cycle first presented by Dr. Foster Cline, founder of the Youth Behavior Program (the predecessor to The Attachment Center at Evergreen). This diagram exemplifies the interaction patterns that take place thousands of times between the human infant and its primary caretaker. The uninterruped repetition of this cycle, from the ages of 0 to 26 months is a crucial factor in the human infant's development of the first and primary attachment.

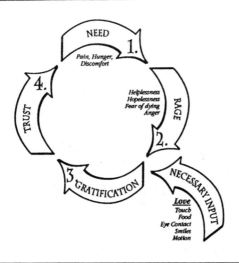

Figure 1. First Year of Life Cycle (F. Cline, 1992)

(Hope for High Risk and Rage Filled Children, Dr. Foster Cline, 1994)

The quality of this attachment will later be the foundation for a lifetime of attachments; if an infant does not make this primary attachment, or the attachment is broken in some way, the effects last the individual's entire life. It is through this primary attachment that the child's ability to have close, long term, sustaining relationships throughout his/her life is determined. The quality and the character of the infant's attachment varies, perhaps, as much as handwoven material, whether it be burlap, cotton, silk, or wool. Mary Ainsworth, through her work with pioneer John Bowlby and her research, was to differentiate five different dimensions of attachment:

- Secure Attachment
- Ambivalent Attachment
- Anxious Attachment
- Avoidant Attachment
- Disturbed Attachment[1]

---

[1] Ainsworth, M., et all, (1978) Patterns of Attachment: A Psychological Study of the Strange Situation. Erlbaum Association, Hillsdale, NJ.

THE ELUSIVE BOND

The elusive bond is referred to by many therapists in the area of attachment as the "Fantasy Bond." This occurs when children who have no conscious memory of their birth parents continue to have a longing to find their birth parents with the hope, dream, or fantasy that -- if their birth mother or father knew where they were, they would come for them. Out of this sense of longing, they develop a belief that they must save their love for their "real" momma, the mom who gave birth to them. This tendency of children to withhold their love, at times, can increase their chances of continuing to disrupt (fail) in their adoptive or foster placements, exasperating their feelings of abandonment and reaffirming their belief that only their birth parents could really love them. Even children who have memories of severe abuse and neglect, when in the care of their birth parents will often, later, deny this experience and fantasize a feeling of close connectedness with their birth parents. This is because they have deeply internalized their experiences of abuse, neglect, and abandonment as being their fault because there was something wrong with them. They fantasize that, if they can go back and act differently, they can then elicit the love from their birth parents that they feel is there for them.

Children have the ability to attach on any level, even a traumatized level. Those who have had the experience of being severely traumatized during the first two to three years of their existence, including (some experts believe) the in-utero experience, are often referred to as "unattached." These are children described as having the following signs and symptoms:

1. Approach strangers easily without apprehension.
2. Show a lack of impulse control and often seem hyperactive.
3. Chronic and constant control issues with their mother and other authority figures. This includes an inability to accept boundaries.
4. Primary process lying.
5. Destructive to material things and self. This includes firesetting.
6. Aggressive, angry, and hurtful with animals and children younger than themselves.
7. An inability to stay in long term relationships with peers.
8. Often diagnosed as having learning disabilities, speech problems, and motor coordination difficulties.
9. Constant need for attention and structure; i.e.: incessant talking, clingy and demanding behavior, and having a hard time "settling".
10 Problems with sustaining eye contact and accepting affection on the parent's terms. They are often described as "tactile defensive" and yet, will seek touch in inappropriate ways on their own terms.

11. Issues with food, including hoarding and gorging.

12. The appearance of normalcy with people they aren't close to; often leading to triangulation of the adults; i.e., teachers, parents, therapists.

These children will often perform differently for teachers and professionals than they do on a regular basis in their home environment. Therefore, the parents often seem unreasonable, angry, and intolerant by the time they seek professional help.

13. Lack of remorse, conscience, and acceptance of responsibility for behavior. The child tends to blame others for what has happened and, in extreme cases makes false accusations of abuse.

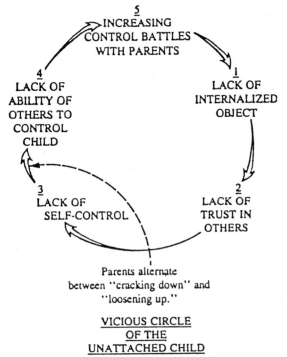

THE VICIOUS CIRCLE OF THE UNATTACHED

5
INCREASING CONTROL BATTLES WITH PARENTS

1
LACK OF INTERNALIZED OBJECT

4
LACK OF ABILITY OF OTHERS TO CONTROL CHILD

2
LACK OF TRUST IN OTHERS

3
LACK OF SELF-CONTROL

Parents alternate between "cracking down" and "loosening up."

VICIOUS CIRCLE OF THE UNATTACHED CHILD

Dr. Foster Cline's description of the dynamics of the "Vicious Circle of the Unattached Child", (above) best shows the parent-child interaction patterns that occur when a child has been severely traumatized by not bonding with their parents.

The human infant's attachment to its primary caretaker may be put at risk by any event that interrupts the infant's bonding cycle with that primary caretaker for a prolonged period of time. This includes any interruptions that the infant might experience over a period of time in its sleeping or eating patterns, such as: severe allergies, asthma, undiagnosed and/or unrelieved pain (i.e., medical intervention and inner ear infections). A break in the bonding cycle is also caused by changes in primary caretakers, maternal depression, early abuse, neglect, and abandonment. The younger the infant when the break occurs, the greater the trauma. Prolonged breaks during the first year of life can cause learning disabilities. Repetitive abuse, neglect, and abandonment in the first year of life can later result in the manifestation of severe aggressive behaviors, including the harming and killing of animals.

In other words, the more helpless and hopeless the infant is when the trauma occurs, the more devastating the later effects of that trauma on the child's life. It is believed that the disruption in the child's bonding cycle during the first year of life can often cause a disruption in the development of the neurological pathways, thereby causing the before mentioned learning disabilities, as well as other associated problems.

RAGE REACTION

When an infant has a rage reaction (rageful crying spell), they are experiencing their only way of communicating to their environment that they have a need that needs to be met. Therefore, infantile rage is a combination of helplessness, hopelessness, and the terror of dying.

When the bonding cycle is broken, and is not resumed in a corrective way, the child internalizes an experience of rage, instead of trust. From that moment on, until there is a positive resolution of the break in the cycle, all of the child's psychological energy becomes organized around sustaining and maintaining deeply internalized rage. This means the child has mistrust for his environment. This is the crucial point, because the child's ability to relate to his outside environment and primary caretakers changes significantly. It has been observed in infants who have experienced this break, that they become delayed in their developmental milestones. "Jenny's" case is an example of this:

JENNY

Jenny, a two-month-old infant, had experienced five different changes in her primary caretaker, including another adoptive placement prior to her being placed with her current adoptive family. At this time, Jenny was described as being a "good baby," because she slept most of the time and seldom cried. She would only wake to eat. Jenny liked being held and touched, as long as there was no eye contact between her and her mother. As the weeks went by, Jenny became more developmentally delayed in her ability to reach and grasp objects, or to even hold up her head and move it from side to side.

Her mother, began to realize that Jenny had attachment issues, so she insisted on always being the one to feed her, hold her, and rock her. When Jenny's mother would give her the bottle, her mother insisted on eye contact before she would let Jenny take the nipple into her mouth. It was noted that as soon as Jenny would start sucking on the nipple, she would look away from her mother and not again resume eye contact of her own accord. At one point, when the mother held Jenny, insisting on eye contact, the baby went into a full blown rage reaction. The only time Jenny would have a rage reaction was when mom would insist on eye contact.

In all, it took five months for Jenny to finally start bonding with her new adoptive mother. At this point, her eye contact with her mother was no longer an issue; and whenever she had a need or felt discomfort, she would go into a rage. At seven months old, Jenny was now showing the signs of an infant that was bonding to her mother. Within a few days, in the weeks following this time, she proceded to catch up with her chronological age group on her developmental milestones and she later surpassed her chronological age group.

GRATIFICATION

Gratification of the human infant needs to occur and this important need involves five factors: eye contact, touch, vestibular movement, smiles, and lactose. There have been many studies, including the Harlow studies, where one of these factors is isolated, showing the essential nature of all five factors in relationship to the infant's need for gratification. A typical scenario, between an infant and his mother, would be the following:

The mother will pick up her crying infant and she is smiling and rocking at the time she proceeds to give the baby food. As the infant begins to suck on the nipple, the infant is gazing up into the mother's eyes. It is as if the baby is drinking in her very essence. The sucking response, along with the eye contact and rocking, are essential interactive factors in the bonding process. It is no accident, then, that children who have had a traumatized attachment often do not even develop a sucking response. If they do, they are often unable to maintain eye contact in the arms of their mother at the same time they are sucking a bottle. It is through this bonding cycle the child learns that touch, eye contact, smiles, and movement, along with food, is associated with well being and love. Later, as a child grows, these elements continue to be an important part of the way the child relates to the people he loves.

On the other hand, children with traumatized attachment are unable to sustain eye contact for long periods of time, along with touch and closeness. They, in fact, are often described as "tactile defensive." Although, these children seek touch, it is often inappropriate and hurtful.

TRUST

Through the repetition of the above cycle, thousands of times, the child develops an experience of trusting not only his primary caretakers, but the world in general. The completion of this cycle during the first year of life, therefore, leads to the child learning that when the child needs help and is vulnerable, they can go to someone and have their needs met. When this cycle has been broken, the child learns the opposite. The child who never learns basic trust then organizes his/her behavior around the feeling that they can never ever give up control, because if they do, things will not work out well.

An example is a young infant girl. Following a difficult delivery that was prolonged and exhausting for mother and baby, this infant was carefully, but tentatively, held by her father. Seeing the anxiety on the young father's face, a nurse reassured the father, saying, "She looks fragile, but she won't break." The infant's mother had to remain in the hospital because of medical complications and severe exhaustion from the hours of prolonged labor. A great aunt of the child moved into the home to care for the infant until her mother could regain her physical strength. The baby appeared responsive to the physical care provided by the aunt and her father during the first month of her life.

When the child was one month old her mother was able to resume care of her. But the baby developed colic and was inconsolable for hours at a time during the next three months. At five months of age, she was no longer being fed with a bottle. She was already on baby food and drinking out of a cup. At seven months, the baby was so mobile that the parents needed to keep her in a playpen for periods of time to keep her from crawling aimlessly away. At one point, the parents found the playpen carefully dismantled. The child was crawling away.

As the girl grew into a toddler, she displayed no sense of physical boundaries and often was found wandering blocks away from her home. Her parents tried many things, including a large fence to keep their child home. Even then, the mother received calls reporting her daughter swimming in the town fountain, or having gotten out anyway. They discovered the little girl had dug under the fence to tunnel away. Over time the interactions between mother and child became permeated with anger and conflict. The girl grew more and more oppositional toward her mother. At one point, the mother turned to her adolescent daughter and said,

"Your father can do no wrong and I can do no right." Her mother referred to the uncommon affinity her daughter had always felt towards her father, but not her mother.

Later, in recalling happy moments in her childhood, the girl always remembered a time that she spent, waiting to meet her dad at a certain spot in the path as he walked home from work each day. She also remembered happy moments she had as a young girl taking long morning walks with her father.

Only as an adult could the child, now a young woman, come to the realization that all her life she'd been searching for a real mother, not recognizing that her mother was there all along. At one point, this young woman was overwhelmed with feelings of never having been loved by her mother, even though she knew, clearly, that her parents had always loved her and provided well for her. Looking at this case, it became probable that the girl had suffered greatly because of: the trauma of a stressful birth; the initial one month separation from her mother after that traumatic birth; and separation from her initial primary caregiver (her great aunt) after the first month. These "breaks" had taken a toll -- leaving her, as an infant and a child, chronically angry at her mother. She never was able to experience the intimacy and joy of a reciprocal relationship with her mother.

Only now, after Thomas R. Verny's book, The Secret of the Unborn Child,[2] can therapists see how the slightest deviation from the normal course of a child's birth and the initial mother-child bonding can have long term effects on the child's ability to be responsive and reciprocal with the primary caregiver. In this case it appears the series of breaks led to a lifetime pattern of chronic angry relationships with other adults.

In light of this revelation, when we look at children who've experienced early neglect, abuse, and abandonment repeatedly in the first two years of life, we have a better appreciation of the extent of the trauma that interrupts and disturbs the process that leads to normal personality development.

ANNA

"Anna" was diagnosed with kidney failure at the age of two and found to be in need of surgery. The toddler was to be flown from her native country to the United States for the surgery. Prior to this time, her mother had placed her in an orphanage, so that Anna would receive the nutrition she needed to make the necessary weight gain for the surgery. When

---

[2] Verney, T. (1981) The Secret Life of the Unborn Child, Summit Books, New York.

sent to the orphanage, Anna was suffering from severe malnutrition and starvation. When Anna's kidney condition was detected, she was not physically strong enough to have the surgery. She stayed several months in the orphanage prior to being flown to the United States. At two and one-half years of age, she weighed a mere 20 pounds and was severely emaciated.

Two to three days prior to her surgery, her American host family interacted with her and started bonding with her. Following her surgery, Anna went home with the host family and they became her primary caretakers, nursing her back to health.

During this initial period, Anna and her host family became very close. Anna made great strides in toning and catching up in her developmental milestones. Shortly after recuperation from her surgery, she began to walk, talk, and recite nursery rhymes in a language that had been, previously, foreign to her. She learned her nursery rhymes and her ABC's within a relatively short time. The bond between Anna and the family was very strong.

The family established communications with Anna's birth mother and, eventually, they received permission from Anna's mother to adopt her. However, this did not occur right away.

Anna had to return several times to the orphanage in her own country before she was allowed to return to her host family for adoption. Anna's new mother later reported that the last time Anna was sent back to the orphanage was the most difficult for her. Prior to sending her back to the orphanage, the adoptive family made a tape of Anna and her new family singing and reciting nursery rhymes and doing ABC's. This tape recording had all the voices of her family and recorded all the exciting things she had learned during her time in America. The family requested this tape recording be played over and over for Anna in the orphanage during the six week period she needed to remain there.

Even though Anna had this tape played frequently for her, and her parents called her every day, the child became more and more lethargic and withdrawn. Finally, she was barely responsive at all during the phone calls. Anna's country finally allowed her to legally leave and be adopted by her host family, and she returned to the family that had cared for her before, during, and after kidney surgery.

However, the child that returned was no longer the spontaneous, joyful, and reciprocal one who had left. Now Anna was demanding, controlling, seemingly insatiable for attention, and non-reciprocal. She talked incessantly, asking questions and constantly demanded adult attention. After this happened, her adoptive mother was taught how to hold her, insist on eye contact, and allow her to rage in her mother's arms. Following several "holding-time" sessions,[3] Anna became much more loving, reciprocal and calm. The difference in her demeanor and her relationships with other family members was remarkable. She continued, however, to have problems with learning, particularly with reading. Her mother, a former teacher, was baffled at her child's resistance to learning her colors and how to read. She remembered Anna as learning quickly and early when she was younger. A therapist evaluating Anna's learning, was able to determine Anna did know her colors, but was refusing to identify them.

A number of years later, in a discussion with an attachment therapist, the mother mentioned the audio tape that she had made for Anna that had been played over and over in the orphanage. Upon a suggestion, the mother was able to find the tape and, holding Anna, played it for her. Within seconds, Anna began to cry and sob uncontrollably. Between her sobs, she asked, "Why did you leave me over and over again?" As the mother held her and rocked her, mother and child cried together over the heartbreaking trauma from their earlier repeated separations from each other.

A few days later, Anna started to learn to read. Even though Anna had been resistant to learning to read, she now asked her mother, "Mom, I want you to help me with my reading."

The experience that Anna and her family had is explained in John Bowlby's book, Loss, Sadness, and Depression. In the book he explores the concept that children who experience a temporary, but physical, separation from their mother, during the first five years of life, go through a bereavement that is not psychologically resolved.[4] Later in life this "break" can result in psychiatric illness, Bowlby says. At one point in Loss, Sadness and Depression, Bowlby gives this example:

"In 1936, Jerrauld reported on two patients suffering from depression. One of them, he concluded, had been 'starved of love' as a child; the other had been sent to a residential nursery and had only returned home when he was three years old. Each showed intense ambivalence toward any person who they loved, a condition which Jerrauld believed could be traced to the early experience.

In the second case, he speaks of both a fixation on the mother and an inability to forgive her for the separation." (Bowlby, 1969)

Breaks in the bonding cycle Bowlby is discussing occur for prolonged periods of time and it's conceivable that the younger the child is at the time of the break, the more they internalize their terror -- an actual fear of physical death, which later changes the quality of their life physically,

---

[3] See Welch, M. Holding Time (1988) Simon & Schuster, New York.
[4] Bowlby, J. Loss, Sadness and Depression, (1969) Basic Books, New York.

emotionally, spiritually, and psychologically. It has been the experience of professionals working with children with severe attachment issues that the child often has the following experiences:

- Deep feelings of uncontrollable anger and rage toward maternal figures.
- A belief that the mother they have now is a bad mother and is, in some way, abusive to them.
- They have their needs and their wants confused and react to limit setting as if they are being deprived of their needs.
- Spiritually, they often identify with the devil and they are, psychologically, not capable of experiencing love, but are fully capable of hate. They sometimes believe the devil is inside of them or that they are the devils child.
- The child is physically rigid and tactile defensive when being held or hugged on the parent's terms. It is as if the child were frozen in terror.

PARENTING TECHNIQUES THAT ENHANCE THE BONDING

Any parenting technique which includes touch, eye contact, smiles, pizazz (movement), along with physical nurturance, will enhance bonding. For parents to do this, it is essential they take good care of themselves, specifically in their relationship to their child with attachment problems. There is a tendency, even among highly trained therapeutic parents, to put the child's needs first because of the child's profound history of severe abuse and abandonment. There are countless books on parenting that actually encourage this. There are strong indications, however, that parents that constantly are able to take good care of themselves are far more effective in their nurturing and as role models for the disturbed child.

When working with the attachment disordered child, attachment therapists employ several therapeutic techniques:

I: REGRESSIVE DEVELOPMENTAL PARENTING

Psychodynamically, children with traumatized attachments are often emotionally fixated at ages far younger than their chronological years. For example, a nine-year-old boy may fluctuate between, emotionally, the ages of two and five. This means, in terms of the developmental tasks, he has not gone beyond five. In most cases, these children will fluctuate between two and three. Therefore, a parenting technique developed at The Attachment Center at Evergreen is called Regressive Developmental Parenting. It has been very effective. Under a therapist's direction, and in accordance with a treatment plan, therapeutic parents will structure the child's life in the home in such a way that he is only allowed to do, and is expected to do, the psycho-social, emotional tasks of a child of a much younger chronological age.

For instance -- Joey is ten, but is fixated, emotionally, at two. So, for specified periods of time he is encouraged to participate in two-year-old activities and is given the structure and limits of a two year old. Once he masters the developmental tasks of two, there will be a celebration party (birthday), at which time it is decided that his "emotional heart" is now three. In the course of the next two years, Joey will have many "birthday celebrations" -- until he catches up to his chronological age. In some cases, the child may continue at chronological age while in public school. In other cases, the child will be kept home and "home-schooled" so there is more latitude in terms of his performance during the reparenting phase. The advantages of this technique are:

1. There are lots of control issues between the parent and child that no longer occur because the child is not expected to handle activities and responsibilities that he is not, emotionally, capable of handling at this point.

2. The child is allowed to regress to a time in their lives they have missed because of the trauma. In essence, this parenting experience allows the child to have part of the child's childhood back, but without the trauma.

3. When this parenting technique is done right, the child is insured a very high level of nurturance and structure that he needs, thereby enhancing and rapidly facilitating, the bonding process with the primary caretakers.

II. STEEL BOX WITH VELVET LINING

The overall philosophy of parenting children with attachment disorder by the parents at the Attachment Center is typified by the analogy of a steel box with velvet lining. The "steel box" is the structure they need to win in their interactions with parental figures and the "velvet lining" is the constant nurturance that must always be available, unconditionally.

To do this, the rules of control issues must be carefully followed. These rules include the following:

1. Avoid all control issues, if you can. No one wants to be into control issues with the people they love.

2. Win. If we expect our children, especially attachment disordered children, to want to internalize us or to look at us as role models, they need to see someone they know is a winner. Because of this, number 3 is particularly important.

3. The parents need to be sure they are the ones that have taken the control issue and it is one on which they can win.

Prolonged lose-lose interactions between parent and child prevents bonding. Therefore, staying out of control issues takes a lot of creativity and sometimes, professional involvement and support. Parents are encouraged to stay out of all issues that don't fall under the criteria of: "respectful, responsible, and fun to be around behavior" while the child is at home or around the parents. For instance, they are encouraged to stay out of food, personal hygiene and school issues. An example:

TONY

Tony is flunking third grade at school. He is a bright child who doesn't do any work, and when he does do his work, he doesn't turn it in. Behaviorally, he's fine and avoids confrontation with the teacher and other students. His therapeutic mother says, "Honey, according to your teacher, you had a very restful day. (Paradoxing him) She says, "since the rest of the family has worked hard all day and needs a rest, it is so good to have someone rested and ready to go to work." Then his mom gives Tony a list of chores, which she later checks carefully and grades. While she is doing this she is assuring Tony in a good way, with hugs and smiles, that a good mom always makes sure that her children are able to do something very well so that they will be equipped to support themselves in the real world. When Tony becomes whiny or angry and belligerent and acts like he can't do the chore, mom continues, in a calm and loving way with her arm around Tony (Tony is extremely stiff at this point), to tell Tony that the good thing about having Tony work on the bathroom all evening long, taking as long as he wants, is that she always knows where she can find a little boy to hug.

Now, many children will drag the task on for hours and hours. When the mom is ready to go to bed, she can always say to him, "Honey, listen. We can continue this in the morning. The toilet will still be here needing to be cleaned. Let's go to bed." She also has the option of going in and saying, "Well, I've had my rest and I'm ready to go to bed. I don't mind helping you out". She then proceeds to give him specific directions in a loving and fun way. At any time, when he seems to moving a little fast or is getting something that she suggested be done quickly, she might even feign a heart attack and fall on the floor or against the wall. Tony will particularly love this, as he has fantasies about his mom, in some way, being devastatingly incapacitated.

This story about Tony exemplifies how parents can find creative and fun ways to love the child, while "playing" with their resistance. When the child's resistance does not elicit anger or rejection, then gradually, the need for it subsides.

III. THE ART OF CONSEQUENCING

It is not considered acceptable or permissible for children with attachment issues to ever treat their parents with disrespect or act irresponsible in their behavior around them. Therefore, the parenting technique that utilizes the basic premises of the art of consequencing become useful in boxing in the behavior and allowing the parents to still be nurturing and loving with their child.

Creative consequencing is an "art" and cannot be done when a parent is angry. Anger and consequencing results in punishment and is contraindicated. Punishment actually reinforces feelings of anger, resentment, blaming, passive-aggressive behavior, a failure to learn from mistakes, and reinforces low self image.

The goal of consequencing is to preserve and strengthen the parent-child relationship, not to necessarily directly change the child's behavior, but to provide the child the opportunity to change. When this is done effectively, the following happens:

1. All units of concern for the child's behavior are picked up by the child.

2. This allows the parents the time and attention to be loving, non-angry, and non-reactive.

3. This then allows the child to regain self image points and promotes a "win-win" interaction.

Many times in the course of parenting, parents fall into the trap of asking themselves the question, "What can I do to make this child change?", rather than asking themselves, "What do I need to do, so that I can continue to love my child, no matter how long he continues to do this behavior?"

When consequences are given in a loving way, the child learns to accept responsibility for his behavior, starts to show thoughtfulness around the ramifications of that behavior, and learns from mistakes. Creative consequencing provides the child with an opportunity to change behavior, while still feeling good about decisions. As the child learns to accept the consequences of behavior, the child starts to allow himself to be in a "win-win" interaction with the parents and this facilitates internalization of them as role models and development of the child's inner voice.

The "Love and Logic" parenting techniques, developed by Jim Fay and Foster Cline, (see the suggested reading list in the Appendixes) are consistent with parenting philosophies thought to be most effective with attachment disordered children. Particularly helpful are the techniques around the "think it over spot", "heart to heart" talk, and the "one-liners".[5] Cline-Fay Institute, Inc., Fay Professional Bldg., 2207 Jackson St., Suite 102, Golden, CO. 80401. Love and Logic Press.[6]

SUMMARY

Finally, let me review what we have discussed in this chapter on Insights into Attachment:

- We have reviewed how the interruption of the bonding cycle from ages 0 to 26 months can have lifetime ramifications for the child and for those who love that child. Early diagnosis of attachment problems is essential, since a good prognosis is dependent on early and affective intervention.
- The causes of a disruption and the signs and symptoms that occur because of it, have also been explored.
- Therapeutic parenting techniques found to be most effective have also been reviewed.

At this point, it is imperative that we, at least, touch on the implications for society, parents, and professionals regarding attachment issues. Unless a new look and approach is taken to the care and permanency life plan of our nation's children, we will continue to have thousands of children disrupting from their families. Children from foster care and in adoptive homes (the majority of children who have attachment disorders) will continue to be placed in psychiatric hospitals and residential care.

In today's America the percentages of children from these groups in these facilities, are greater than their number in the general population.

Professionals in the field of attachment have noted again and again in various publications, including the book, High Risk: Children Without a Conscience[7], how continued professional neglect and lack of attention to this problem, will lead to more and more violence being perpetrated by younger and younger children. Foster Cline's Conscienceless Acts, Societal Mayhem, also addresses these concerns.[8]

The DSM-IV, as it is currently written, is a disservice to these children and the parents who raise them, and the professionals who treat them.

---

[5] (See the publications on "Love and Logic" put out by the Cline-Fay Institute, Love and Logic Press.)

[7] Magid, K. & McKelvey, CA, (1988) High Risk: Children Without a Conscience, Bantam Books, New York

[8] Dr. Foster Cline, (1995) Consciousless Acts and Societal Mayhem, Golden, Colorado: Love and Logic Press.

The limited criteria and selection for diagnosis actively inhibits profession-als from accurately assessing, diagnosing, and effectively treating these children.[9]

THE IMPLICATIONS FOR PROFESSIONALS:

Professionals who work with placing children for adoption need to be better informed and better able to inform perspective parents of the possibility of attachment problems and symptoms of these problems, and the severe ramifications if this disorder is not identified early and goes untreated. Many professionals, foster and adoptive parents continue to be in denial, for long periods of time, that their child or the child they're working with has attachment issues. This leads to the dissipation of funds for treatment that is ineffective, while the parents continue to become more and more traumatized and exhausted in the course of their caring for the child. When a proper diagnosis of the overall problem is given, it is often too late, as all financial and emotional resources have been ex-hausted. It is important for professionals and parents to realize that, in most of the cases, children with attachment issues have a higher success rate if they are being parented by a full-time mom.

There continues to be a need for professional organizations to provide training and support to families and professionals working with these children. It is a continuing sad statement, regarding the professional com-munity, that this community is chronically concerned with political power plays and territorial issues, making it difficult for the individual practitioner to address attachment issues of the children they treat safely.

Professionals in foster care need to become more cognizant that every time they move a child from one home to another, they are inducing loss. The younger the child, the greater the trauma. More funds and support systems need to be directed at the foster care system and adoptive place-ments so it is financially viable to provide the resources and services necessary for there to be more successful and permanent placements.

It is imperative that there be more opportunities for professionals and parents to work together towards preventative measures. To help with effective prevention an important step is education in our schools of future parents, particularly about the causes and ramifications of attachment issues in children. Every year in the United States thousands of babies are born to mere children themselves, teen age mothers.

"Every year more than one million young women between the ages of 12 and 19 become pregnant. Less than 3 percent of all babies born out

---

[9] DSM-IV, Diagnostic and Statistical Manual, 4th ed., American Psychiatric Association, (1994), Washington, D.C.

of wedlock go to adoptive homes directly; 95 percent of all unmarried women opt to raise their own children. Teenage mothers who keep their babies are a major contributor to what has been called the "feminization of poverty" in the United States, and according to the Ms. Foundation in 1991, 'their children comprise the single largest group of people in the United States living in poverty.'"[10]

In addition, mental health professionals need to be particularly mindful of the responsibility they have to be knowledgeable and supportive in working with families who have made a commitment to raise these children to become productive members of society.

REFERENCES:

Cline, F.W., M.D. (1994) Hope for High Risk and Rage Filled Children: Reactive Attachment Disorder, p. 17.

Bowlby, J. (1969) Attachment and Loss, vol. 1. New York: Basic Books p. 223-228.

Verny, T., M.D. & Kelly, J. (1981) The Secret Life of the Unborn Child, New York: Delta Books.

Cline, F.W., M.D. (1994) Consciousless Acts and Societal Mayhem, Golden, Colorado: Love and Logic Press.

Magid, K. & McKelvey, C.A., (1988) High Risk: Children Without a Conscious, New York: Bantam Books.

McKelvey, C.A. & Stevens, JE. (1994) Adoption Crisis: The Truth Behind Adoption and Foster Care, Golden, Colorado: Fulcrum Press.

---

[10] A survery by the Ms. Foundation for Women in 1991 as quoted in the book, Adoption Crisis: The Truth About Adoption and Foster Care, Carole A. McKelvey and Dr. JoEllen Stevens (1994), Golden, Colorado: Fulcum Press. pp. 30-31.

4

Does Attachment Disorder Exist?

Statistics, Research, Rationale

Elizabeth Randolph, RN, PHD.

No one knows for sure when the term "attachment disorder" first began to be used. Certainly it was not a part of the Diagnostic and Statistical Manual (DSM) of the American Psychiatric Association (1968) until the third edition was published in 1980.

The closest description in the second edition of DSM is "unsocialized aggressive reaction of childhood," whose symptoms include overt or covert hostile disobedience, quarrelsomeness, verbal and physical aggressiveness toward others, vengefulness, destructiveness, temper tantrums, stealing, lying, and hostile teasing of other children.[1] In addition, there is no consideration given as to possible causes of this disorder. In DSM-III (1980), we see the first mention of attachment problems, under the category "Reactive Attachment Disorder".

This disorder refers primarily to infants younger than eight months of age and is characterized by failures to make eye contact, to smile, to vocalize reciprocally, to turn to the mother's voice, to spontaneously reach for the mother, to anticipate being picked up by the mother, and to engage in playful activities with the mother. It is presumed to be due to a lack of adequate maternal care during the first eight months of life.

When DSM III was revised in 1987 (DSM III-R), the age of diagnosis of Reactive Attachment Disorder was expanded upward to age 5 (as opposed to 8 months in DSM III). The primary symptom of reactive attachment disorder was a marked disturbance in social relations as evidenced by either a persistent failure to respond to social interactions, or an indiscriminate sociability with strangers.

However, there is no mention of the disturbed and aggressive behavior that therapists familiar with attachment disordered children so frequently see. Thus, it appears that the understanding that therapists have of reactive attachment disorder differs considerably from what therapists experienced in treating children with attachment problems mean when they discuss "attachment disorder".

Child therapists have long known that children who experience early abuse and neglect have difficulty adjusting in both later childhood and adulthood. In 1940 Lowrey noted that children who had been raised in institutions for the first three years of their lives "undergo an isolation type of experience with resulting isolation type of personality, characterized by unsocial behavior, hostile aggression, lack of patterns for giving and receiving affection, inability to understand and accept limitations... delays in development ... egocentricity is marked, and they do not recognize the individuality and needs of others" (p. 250). In addition, Goldfarb (1942) notes that "case workers have for a long time noted the hyperactivity, destructiveness and aggressive which seemed to be especially characteristic of foster children whose babyhood had been spent in institutions" (p. 251). However, neither of these authors referred to such children as attachment disordered.

Probably the first published concept of the term attachment disorder was in 1979 in the book <u>Understanding and Treating the Severely Disturbed Child</u> by Foster Cline, M.D.

Dr. Cline hypothesized that attachment is a process that develops between a mother and child during the first year of life, in repeated cycles in which the child first feels a need of some kind, experiences rage when that need is not immediately responded to, calms when the need is met, and develops a sense of trust as the rage lessens.

When this cycle is repeated thousands of time during the first year of a child's life, a secure sense of trust develops and a child is said to be securely attached. When a mother fails to respond to a child's needs on a consistent basis (either because of problems in the mother or chronic pain in the child), the child's rage increases, trust does not fully develop, and the child is said to be insecurely attached.

In situations where there is grossly inadequate care by the mother (or severe, chronic pain in the child), the child experiences intense rage for prolonged periods of time, trust fails to develop, and the child is said to have an attachment disorder. Thus, when we talk about children who have attachment disorder, we are talking about children who experience great amounts of rage, who do not perceive other people as being trustworthy (or even as being of interest), who lie constantly, who lack a conscience for their misbehavior (because they lack an internalized object), and who abuse and mistreat other people.

Dr. Cline (1992) describes the following symptoms as characteristic of the attachment disordered child: lack of ability to give and receive affection, self-destructive behavior, cruelty to others, phoniness, stealing, hoarding, gorging on food, speech problems, extreme need for control, lack of long-term friends, difficulty making eye contact on adult terms, parents who seem unreasonably angry, preoccupation with blood and gore, fire setting, superficial attractiveness and friendliness with strangers, learning problems, and a pathological type of lying that flies in the face of reality.

However, many child therapists dispute the notion that a disorder of attachment is responsible for the problem behavior of neglected and abused children. Those who disagree with a syndrome of attachment disorder often argue that there is no research to support that such a disorder exists; there are only the anecdotal reports of Dr. Cline and others (actually, many others).

They seem to overlook much of the early research conducted by people like Goldfarb and Tizard. Goldfarb's (1942) study comparing the behavior of 20 children raised in institutions for three years before being placed in foster homes with the behavior of 20 children raised only in foster homes provides quite clear evidence that there is a syndrome of specific behaviors that characterizes neglected children. All of the children in this study had lived in foster homes for at least three years before being tested. The only difference between the two groups of children was that one group had lived in foster homes for at least six years, while the other had lived in an institution for three years, and then in foster home for three years.

None of the institution children were free of any behavior problems, while 25% of the children raised in a foster homes were free of any behavior problems. Institution children were noted to have frequent temper tantrums; to lie, steal, and be dishonest; to talk back to and argue with adults; to be destructive of property; to abuse other children; to consistently fail to regard the rights of others; to be overly excitable, easily upset, and easily overstimulated; and to be distractible, hyperactive, and flighty.

Barbara Tizard is another child therapist who devoted considerable research to the effects of institutional care on the behavior of children. In particular, she conducted a longitudinal study of the behavior problems and interpersonal relationships of 26 children raised in an institution with a group of children raised in working-class homes in London, and with a group of children raised in an institution for two years and then returned to their birth mothers (Tizard & Rees, 1975). She then followed-up with these same children four years later (Tizard & Hodges, 1978) to determine more long-term effects of institutionalization. At age four, the institutionalized children were noted to have greater problems with poor concentration, food fads, problems getting along well with peers, temper tantrums, and excessive clinging to adults. The children's caretakers (only two children had fewer than 10 caretakers) noted that, despite being clingy, the institutionalized children's affectionate behavior was markedly shallow, and the children did not protest when favorite caretakers left the institution for another job. Ten of these children were noted to be willing to follow anyone around and to try to go home with strangers. All of the institutionalized children were far more self-sufficient than children in the two comparison groups, often refusing to let adults help them with self-care activities.

At follow-up four years later, only eight children remained in the institution (the other 18 had been placed in foster or adoptive homes). The behavior of these eight children was compared with the behavior of the 18 children who had been placed to determine the long-term effects of institutionalization.

Significant differences were found in the areas of cooperativeness, friendliness, and attention-seeking, with the institutionalized children having more problems in these areas than the children who had been placed. They continued to be indiscriminately affectionate with strangers, had many more antisocial behaviors, and were noted to chatter incessantly as a way of getting attention from others.

Those familiar with attachment disordered children will have noted the strong similarities between the behavior noted to be characteristic of attachment disordered children and the behavior described in the studies reported above.

Despite these similarities, there continues to be a large number of child therapists who doubt that there is a strong connection between early abuse and neglect and certain behavior problems. Therefore, the purpose of this research was to provide validation of the theory that it is disruptions in the attachment cycle that cause certain behavior problems in children, and that children with disrupted attachment do show inordinate amounts of rage, impaired reality testing, and impairments in their ability to relate to other people.

One major impediment to doing such research is finding a tool that measures these disparate characteristics in a manner that is reliable and valid. Fortunately, the Exner Comprehensive System (1990) for using the Rorschach Inkblot Test provides such a tool.

The Rorschach Test was initially developed as a projective test that measured themes and issues in psychopathology. Many different scoring systems were developed to be used with the Rorschach over the years, but none of these scoring systems was based upon controlled psychological research (all were subjective measures). The Exner scoring system was based upon years of extensive, well-controlled research and has provided an objective scoring system for understanding the way a person perceives, interprets, and interacts with the world. Of particular interest for this study are the indices that measure perception of human figures, humans cooperating with each other, the ability to delay getting one's needs met, the ability to process and cope with emotions, and the ability to accurately perceive the world the way other people do.

Several research studies have used the Exner Rorschach to assess behavior problems in children, most often in children who have conduct disorders, and several have used the Exner Rorschach with psychopathic and incarcerated adults. Some of the earliest of these studies use different scoring systems, as the Exner system only became available in the 1970's.

Of particular interest is Goldfarb's (1943) study of the effects of early institutional care on adolescent personality development as measured by the Rorschach. He studied 15 children between ages 10 and 14 who had spent the majority of their lives in an institution or foster home setting, and 15 children who had lived only in foster homes (not in institutions). Goldfarb notes that previous researchers who studied children raised in institutions until age three demonstrate "a conspicuously unique type of personality development ... he is markedly different (in being) less socially well adjusted, less secure, more likely to demonstrate problem behavior, and more retarded in social maturity. He is more removed and isolated in his relationships with people, although there is an excessive craving for attention... His speech remains defective through adolescence. His school performance is consistently poor" (p. 215).

Goldfarb found that institutionalized children give significantly more pure color, irrational, primitive, and self-oriented responses than children raised in foster homes.

He concluded that institutionalized children had more primitive defenses and lacked common social judgements when compared to children raised in foster homes. In addition, the institutionalized group gave significantly more responses that are commonly seen in schizophrenic or brain damaged subjects.

Carl Gacono has been involved in several studies using the Exner method for scoring the Rorschach to examine a variety of personality traits. He first published a report that examined the frequency of human responses, and the egocentricity index (a measure of self-focus) in incarcerated men diagnosed as severe and moderate psychopaths (1990). He found no significant differences between these two groups in the number of human responses, but both groups were significantly more self-focused than the normal adult population. Gacono also examined the object relations of psychopathic individuals as part of this study, using the Self-Focus Sentence Completion Test (SFSC) to assess what are called "borderline object relations" (immature ways of relating to other people by splitting them into parts). There were no significant differences between severe and moderate psychopaths in terms of the frequency and types of borderline defenses used, but both groups had significantly higher scores than the normal population, indicating a greater tendency to have difficulty relating to others as whole people, not split-off parts.

Gacono, Meloy, and Heaven (1990) examined the frequency of pair and reflection responses (an indication of narcissism and self-focus), and of personalized (PER) responses (when asked why the card looks the way it does, the subjects says something to the effect of "because I've seen one that looks just like it") to the Rorschach cards with adults incarcerated and diagnoses with antisocial personality disorder.

They had two subject groups:
- One with 21 men who had severe psychopathy, and
- One with 21 men who had moderate psychopathy (as measured by Hare's Psychopathy Checklist).

They found that severe psychopaths produced significantly more reflection (but not pair) responses, indicating a greater degree of self-focus.

Forty-eight percent of severe psychopaths, 31% of an out-patient character disordered group, 14% of the moderate psychopathy group, and 8% of non-patient adults produce reflection responses. The severe psychopaths also produced significantly more PER responses (81%) than moderate psychopaths (66%), or an out-patient character disordered group (41%). The authors concluded that Rorschach responses in psychopathic adults are consistent with the hypothesis that such individuals are more narcissistic and self-focused than people with other psychiatric disorders, and than the general population.

In 1991 Gacono and Meloy used the Exner Rorschach to study anxiety and its relationship to attachment in 42 incarcerated adult males diagnosed with antisocial personality disorder, comparing subjects with moderate psychopathy with subjects with severe psychopathy. In this study, they examined the frequency of vista (introspection), shading (helplessness), and texture (desire for human contact) responses to the Rorschach cards, as well as scores on an adjustment index.

They found no significant differences between groups in the frequency of vista responses, but the moderate psychopaths did produce more texture and shading responses that the severe psychopaths. Only 5% of the severe psychopaths (as compared to 33% of the moderate psychopaths) had a texture response. In addition, only 29% of the severe psychopaths had a shading response, in contrast to 47% of non-patient adults, and 89% of a character disordered group. The authors conclude that the almost lack of texture responses indicates a lack of the capacity to bond with others, and that this trait is much more characteristic of severe psychopaths than moderate psychopaths.

Weber, Meloy, and Gacono (1992) studied the frequency of text (desire for contact with others), shading (helplessness), and human (interest in other people) responses to the Rorschach cards in 48 adolescents who were diagnosed with conduct disorder, and in 30 adolescents who were diagnosed with chronic depression. They also examined the differences in the frequency of these responses between subjects who have mild, moderate, and severe degrees of conduct disorder.

The results of this study showed that depressed subjects made significantly more texture (desire for human contact), shading (helplessness), and human (interest in people) responses than subjects who had conduct disorder.

In fact, only 29% of conduct disordered subjects had a texture response, compared to 85% of normal subjects.

In depressed subjects, 63% had a texture response.

Only 67% of conduct disordered subjects had a human response, while 97% of depressed subjects had a human response.

There were no significant differences between groups when subjects were divided up according to the severity of their conduct disorder symptoms, probably because this division made the group sizes too small for accurate statistical comparison. Finally, Greco and Cornell (1992) studied aggression and human responses using the Exner Rorschach with 110 adolescents. Thirty-three of these subjects had committed murder during a conflictual interaction with someone, 22 had committed murder in the course of another crime (burglary or robbery), and 55 were convicted of robbery or burglary that did not involve murder. They found significant differences between groups only on the number of human responses, with subjects who murdered as an adjunct to another crime producing more human responses than either of the other two groups.

Thus, the Rorschach test has previously been used to measure a variety of traits, with subjects with a variety of disorders. Basically, its use has shown that subjects who have conduct disorders (as children) or antisocial personality disorder (as adults), and who are presumed to have deficits in their attachment to others, make more frequent pure color, aggressive, self-focused, reflection, and personalized responses, and fewer human, human movement, texture, and shading responses to the Rorschach cards.

However, none of these studies actually attempted to assess levels of attachment in their subjects; they simply presumed that lack of attachment was present because psychopathic behavior was present.

These findings are supported by research done by Exner and his colleagues, a compendium of which is reported in the latest edition of using the Exner Comprehensive System with children (1995). Exner describes character disordered or psychopathic children as being people who have an underdeveloped conscience and a disinclination to identify with other

e loveless people who seldom form deep relationships
rarely are they able to feel or express sympathy, support,
Other people exist primarily to be manipulated and taken
They are highly self-focused people who blame others for
their pro.... and limitations, feeling totally justified for taking whatever
actions they deem necessary. They lack concern for the welfare of others,
so they are usually very selfish, self-aggrandizing, and heartlessly exploitative of others. These children lie, cheat, steal, and behave cruelly toward
others. They bully other children, mistreat animals and people, and display
a demanding and self-centered lifestyle. They are likely to lack friendships,
and to be argumentative and disobedient at home. They are likely to
engage in delinquent behaviors, including truancy and running away
from home.

After conducting a number of studies with conduct disordered children,
Exner reports that a lack of texture responses indicates early life depriva-
tions that have interfered with the development of a basic sense of attachment to others.

In addition, the absence of human responses indicates a lack of attachment in early childhood. Finally, the excessive self-focus of conduct disordered children is likely to be seen in elevated egocentricity scores. Exner
lists several Rorschach measures that are common in conduct disordered
children: no texture responses, low human responses, elevated isolation
index, no cooperative human movement, no food responses, high color
responses, poorly modulated expression of emotions through avoiding
complex situations, low animal movement responses, low popular responses, a high number of unusual responses, and low scores on variables
that measure introspection and feelings of vulnerability. In fact, when
there is an absence of texture responses along with few human responses,
this should suggest the presence of a characterological disorder.

These children are often resentful, bitter, and oppositional, traits that
show up as a high number of space responses. Character disorders are
also typified by a high Lambda ratio and few animal movement responses
(because they want their needs gratified immediately, rather than allowing
negative feelings to intrude into their consciousness as irritants). Because
they feel so confident of their abilities to take whatever they want from
the world, these children usually show little distress to contrast with their
limited coping skills, so they often appear to be functioning quite well.

The findings of Exner and others provide intriguing questions for those
of us who treat attachment disordered children, such as:

Is attachment disorder simply a variant of conduct disorder, as many
therapists believe? Or is attachment disorder a separate entity that differs
in significant ways from conduct disorder?

Is attachment disorder the same thing as psychopathic behavior?

Do attachment disordered children actually have different ways of perceiving and responding to events around them than do conduct disordered children?

To answer these questions (and a few others), the purpose of the present study is to examine attachment and its relationship to various types of Rorschach responses, and to determine whether or not there are differences between children who have attachment disorders and those who have conduct disorders, schizophrenia, and depression in terms of their Rorschach responses. In order to accomplish this task, this study will examine the following clusters of Rorschach responses and indices:

- human interactions,
- willingness to experience and try to cope with emotions,
- ability to cope with emotions (includes impulsivity),
- cooperation,
- reality testing, and
- egocentricity.

For this study it was hypothesized that attachment disordered children would score differently on most of the values in these clusters than will children with conduct disorders, depression, or schizophrenia.

A second part of this study examined the differences in responses to the Rorschach between attachment disordered children and children who were abused/neglected but who do not have behavior problems.

It was hypothesized that the children without behavior problems would produce more human, human movement, and cooperative human movement responses; would be less self-centered; and would be more cooperative with the Rorschach task. They were not expected to differ on measures of reality testing because both groups had experienced about equal degrees of abuse and neglect.

Method

Subjects

The subjects were 95 children between ages 6 and 17 who were referred to a private practice clinic that specializes in treating children with severe emotional problems. All subjects had a minimum IQ of 80 (only one subject had IQ<90), and were free of major neurological and physical disorders.

These subjects were divided into two groups:

1) children with severe behavior problems who had a history of abuse/neglect in the first year of life (DBD; N=70; 37 males and 33 females); and

2) children who were abused/neglected but who do not have behavior problems (ABN; N=25; 7 males and 18 females).

The scores of these two groups of children were separated into two different studies as described above. For the first study, the scores of the 70 abused/neglected children with behavior problems were compared with the norms reported by Exner (1995) for depressed children (DEP; N=100) ranging in age from 13 to 16, and about half of whom were hospitalized for depression for the first time; conduct disordered children (CD; N=140) ranging in age from 12 to 16, and who had a diagnosis of conduct disorder with a history of aggressive behavior toward others; schizophrenic children (SCZ; N=110) ranging in age from 12 to 17 who were diagnosed as schizophrenic following their first psychiatric hospitalization; and normal children (NORM; N=1300) ranging in age from 6 to 16.

For the second study, the two groups of abused/neglected children (with and without behavior problems) were compared.

Procedure

All subjects completed the Rorschach Inkblot Test (using the Exner Comprehensive System for administration and scoring) as part of a more complete psychological evaluation. Rorschach protocols were scored by an examiner who was blind to the diagnosis and presenting problems of each child. Parents or primary caretakers (some children were placed in group homes or residential treatment programs) of each child completed the Children's Behavior Questionnaire, a 30-item test designed to measure symptoms of attachment disorder using a 5-point Likert scale (usually, often, sometimes, occasionally, rarely) for each behavior. (see Appendix II).

Results

Study 1

T-tests for independent means were conducted on all measures to compare scores of male and female subjects. No significant differences were found to be due to gender, so results for males and females were combined for all subsequent statistical analyses.

Table 1 depicts the mean scores for the five groups on variables related to attachment to, and perceptions of others. In Table 1, the DBD group:
   • gave significantly fewer human (H-interest in other people), human movement (M-interest in interacting with other people), and cooperative human movement (COP-ability to trust others) responses than the comparison groups.
   • gave significantly more human part and mythical human responses (Hd-the tendency to split people into parts) and personalized (PER -

defensiveness and rigidity in interpersonal relationships) responses than the comparison groups.
- made significantly fewer texture (anticipating that intimate and mutually supportive relationships can be developed with others) responses than the NORM group and DEP group, but was not significantly different from the CD or SCZ groups.

Table 1
Attachment and Human Relatedness

variable	DBD	CD	DEP	SCZ	NORM
H	1.5	2.4	2.6	1.7	2.9
M	1.7	4.3	5.0	4.8	3.7
COP	0.2	0.9	0.9	0.6	1.9
Hd	2.6	1.3	1.4	1.6	1.3
PER	2.0	1.6	1.2	1.0	1.0
T	0.4	0.5	0.8	0.5	1.0

Table 2 depicts the mean scores for the five groups on variables related to willingness to experience and try to cope with emotions, as well as the ability to modulate and control one's emotions. On some variables there were clear differences. The DBD group:
- made significantly fewer diffuse shading (Y-feelings of helplessness, insecurity, and anxiety) and Blend (willingness to do more than the minimum required to cope with one's emotions) responses than the other groups. The DBD group also made more pure color (C- propensity for unrestrained emotionality and inadequate emotional control) responses than the other groups.

Table 2
Emotionality

variable	DBD	CD	DEP	SCZ	NORM
C'	2.1	2.4	2.1	1.2	1.2
S	2.5	3.6	4.1	2.6	1.5
Blends	2.4	4.1	5.4	3.9	5.4
Y	0.5	0.8	0.9	1.3	0.8
C	1.2	0.7	0.1	0.5	0.3
Afr	.49	.57	.50	.56	.70
L	1.10	.91	.74	1.31	.69

On the other hand, for the other variables, the results were mixed. The DBD group made significantly more achromatic color (C' - willingness to experience feelings, leading to tenseness and irritability) than the NORM and DEP groups, but not more than the CD and SCZ groups.

For space (S-willingness to experience anger) responses, the NORM group made the fewest responses, while there were no differences between the DBD and SCZ groups. Both the DEP and CD groups made significantly more space responses.

Afr is a ratio of the number of responses to the colored cards. It measures willingness to deal with emotionally charged situations.

There were no differences on Afr between the DBD and DEP groups, but the DBD group scored significantly lower on this variable than the NORM, CD, or SCA groups. Lambda (L) is a ratio of responses that use only the form features of the cards, divided by all other responses. It also measures willingness to process emotionally charged material (among other things).

The SCZ group scored the highest on this variable, indicating the least willingness to experience emotions.

The next highest score was for the DBD group, which was significantly higher than the NORM, CD, or DEP groups.

Table 3 depicts variables related to willingness to put effort into cooperating with others. On several of these variables, the DBD group scores significantly higher than the comparison groups.

On Lambda (L- willingness to cooperate with others, among other things) and perseveration (PSV-willingness to put effort into complex tasks) the SCZ group scores higher then the DBD group, but otherwise the DBD groups scores higher than the DEP, CD, and NORM groups.

On this particular variable, the SCZ group probably scores higher because PSV is also an indication of psychotic thinking.

Table 3
Cooperativeness

variable	DBD	CD	DEP	SCZ	NORM
L	1.10	.91	.74	1.31	.69
DQ+	4.5	6.0	7.0	5.2	7.3
Zf	11.0	10.5	13.2	9.6	11.3
PSV	0.6	0.3	0.1	1.5	0.2

Good developmental quality (DQ+) is also a measure of willingness to put effort into solving complex tasks. On this variable, the DBD group scores consistently lower than comparison groups. Finally, on a variable called Zf, which measures cooperation with the Rorschach task, the results are more mixed. The DEP group made significantly more Zf responses, and the SCZ group made significantly fewer, but there are no differences between the DBD, CD, and NORM groups.

One observed trait of attachment disordered children that has not been documented by research is a particular kind of impaired ability to view the world the way other people do that approaches being distorted thinking, but falls short of actually being psychotic thinking. Table 4 depicts scores on the various reality testing measures of the Rorschach. Interestingly, the results support the clinical opinions of those child therapists who specialize in treating attachment disordered children; their thinking is highly distorted, but falls short of being psychotic. If anything, the thinking of attachment disordered children most closely resembles that of schizophrenic children, but it lacks the severe distortions of reality that are common in schizophrenic children.

Table 4
Reality Testing

variable	DBD	CD	DEP	SCZ	NORM
X+%	.36	.56	.57	.36	.77
F+%	.40	.52	.64	.43	.64
X-%	.38	.18	.21	.39	.09
S-%	.16	.21	.38	.30	.15
Xu%	.23	.24	.22	.24	.15
P	4.0	5.2	5.5	3.9	6.0
Level 2	1.1	1.3	0.8	2.5	0.2

As can be seen, there are no significant differences between the DBD and SCZ groups on X+% (the ability to see the world the way others do), F+% (good thinking quality when emotions are absent), X-% (distorted thinking quality), Xu% (highly idiosyncratic ways of viewing the world, and the number of popular responses (P- ability to see what others see).

However, the SCZ group scores significantly higher than the DBD group on the variables that measure frankly distorted perception of reality; S-% (severely distorted thinking) and Level 2 special scores (psychotic thinking).

The DBD groups scores significantly lower than the CD, DEP, and NORM groups on X+5, F+5, S-%, and number of popular responses, and about the same as the other groups on Xu%. The DBD group also scores significantly higher than these groups on X-%.

Other researchers have commonly found that children with behavior disorders are excessively self-focused, using the number of reflection (Fr) and pair (2) responses (as well as the egocentricity (ego) index that is based on those two variables) to indicate higher levels of self-focus in conduct disordered children, and antisocial and psychopathic adults.

Table 5 depicts the scores on these variables. These results clearly show that the DBD group is significantly lower on the egocentricity index, and made significantly fewer pair responses than the comparison groups.

The only significantly different group in terms of reflection responses is the DEP group. Thus, the results of this study clearly show that children with the kinds of disruptive behaviors that are often classified as attachment disorder are not overly self-focused in the same way that children with conduct disorders are.

Table 5
Self-Focus

variable	DBD	CD	DEP	SCZ	NORM
(2)	5.9	9.1	6.2	7.9	9.1
Fr	0.4	0.3	1.0	0.4	0.4
ego	.31	.41	.47	.45	.54

There are three other variables measured by the Rorschach that are pertinent to this study and that can only be represented through percentages. These are the problem-solving style (how a person approaches problems and tries to cope with them), the D score (whether or not a person has sufficient coping skills to deal with the problems and stressors in his/her life), and the Zd score (how the person takes in information about the world and then decides how to respond).

Table 6 depicts the percentages of each group on these variables. There are three types of problem-solving styles; extratensive, ambient, and introversive.

Extratensive people rely heavily on their emotions for interacting with the world around them and solving the problems it presents to them.

Introversive people, on the other hand, prefer to delay responding to situations, to think things over carefully before responding, and to worry and ruminate about problems. Ambient people vacillate between these two poles, showing no clear problem-solving style. Most people with life-long problems have an ambient problem-solving style. In terms of Zf scores, there are two possibilities; overincorporators and underincorporators.

People who are overincorporators cautiously scan the environment for cues as to how to act before responding, and usually have impaired thinking abilities as a result. Underincorporators are people who scan the environment quickly, responding impulsively without giving due consideration to the demands of the situation.

Well-functioning people generally fall somewhere between these two poles. People who obtain a minus score on the D scale are facing more problems than they have the ego strength to deal with. People who obtain a positive D score are usually functioning well, although people with conduct disorders and psychopathy often have positive D scores because they are in denial about or oblivious to the problems in their lives.

As can be seen in Table 6, there is very little similarity between the DBD group and the comparison groups. Although there is similarity between the

DBD and CD groups on the extratensive variable, this is the only variable that is similar between these two groups.

It should also be noted that both the DBD and CD groups are similar to the NORM group on this variable. However, what is most noteworthy about the DBD group in the problem-solving realm is the relative dearth of subjects in the introversive group (3 out of 70 subjects).

This finding suggests that rarely do DBD subjects take their time to think things through before deciding how to act.

Another word for such behavior is impulsivity.

Table 6
Additional Variables

variable	DBD	CD	DEP	SCZ	NORM
extratensive	49%	50%	26%	19%	45%
ambitent	47%	24%	40%	29%	29%
introversive	4%	26%	34%	52%	25%
overincor	17%	26%	41%	66%	18%
underincor	26%	4%	21%	9%	17%
D>0	17%	33%	12%	35%	5%
D<0	39%	26%	24%	21%	21%

The DBD group is similar to the NORM group in terms of overincorporation, and there are significantly fewer overincorporators among the DBD group than the comparison groups. There are significantly more underincorporators among the DBD group than in the CD group, again pointing out the differences between subjects in these two groups. The results of the D>0 category (adequate coping skills) are mixed. However, significantly more DBD subjects have deficient coping skills (D<0) than the comparison groups.

Finally, the Rorschach has six clusters of scores that identify subjects at risk for specific problems. Only three of these clusters will be discussed here, as too few subjects had positive scores on the other three. The clusters to be considered are the schizophrenia index (SZO), the depression index (DPR), and the coping deficit index (CDIO.

Table 7 depicts the percentages of subjects in each group who had significant elevations on these indices.

Table 7
Significant Cluster Scores

variable	DBD	CD	DEP	SCZ	NORM
SZO	59%	14%	12%	90%	0%
DPR	36%	39%	69%	12%	0%
CDI	39%	17%	41%	29%	11%

It is important to note that the DBD group has a significantly larger percentage of subjects who have a positive score on the schizophrenia index, consistent with their performance on the measures of reality testing.

The DBD group and CD group are essentially equal on the depression index, and significantly more subjects in these two groups are positive on this index than in the SCZ and NORM groups. Only the DEP group has a higher percentage of positive scores on this index.

STUDY 2

The other comparison that was made in this study was between the DBD group and the group of 25 subjects who had been abused/neglected, but who did not have behavior problems (ANB).

This comparison is important when considering the issue of why some abused/neglected children develop serious behavior problems and others do not. What is it that distinguishes between these two groups?

In terms of living situations, 13% of the DBD group were living with their birth families, 10% were living with adoptive families, 29% were in foster homes, 34% were in group homes, and 14% were in residential treatment facilities.

In the ABN group, 42% of the children were living with their birth families, none had been adopted, 46% were in foster homes, 8% were in group homes, and 4% were in residential treatment facilities.

There was a significant difference between groups in terms of gender. The DBD group was 53% male and 47% female, while the ABN group was 25% male and 75% female, However, when scores were compared for differences between genders, no significant differences were evident.

In terms of ethnic background, 81% of the DBD group were Caucasian, 12% were African American, 5% were Hispanic, and 2% were Asian. In the ABN group, 83% were Caucasian, 4% were African American, 8% were Hispanic, and 4% were Asian. There were no significant differences between groups in terms of ethnicity.

The scores of these two groups on all of the variables discussed in Study 1 were compared using t-tests for independent means.

* * * * * * * * * *

Significant differences were found for only a few variables, primarily related to human relationships and levels of cooperation with others. The following Table 8 depicts those variables that were significant between these two groups.

* * * * * * * * * *

Two of the variables in this table were not previously mentioned because they were not found to be significantly different between the groups in Study 1; whole (W-ability to organize the environment in a meaningful way), and common detail (D- ability to perceive and react to obvious characteristics of the environment) responses.

The DBD group made significantly fewer whole responses, and significantly more common detail responses than the ABN group. This combination indicates an unwillingness on the part of subjects in the DBD group to deal with complex situations and a preference to choose the easiest path to solving problems.

Table 8
Differences Between DBD and ABN Groups

	t	P
M	6.38	.002
H	8.21	.001
COP	23.5	.001
C	2.97	.05
W	4.77	.01
D	4.05	.02
DQ+	3.65	.02
Zf	3.45	.03

On the Rorschach, the DBD group made significantly fewer human, human movement, and cooperative human movement responses, indicating a lack of interest in forming relationships with others. They also made fewer DQ+ and Zf responses, indicating a lack of cooperation. The DBD group also made significantly more pure color responses, indicating a lack of adequate emotional controls and a tendency to discharge emotions as soon as they are felt.

As discussed in the introduction to this book, it can easily be seen from the above discussion that there are many similarities between attachment disordered children and psychopaths, conduct disordered children, and children with oppositional defiant disorder. How, then, can we tell the difference between a child who has an attachment disorder, one who is a psychopath, or one who has either conduct disorder, oppositional defiant disorder, or both?

For the purposes of this book, this question was researched.

- Our first area of interest was to investigate the behavioral traits of children with attachment disorder, disruptive behavior disorders (includes conduct disorder and oppositional defiant disorder), depression, and no disorder using the Children's Behavior Questionnaire (CBQ). (See Appendix II)

The CBQ is a 30-item inventory, designed specifically to assess for the presence of attachment disorder. This study also examined the scores of these four groups on selected variables, as measured by the Rorschach Inkblot Test (Exner, 1990) to determine if this test differentiates between groups.

We have noted that there is a considerable amount of research in the area of attachment, but virtually no research in the area of attachment disorders.

A number of studies on attachment have explored the effects of abuse, neglect, maternal depression, prematurity, and physical illness on the child's ability to attach. Many of these studies have used Ainsworth's (1978) strange situation

- A second area of interest to this study is that of research using the Exner Comprehensive System for administering and scoring the Rorschach, particularly as it relates to children with conduct disorders.

There are two previous studies on this point:
- Weber, Meloy, and Gacono (1992) studied the relationship between attachment and anxiety in conduct disordered and depressed children admitted to an inpatient psychiatric unit for treatment. They assumed that conduct disordered children had experienced disruptions in attachment (without measuring this) because failures to attach have been linked to psychopathy in other research. They found that conduct disordered adolescents made significantly fewer human, texture, and diffuse shading responses to the Rorschach cards than depressed adolescents. Their conclusion -- conduct disordered adolescents showed a lack of attachment to, and empathy for others.[2]
- The second study on this point was done by Greco and Cornell (1992) who also studied the frequency of human responses to the Rorschach cards, with a group of adolescents who had been convicted of homicide. They found that subjects who murdered produced significantly fewer human responses than subjects incarcerated for other crimes. They concluded that juveniles who committ murder have more serious impairment in their ability to relate to others than do juveniles convicted of lesser crimes.[3]

This is the first study, however, to actually examine the attachment classifications of children with various psychiatric diagnoses to determine whether or not there are differences in their social relatedness and the types of behavior (and behavior problems) they exhibit.

This study's purpose is to present the Children's Behavior Questionnaire (See Appendix II of this book) as a means of assessing behavior problems known to be present in attachment disordered children. It was also our hope to be able to compare the results of that test with the frequency of human, human movement, texture, and cooperative human movement responses to the Rorschach cards. This is the first examination of its kind in the literature. As noted in the introduction, the results were interesting.

CBQ/RORSCHACH STUDY

Method:

Subjects:
The subjects for this study were 145 children between ages 6 and 16 who had been referred to a clinic for treatment of a variety of psychological problems. All children had a minimum IQ of 90, and were free of major neurological and physical problems. Subjects were divided into four groups: 1) children with severe behavior problems consistent with attachment disorder (ADS; N=63), and with a history of severe abuse/neglect; 2) children with severe behavior problems not consistent with attachment disorder (DBD; N=28), and without a history of abuse/neglect; 3) children who met the diagnostic criteria for major depression (DEP; N=34) who had no history of abuse/neglect; and 4) children with no apparent problems and who had never been referred for therapy (NORM; N=20).

Procedure
All children completed the Rorschach inkblot test using the Exner method, and the parent bringing them for the evaluation (usually the mother) completed the CBQ. Rorschach results were scored by an examiner blind as to the diagnosis of each child. The CBQ was scored by this researcher using the scoring guidelines for that test.

RESULTS
Scores for male and female subjects on the CBQ were compared, and no significant differences were found to be due to gender. Data for both genders was thus combined for all subsequent statistical comparisons. We present that data here:

Table 1
CBQ Scores

group	mean score	s.d.	low	high
ADS	83.1	9.4	64	110
DBD	48.9	6.6	35	58
DEP	25.6	14.2	10	53
NORM	9.4	5.6	0	23

Table 1 (above) depicts the mean scores, standard deviation, low score, and high score for each group on the CBQ. It is easy to see that there is a highly significant difference between groups in terms of their CBQ scores. In addition, there is no overlap of scores between the attachment disordered and conduct disordered groups.

Cronbach's alpha coefficient was used to determine split-half reliability for the CBQ (using all scores in a combined group). The alpha coefficient was $r=.82$, which demonstrates acceptable reliability for this instrument.

One-way analyses of variance (ANOVA) were conducted on each of the items on the CBQ to determine if there were significant differences between groups. All items differentiated highly between groups (all F's> 19.85, p<.001). T-tests for independent means were conducted for each item of the CBQ to compare scores of the attachment disordered and conduct disordered groups. An important issue, in terms of validity for the CBQ, is whether or not it successfully differentiates between children with different types of behavior problems.

Since attachment disordered children have traditionally been viewed by child therapists as simply being conduct disordered, if subjects in these two groups score differently on the CBQ, this will demonstrate that attachment disorder is a separate entity from conduct disorder.

Twenty-seven of the thirty CBQ items were significantly different between these two groups, and thirty-three of the items were highly different (all t's>3.00, p<.001).

The three items that did not differentiate between groups were as follows:

- My child responds with prolonged arguing when asked to do something.
- My child becomes overly upset if he/she is asked to wait before someone responds to his/her needs or wishes.
- My child is surprised when others are upset by his/her actions.

The four items that were significantly different between groups, but at a lower level of significance were as follows:

- My child refuses affection and pushes me away unless he/she is in control of how and when that affection is received. (t=2.33, p<.025)
- My child needs to be in control of events in his/her life, tending to boss others. (t=2.12,p<.039)
- My child tries to get my attention by demanding things instead of asking. (t=2.35, p<.02)
- My child is fascinated with or preoccupied by fire, blood, or morbid activities. (t=2.49,p<.01)

Thus, 93 percent of the items developed for the CBQ (based on attachment disorder theory) significantly differentiate between the two groups of behavior problem subjects, lending strong support to the instrument's usefulness in correctly identifying attachment disordered children (there were no false positives-- subjects who are not attachment disordered, but who are identified as such by the instrument).

Table 2 (below) presents mean scores for the Rorschach variables under consideration in this study.

Table 2
Rorschach Variables

variable	ADS	DBD	DEP	NORM
H	1.5	3.2	2.4	2.9
M	1.7	3.0	2.8	3.7
COP	0.2	1.1	1.4	1.9
T	0.4	0.6	0.6	0.4

One-way analyses of variance were conducted for each of these variables:

- For H (number of human responses), $F=5.60, p<.001$.
- For M (number of human movement responses), $F=4.62, p<.004$.
- For COP (humans cooperating with each other), $F=15.9, p<.001$.
- For T. (texture responses, presumed to indicate a desire for closeness with others), there were no significant differences between groups ($F=1.31$, n.s.).

Each of the four Rorschach variables was correlated with the total score of the CBQ to determine if there was a relationship between human perceptions and CBQ score. The only significant relationship was found for the depressed group, where there was a significant negative correlation between human movement and CBQ score ($r=-.32, p<.01$).

This indicates that, for depressed subjects, the more human movement responses a subject makes, the fewer attachment disordered symptoms he has.

There was a trend for a relationship between human responses and CBQ scores for the attachment disordered group ($r=.19, p<.10$), but because so many of the attachment disordered subjects made no human responses, this was likely to be an underestimate of the actual relationship between these two variables.

Table 3 presents the percentage of subjects in each group who made certain responses to the Rorschach:

Table 3
Percentage of Responses

variable	ADS	DBD	DEP	NORM
H=0	27%	4%	8%	2%
M=0	26%	18%	17%	3%
COP=0	83%	43%	17%	9%
T=0	67%	57%	58%	11%

A significantly higher percentage of attachment disordered subjects made no human, human movement, and cooperative human movement responses than in the other groups.

More attachment disordered subjects had no texture response, but this was not significantly higher than in the conduct disordered or depressed groups, indicating that attachment disordered subjects have a desire for contact with others. They simply lack the skills to pursue such contact because they lack interest in others.

SUMMARY

As previewed in the Introduction, the results of this study show strong support for the usefulness of the CBQ in assessing attachment disorders. The results of this study completed for this book clearly show it as a reliable instrument that has excellent differential validity in separating out children with attachment disorders from children who have conduct disorders, or depression, or who have no disorder.

These results also demonstrate the considerable differences between conduct disorder and attachment disorder. It is interesting to note that this finding was true with the results of the Rorschach -- as well as the CBQ.

It also provides strong support for the theory that attachment disorder is a separate entity from conduct disorder or psychopathic behavior.

Finally, a comparison was made between scores on the Children's Behavior Questionnaire between these two groups. Table 9 depicts the details of that analysis:

Table 9
CBQ Scores

group	mean score	s.d.	low score	high score
DBD	83.1	9.4	64	110
ABN	25.6	14.2	10	53

It is evident that there are highly significant differences between the two groups on the CBQ. The highest score obtained by a subject in the ABN group is 11 points lower than the lowest score obtained by a subject in the DBD group. Thus, there were no false negatives (children identified as not being attachment disordered when they are) or false positives (children identified as being attachment disordered when they are not) using the CBQ. These results indicate that the CBQ is a highly useful tool for diagnosing attachment disorders in abused/neglected children. A study of its ability to distinguish conduct disordered children from attachment disordered children is currently being conducted.

Discussion

The results of these two studies clearly and repeatedly show that there exists a set of characteristic responses to the Rorschach given by a group of children with severe behavior problems who also have a history of abuse/neglect, and that these children are distinctly different from other abuse/neglected children who do not have behavior problems. These differences are primarily in the realms of relating to other people, as well as with cooperation, ability to experience and manage emotions, and reality testing. These results strongly support the theories of Cline and others that such children failed to attach to others in infancy as a result of abuse/neglect, and so to refer to them as attachment disordered is an appropriate term.

Obviously, additional research is needed to add to this data base, particularly in terms of additional abused/neglected subjects who do not have behavior problems, but also in terms of being able to separate out children in various types of placements to determine if there are different characteristics in children who require different types of placements.

In the meantime, however, the results of this study should be considered as exciting evidence to support the theory of attachment disorders, since virtually all differences between groups were beyond the .001 probability level (one chance in a thousand of that your hypothesis is incorrect).

Since research is usually considered to be significant if differences are found at the .05 level (5 chances in 100 that your hypothesis is incorrect), the results of this study are highly significant. The final result?

The answer to the question -- Does attachment disorder exist?

Although further study of the issues considered in this research is necessary, the answer at this point in the research is an unequivicable YES. Attachment disorder does exist and this fact is provable through research.

RESOURCES:

Ainsworth, M.D., Blehar, M.C., Waters, E., and Wall, S. (1978). Patterns of Attachment. Hillsdale, N.J.: Erlbaum.

American Psychiatric Association (1994). Diagnostic and Statistical Manual (4th ed.). Washington, D.C.: Authors.

Cline, F.W. (1979). Understanding and Treating the Severely Disturbed Child. Evergreen, CO: EC Publications.

Cline, F.W. (1992). Hope for High-Risk and Rage-Filled Children. Evergreen, CO: EC Publications.

Crittenden, P.M. (1985). "Maltreated infants: Vulnerability and resilience." Journal of Child Psychology and Psychiatry, 26(1), 85-96.

Delaney, R.J. and Kunstal, F.R. (1993). Troubled Transplants. University of Southern Maine.

Exner, J.E. (1990). The Rorschach: A Comprehensive System (Vol. 2, 3rd ed.). New York: John Wiley & Sons.

Fagot, B.I. and Kavanagh, K. (1990). The prediction of antisocial behavior from avoidant attachment classification. Child Development, 61, 864-873.

Greco, C.M. and Cornell, D. G. (1992). Rorschach object relations of adolescents who committed homicide. Journal of Personality Assessment, 59(3), 574-583.

Harrington, A. (1972). Psychopaths. New York: Simon & Schuster.

Lamb, M.E. (1987). Predictive implications of individual differences in attachment. Journal of Consulting and Clinical Psychology, 55(6), 817,824.

Lewis, M., Feiring, C., McGuffon, C., and Jaskir, J. (1984). Predicting psychopathology in six-year-olds from early social relations. Child Development, 55, 123-136.

Magid, K. and McKelvey, C.A. (1988). High-risk: Children Without a Conscience. New York: Bantam Books.

Main, M. and Cassidy, J. (1978). Categories of responses to reunion with the parents at age 6: Predictable from infant attachment classifications and stable over a 1-month period. Developmental Psychology, 24(3), 415-426.

Randolph, E.M. (1995). Does attachment disorder really exist? Unpublished manuscript.

Shaw, D.S. and Emery, R.E. (1987). Chronic family adversity and school-age children's adjustment. Journal of the American Academy of Child and Adolescent Psychiatry, 27, 200-206.

Weber, C.A., Meloy, J.R., and Gacono, C.B. (1992). A Rorschach study of attachment and anxiety in inpatient conduct-disordered and dysthymic adolescents. Journal of Personality Assessment, 58(1), 16-26.

PART TWO

The Attachment Center at Evergreen Therapy

**Give Them Roots,
Then Let Them Fly**

5

Placing Parents - Life In The Trenches

Paula Pickle, LCSW
& Dianne Allred

"If I had only known what I was getting into..."
"I feel like one of us should be hospitalized, but which one?"
"I don't even like this child anymore."
"Our marriage is in trouble."
"My spouse doesn't see how serious the problems are."
"I'm so tired."
"I have no life anymore."
"We're not safe in our own home."
"Everyone's blaming me for the child's problems - maybe it is my fault..."

How many of us, as parents of Attachment Disordered children, have found ourselves saying or thinking these words?

Whether we are foster, adoptive or birth parents, if we are living with an attachment disordered child, we are having similar experiences and feelings. We are constantly being faced with situations and stresses that no "normal" parenting could even begin to address. We feel isolated, due to loss of friends and family who either don't understand or don't want to be around it. We can't find appropriate help or the financial resources to get to it. We develop symptoms in ourselves that resemble those of prisoners of war, symptoms of Post Traumatic Stress Disorder (PTSD). We give over control of our parenthood, our lives, our self worth, out of fear of this child and sheer exhaustion. We have thoughts of relinquishing and then feel guilty about that. We have to fight so hard for help that soon we take on an adversarial attitude in most areas of our lives - and it doesn't feel good to us. We don't like what we have become. So why do we do it?

For the answer, we have to go back to the reasons why we brought this child into our lives in the first place. We wanted a family. We had a lot of love to share. We believed we could help to make a difference in the life of a child.

And we don't want to let go of the hope that something could make a difference. "There must be help for a six-year-old child."

There is help! There is hope!

Let's take a look at the story of "Sue and Jerry" and the little girl who would change their lives forever:

Annie

Sue had come from a farm family with six children. Sue was the oldest child in the midwest family, and took care of the other children during most of her own childhood. Her parents worked hard and fought hard. Sue was the peacemaker.

Jerry was an only child. His father worked two jobs and was hardly ever home. Jerry's mother was a full-time home-maker whose whole life revolved around her family.

Shortly after high school, Sue and Jerry married. As with most young couples, money was scarce, but they worked hard and were determined to build a happy life together. They both wanted a family, but found out that Sue was not able to have children of her own. After years of trying, they finally decided to adopt. Adoption workers told the couple it was almost impossible to adopt a baby and they would have to wait a long time; they consented to consider an older child -- maybe a toddler.

Sue and Jerry endured all the home studies and scrutiny that adoptive parents must pass and then, they waited, and waited, and waited.

Finally, a call came one night, saying there was a six-year-old girl who needed a home right away. Would they take her? The caseworker said the girl had a rough start in life, but she was bright and very likeable.

"She's so affectionate - she'll go to anyone. She shouldn't have any trouble at all adjusting," they heard. They were so excited at the thought of being parents. Soon everything became sort of a whirlwind, and within two weeks, Annie moved in. The caseworker dropped her off at their home with only a small bag of clothes (most of which didn't fit) and a doll with missing eyes and with broken arms and legs. The worker told Annie, "This is your new mom and dad."

Annie immediately ran up, threw her arms around Sue and said, "I love you, Mom." Sue later remembered that Annie squeezed her pretty hard, but thought she was probably just happy to have a loving, permanent home.

Sue and Jerry decided to go out for pizza, to celebrate their new family. On the way, Annie rolled down the car window and started throwing things out. Sue thought she noticed a peculiar expression on Annie's face, whenever the child looked at her, but Jerry said she was probably just excited.

Once at the restaurant, Annie got food all over herself, from head to toe. "Oh, it was an accident," she said sweetly. Tucking her into bed that night, Sue thought to herself, what an angelic little face Annie had. It was going to be so much fun making up for the hard times she had before now. As she leaned over to tuck her in, however, Annie pulled Sue's hair really hard, then said, "Oh sorry Mom. It was an accident."

During the course of the next several months, Annie had plenty of "accidents"; she was kicked out of three day care centers for hurting other children; totally destroyed her bedroom, including doors, dressers and book cases; she shredded all of the new clothes Sue bought her. Annie also lied about everything. She was very charming with strangers and with Jerry, but went into terrible rages at home with Sue, screaming, kicking, biting.

Soon Sue and Jerry began taking Annie to a therapist. The therapist saw Annie for one hour a week. During the sessions, Annie would run around the room getting into everything. She either didn't answer the therapist's questions or told him lies; she wanted to sit in his lap and rub her hands on his neck. A traditional therapist, the man began asking the family questions, such as: "What are you feeding her for dinner?"

Finally, he came right out and said he thought Sue and Jerry were the ones with the problems. Maybe they should just love her more? Perhaps they should just learn to accept her the way she is? Could the problems be because they had never been parents before? He suggested they put a chart up on their refrigerator with stars on it, for when she did something right. There weren't any stars, because they couldn't find anything Annie did right.

As time went on, Sue became more and more irritable. She couldn't sleep, couldn't concentrate, found herself crying alot and distancing herself from Jerry. Jerry was confused, he couldn't understand what was happening.

Why couldn't Sue control Annie? Maybe she just wasn't a good mother after all. Why was she so angry all the time? Annie didn't act that bad with him.

Then, something mysterious happened to the pet hamster, it was found dead in its cage. At first, they didn't make a connection with Annie, until she started commenting about the "accident."

Sue and Jerry began to ask questions, in an attempt to find out more about Annie's background. They thought this might be the clue to understanding her behavior, so they turned to the case worker. After pressing and insisting on answers, they finally discovered Annie had been severely abused (physically and sexually), neglected, and had been moved many times during her first two years of life. The couple was angry they had not been given that information from the beginning. Sue and Jerry felt betrayed and even considered relinquishing the child. But that made them feel guilty, because it would just be another abandonment for Annie. Also, they were told that in their mid-west state, relinquishment was legally considered the same as abandonment.

They began their long search for help. Their friends had stopped coming over; even their families didn't want to be around them anymore. They couldn't find babysitters who would stay with Annie.

Because she would create terrible scenes, they couldn't take her out in public. They were getting pressure from school to "do something" about her behavior. When they tried to control Annie and discipline the child, they found themselves criticized for being too strict or overly suspicious of her.

Then, one night on television, Sue saw a program about attachment disorder. As the narrator described the symptoms, Sue thought, horrified, "They're talking about Annie!" She wrote down the phone number and address of a place in Colorado that knew something about helping these children.

The next day, Sue called The Attachment Center at Evergreen, Inc., and talked at length with the intake manager, who reassured her that what she was feeling was normal under the circumstances. Finally, there was someone who understood!

Sue found out that attachment disordered children decide at a very early age that they need to be in control of everything and everyone, in order to survive. This is often the result of some kind of trauma, neglect or illness with chronic pain during the first two years of life. Sue learned this kind of trauma can interrupt the bonding process and the child doesn't learn to trust. She was told there is hope for these children, but it takes a specific kind of help. Traditional therapy doesn't work with them, just as normal parenting doesn't work.

Sue also found out that many foster and adoptive families who take these children into their homes end up developing symptoms of PTSD, from living under the constant stress of attacks by the children, either physically or emotionally. No wonder she felt the way she did, Sue thought.

These children, Sue discovered, often have more issues with mothers than anyone else, since bonding begins in-utero and they've had that bond severed; the children are angry and hurt.

The intake manager sent Sue a packet of information about attachment disorder and the available services. To begin treatment, an intake process takes place, involving an evaluation of the child and family accomplished through information Sue and Jerry would send back to the Center. A lot of information was requested, including:

- Social history (birth family data and what happened to the child in the first two years of life):
- Reports on previous psychological testing and treatment already completed;
- Medical information;
- School information;
- Descriptions of the child's behavior.

Sue and Jerry were also asked to take a Minnesota Multiphasic Personality Inventory (MMPI) and write personal autobiographies. It was explained this information would help the Center to understand family dynamics, and any individual issues the parents might have that might get in the way of the treatment process. The more Sue and Jerry learned about the treatment, the more they thought this was what Annie needed. But how were they going to pay for it? By this time, they had already exhausted their savings trying to get help. They did not have an adoption subsidy for Annie to help with therapy expenses. They were ineligible for medical funds from their state, unless they chose to relinquish their child. (If they chose to pursue this, there was no guarantee Annie would then receive the help she needed.)

With the help of an attorney and their therapist, they fought for and received an agreement from the county, who had placed the child with them, to pay for attachment treatment.

After Sue and Jerry completed the admission requirements an initial evaluation determined that a Two Week Intensive was indicated for Annie. The treatment team was assembled and a date was set for Sue, Jerry and Annie to come to Colorado. Their home-town therapist, who was interested in receiving training in attachment therapy, agreed to accompany the family for the Two Week Intensive.

The big day had finally arrived. As they flew into Colorado, Sue and Jerry felt like an enormous weight had been lifted from their shoulders. There were actually people here who understood their child and their family and who knew what to do to help. They found the entire treatment team very understanding and supportive. They were ready to begin the work!

Initially apprehensive about the therapeutic treatment family who would parent their child throughout the treatment process, Sue and Jerry wondered about their child being required to call the therapeutic parents "mom and dad". At first they questioned the necessity of the extreme structure of the program and the different parenting techniques being utilized by the therapeutic family. As the week progressed, however, they began to see the rationale for the structure and parenting techniques. By the end of the two weeks, they had become very close to their therapeutic family. By design they spent much time in the therapeutic home, observing and learning from the therapeutic parents. This family soon became a major source of support to Sue and Jerry.

Even with all the initial preparation, and information sharing, Sue and Jerry were surprised at the intensity of emotions they felt. They saw aspects of their child that had never been revealed to them before. Annie began honestly describing "killing feelings" and revealing how calculating her behavior had been and how distorted her thinking was. They saw the depth of their daughter's pain, fear, sadness and rage and they ached for her. Their hearts, numb for sometime, began to feel a full range of emotions -- empathy for their child, reactions to what they were discovering about her.

During several sessions focusing on Annie's previous abuse, Sue began to remember her own previous abuse, and became very distraught. A secondary therapist accompanying them in the observation room began to comfort Sue, asking her to share what was happening with her. This began a healing process for Sue, as well. The therapeutic process was working well.

During the intensive Annie was learning how to love and live in a family, with the help of her therapeutic family. She was becoming open to her parents' love. Sue and Jerry also began to recognize some of their own issues and worked on them.

This family that had been without hope, began to feel hopeful about the future. The home-town therapist was excited about what he was learning and planned to continue his education in attachment therapy, so that he could help more children like Annie. Everyone felt the Two Week Intensive had been successful. When a follow-up treatment plan was formulated by the team, Sue, Jerry and Annie could return home to continue their work with their therapist. Included in the recommendations were respite care (to give the parents a break) and a support group.

This family returned home, exhausted but happy. At first Annie tried some testing behaviors (she was testing the limits), but Sue called the therapeutic family and received the support and suggestions she needed to feel effective as a parent. On a weekly basis she also received a call from the secondary therapist, asking how things were going. Sue and Jerry were beginning to believe in themselves as parents again and Annie, for the first time, was beginning to be reciprocal in her relationship with her parents. After several months, they felt so confident they didn't need weekly contact from The Attachment Center; they suggested monthly calls.

The changes that were made proved long-lasting for Annie. She was able to develop reciprocal relationships with school personnel and friendships with peers. She and her family looked forward to attending a reintegration conference (discussing dynamics of the return of a child to their family after treatment) at The Attachment Center as part of their summer vacation. Sue and Jerry wanted their treatment team to see the progress Annie had made.

Finally they were confident in the future, knowing that if Annie experienced difficulties during any of the developmental milestones of her life, she would be welcome to return to the Center for additional help.

The experience of this family is typical of many families dealing with attachment disordered children. There are many levels of attachment disorder, from mild to severe, (attachment disorders run on a continuum) and problems that correlate to the severity of symptoms, but most families experience the same feelings, issues and problems. All families, however, do not have the same outcome and sometimes further work is required. This, understandably, depends upon the child's previous history and the severity of the attachment disorder.

Following is a discussion of many aspects of the parenting experience, as it relates to attachment disordered children.

THE PARENTING EXPERIENCE

PARENTING EXPECTATIONS

Parents have many similar expectations when it comes to parenting. Most parents want to see their children grow up to be happy, productive, well-adjusted adults. They look forward to spending enjoyable time with their children through the years. Certainly, they look forward to enjoying their grandchildren. They are curious about the career choices their children will make, what kind of adults their children will be. Most anticipate a guiding role in their children's lives, hoping to pass on something of their own history and values to their children.

Parents usually believe that they, themselves, have something to offer a child -- perhaps to pass on. They hope to give their children a similar family life to that they enjoyed as children. Perhaps, to improve on the family life they experienced.

Most surveys of parents find the following responses to the question, "What do you like most about parenting?"

- The love I get from my children;
- Watching my children grow up into the adults I would like them to be, and;
- Knowing I am doing the right thing for my child.

To the parent of an attachment disordered child, these are three areas that are not particularly rewarding to them as parents. Parents seeking therapy or their children hope that eventually these responses will be true for them as well.

Approximately 80 percent of the children seen at The Attachment Center at Evergreen, Inc., are living with adoptive parents or foster parents. Another 10 percent are living with blended families, but have spent some time living with the other birth parent and perhaps various non-relatives. The remaining 10 percent live with their birth parent(s).

There are many possible explanations for the development of attachment disorder, some of them beyond any parent's control. The end result is very much the same -- a child who is extremely difficult to parent; a parent who feels blamed and who blames himself/herself; a home that is in a constant turmoil, due to the child's relentless behavior; and frequently, a community that is neither understanding nor supportive. This picture definitely does not fit what most expect of parenthood.

REALITIES

Most of the parents at The Attachment Center would not seem to have any particular difficulties were they to parent an average child. The extreme difficulty of parenting an attachment disordered child tends to magnify imperfections and focus attention on any "unfinished business" an individual may have left unresolved. This frequently results in parents being targeted as "the problem" by well meaning, but ill-informed professionals.

By the time a parent contacts The Attachment Center at Evergreen, most have all but given up hope of finding anyone who understood their experience. Each family is unique, but there stories are all too familiar:

- These are families under a great deal of stress.
- They feel they have lost all control in their own home.
- All methods have been tried and all have failed.

- Everything that they once held dear has been "trashed."
- They are isolated.
- Family relationships have reached the breaking point.
- They fear their own children.
- They question their sanity.
- They have been blamed for the problem by family, friends, school personnel, social services and the very professionals from whom they sought assistance.
- They blame themselves.
- They question their worth as individuals.
- They secretly wonder if they are "being punished for some past mistakes."
- Siblings hesitate to bring friends home.
- There is always so much tension.
- It is impossible to predict what might happen next.
- Other children in the home begin to feel jealous of the time and energy required of their parents by the troubled child.
- Finally, there seems to be no relief available and life becomes very confusing. Parents even begin to question the very meaning of life.

All of the above are normal responses to parenting an attachment disordered child. Because of these factors, many parents of these deeply disturbed children have symptoms of PTSD as a result of living with the continuing severe and chronic stress. This on-going stress and the changes they go through as individuals can happen over time, almost imperceptibly.

Many parents are unaware of how severely they have been affected. And yet, the symptoms are there:

SYMPTOMS OF POSTTRAUMATIC STRESS DISORDER

PRIMARY TRAUMA SYMPTOMS
(Diagnostic Criteria for 309.81 Post Traumatic Stress Disorder, Diagnostic and Statiscal Manual, DSM-IV)

> A. The person has been exposed to a traumatic event in which both of the following were present:
> (1) the person experienced, witnessed, or was confronted with an event or events that involved actual or threatened death or serious injury, or a threat to the physical integrity of self or others.
> (2) the person's response involved intense fear, help-lessness, or horror. (NOTE: In children, this may be expressed instead by disorganized or agitated behavior.)

B. The traumatic event is persistently re-experienced in one (or more) of the following ways:

(1) recurrent and intrusive distressing recollections of the event, including images, thoughts, or perceptions. (NOTE: In young children, repetitive play may occur in which themes or aspects of the trauma are expressed.)

(2) recurrent distressing dreams of the event. (NOTE: In children, there may be frightening dreams without recognizable content.)

(3) acting or feeling as if the traumatic event were recurring (includes a sense of reliving the experience, illusions, hallucinations, and dissociative flashback episodes, including those that occur on awakening or when intoxicated). (NOTE: In young children, trauma-specific reenactment may occur.)

(4) intense psychological distress at exposure to internal or external cues that symbolize or resemble an aspect of the traumatic event.

(5) physiological reactivity or on exposure to internal or external cues that symbolize or resemble an aspect of the traumatic event.

C. Persistent avoidance of stimuli associated with the trauma and numbing of general responsiveness (not present before the trauma), as indicated by three (or more) of the following:

(1) efforts to avoid thoughts, feelings, or conversations associated with the trauma

(2) efforts to avoid activities, places, or people that arouse recollections of the trauma

(3) inability to recall an important aspect of the trauma

(4) markedly diminished interest or participation in significant activities.

(5) feeling of detachment or estrangement from others

(6) restricted range of affect (e.g. unable to have loving feelings)

(7) sense of foreshortened future (e.g. does not expect to have a career, marriage, children or a normal lifespan)

D. Persistent symptoms of increased arousal (not present before the trauma), as indicated by two (or more) of the following:

(1) difficulty falling or staying asleep

(2) irritability or outbursts of anger

(3) difficulty concentrating

(4) hypervigilance

(5) exaggerated startle response

E. Duration of the disturbance (symptoms in Criteria B, C, and D) is more than 1 month.

F. The disturbance causes clinically significant distress or impairment in social, occupational, or other important areas of functioning.[4]

Don R. Chaterall, Ph.D., takes this description further in his book, Back From the Brink, A Family Guide to Overcoming Traumatic Stress:

> "**Primary trauma** refers to the direct effects of the trauma on your thoughts and emotions -- the re-experiencing, the emotional numbing, and the hyperarousal. **Secondary trauma** refers to the changes in your relationships and the way in which you view yourself, which is influenced by your relationships".[5]

Some of the following symptoms, in outlined form, have been paraphrased from Chaterall's book:

SECONDARY TRAUMA SYMPTOMS
- You realize that your relationships with others have changed.
- You experience stress in significant relationships, e.g., marriage, friends, family, etc.
- You realize that you have changed.
- You realize you no longer experience the same enjoyment in your relationships with others.
- You may experience a decrease in sex drive.
- You feel different from other people.
- You feel disconnected from others, alienated and lonely.
- You experience a damaged sense of self.
- You feel out of control emotionally.
- You may experience helplessness, hopelessness and anger (rage).
- You may develop health problems.
- You may become excessively immersed in work.

ADDITIONAL TRAUMA SYMPTOMS
- Your perception of yourself in relation to the world changes.
- You develop selective perception

---

[4] Diagnostic and Statistical Manual (DSM-IV), American Psychiatric Association, 4th ed., 1994

[5] Don R. Chaterall, Ph.d., (1992) Back from the Brink, New York: Bantam Books, p. 30

- You become more aware of dangers and feel more vulnerable.
- You question the meaning of your existence.
- You feel that your life is out of control and you take on a victim identity.
- You feel fatigued, depressed and guilty.
- You may deny to yourself or others the severity of the problems.
- You alternate between trying harder and giving up.

LIVING WITH A TRAUMA SURVIVOR

"Now you have an idea of how far-reaching the effects of traumatization can be on a trauma survivor. His or her life can literally be torn apart. But the effect of traumatization do not stop with the trauma survivor. The survivor's loved ones, those who are emotionally close to (him/her) can also pay a mental, emotional or even physical price. The effects of traumatization are easily passed on from parent to child, from child to parent, from spouse to spouse, or even from friend to friend. An entire family can be affected by one member's traumatization."[6]

It is true that children with attachment disorder also have many of the characteristics of Post Traumatic Stress Disorder. Parents of attachment disordered children thus suffer the effects of living with a trauma survivor, as well as having legitimate PTSD, as a result of the tremendous stress created each day by living with their child's behavior.

Parents must recognize that they are essential to their child's well-being. They are the most important element in their child's future. The task they face is extremely challenging. They must be at their very best to accomplish the goal of reaching and healing their child.

Parents of children with attachment disorder must understand the first and second important rules for parents are:

* * * * * * * * * *

1) TAKE GOOD CARE OF YOURSELF, and
2) TAKE GOOD CARE OF YOURSELF.

* * * * * * * * * *

---

[6] Op.Cit., p.59.

For these parents this means recognizing the symptoms of PTSD in yourself and taking essential steps to resolve these issues. This means:
- allowing yourself to grieve the loss of dreams and expectations.
- establishing realistic goals and setting appropriate boundaries.
- allowing your child to make mistakes and to learn from these mistakes.
- letting go of responsibility for another human being and assuming responsibility for yourself and your efforts.

If a child can internalized this behavior from a parent, that parent has given that child a great gift!

PITFALLS

There are several typical pitfalls that parents of attachment disordered children encounter. Knowledge of these areas will assist parents in recognizing them and avoiding them. A proactive stance in these situations is always better than a reactive stance:
- Lack of family understanding. Frequently extended family members do not see your child acting in the ways that you find so distressing. They find it difficult to believe that a child so young could have such destructive tendencies. To be honest, most of us would rather hold on to our beliefs about the innocence of children. Families frequently see a charming, though somewhat manipulative child. Hidden from their eyes are the murderous looks, the calculating "fuck you" behaviors, the lack of any reciprocal relationships, the oppositional-defiant responses to any reasonable requests, the out-of-control rages that keep a family on edge -- always waiting for the next storm. It is little wonder that parents of attachment disordered children feel isolated. Their damaged sense of self worth is worse if they get a poor response from others, particularly from those closest to them.
- A lack of appropriately trained treatment professionals often forces parents to spend fortunes and years seeking assistance. They can end up with little to show for their efforts except discouragement and increased self-doubt. Many of these children exhaust family financial resources and insurance benefits, spending months and years in hospitals, institutions, group residential facilities. Families are told that they must "love the child more" or "not be so strict". Families are frequently blamed for the child's problems. Traditionally, therapy is based on mutual trust and reciprocity in relationships, two qualities that are lacking in attachment disordered children. Since children have little cognitive awareness of their initial two years of life, they have no frame of reference for their

intense feelings. It has been found that traditional therapy will not break through the thick defensive walls these children use to block the healing feeling and expression of their pain and the resolution of their trauma. Identifying the problem and understanding the issues go a long way toward empowering families to continue their efforts with a child. Asking families to go through years and years of therapy with no results, while they live in daily hell, is cruel and unusual punishment -- not only for the family, but for the child whose childhood is quickly slipping away.

An attachment disordered child who had not had successful treatment is unable to receive the nurturing that is every child's due, is unable to playfully relax and experience the joys of childhood. (For more information on how to find a therapist who cares and understands the difficulties of parents with attachment disordered children, see Appendix IV.)

- A lack of trained respite care. Babysitters are hard to recruit and hard to retain. The behaviors exhibited by an attachment disordered child requires a mature, insightful caretaker. Teenagers do not typically have the maturity and judgment required for the care of these children. A caretaker who experiences a particularly difficult situation with a child is unlikely to volunteer for such in the future. A tendency by parents to hesitate to ask for assistance and are unable to relax while away, wondering what their child might be doing.

- A lack of adequate funding to provide needed services. No child comes with a guarantee. The responsibility for children has always rested with their parents. Therapy costs can be a burden when not covered by health insurance. Hospital costs are astronomical. Most parents of attachment disordered children are looking at a lifetime of expenses and risks associated with helping their child reach adulthood with some capacity to live in society. Adoption subsidies are the exception rather than the rule, but are essential to parents of adopted children, especially special needs children. Many of these children are in the foster care system and have Medicaid coverage. Unfortunately, these severely challenged children require the most experienced therapists. There are few therapists with the level of skill required who will accept Medicaid. Therefore, many of these children are treated by therapists fresh out of school, who may not recognize the problem and who are unlikely to have the knowledge and skills to provide effective help.

- Triangulation and Splitting: Between husband and wife, being parents and siblings, between parents and schools, between parents and therapists, leaves parents constantly on guard and denies them the support that they need to effectively parent these children. Parents find themselves constantly explaining, "putting out fires," trying to stay one step ahead of the child. Driving a wedge between husband and wife because of the child's differential treatment of parents can eliminate the parents primary source of support -- each other. The ultimate triangulation and power play can involve the child making false allegations of abuse as a way to "pay back" or "get even" with their parent's legitimate use of authority. Due process is typically not a consideration for parents when the possibility of a child being abused is raised. To lose one's self-respect and reputation in addition to all else, is more than some parents can bear, particularly when it comes in the guise of the child you love.

- Fears: The fear of what your child might do or might be capable of doing is never far from a parents thoughts. Many parents fear for the safety of family members, neighbors, extended family and society as a whole. Fear of what the future holds for your child, and whether your child will ever be able to be productive and self-supporting. These fears can be overwhelming and at times "paralyzing" in their power to block constructive action.

- Lack of appropriate training for parenting attachment disordered children. Parents of these children have found that normal parenting strategies do not work. Most parent training classes are based on what might be effective with normal children. When these techniques are attempted to no avail, parents feel they have no means to establish control in their own home. These children do not typically respond to external reinforcements in the way normal children do. They are internally motivated. They, in fact, lack: the desire to please parents; basic cause and effect thinking; as well as, the judgment to make logical decisions. They are motivated by the desire to control and to "do onto others before they do onto you". They respond to requests with oppositional behavior. Such characteristics make standard parenting practices ineffective.

- Lack of full disclosure of records so that parents, adoptive and foster, are frequently not given the information they need to adequately parent these children. Much valuable time and energy is lost. The relationship between the placing agency caseworker and the parent that begins with inaccurate information is based on mistrust. The caseworker who could be a supportive resource is thus not available because of this lack of partnership based on mutual trust and respect.

Full disclosure of records must become routine, if adoptive and foster parents are to have a chance understanding how to parent these children.

- Often with attachment disordered children the parents assume too much responsibility for child - - the parents are working harder than the child on the child's life and "owning the child's problems." As long as parents have all the "units of concern" for a child's behavior, the child will not find it necessary to make changes. The child controls by being "out of control".

We address these pitfalls here, not to discourage parents, but to point out some typical areas of difficulties so that effective strategies can be developed to address them.

POSSIBILITIES

Every "pitfall" represents a "possibility" for positive change. Some strategies in each of these areas will help:

- It is essential to find the right therapist -- one who has an understanding of attachment disorder and of effective treatment. It is important for parents to check out a therapist's knowledge and experience relative to attachment therapy. Parents and therapists must develop a working relationship, so that children are unable to triangulate between parents and therapist. Parents should be members of the treatment team. That is not to say that parents should not also work on their own issues. Parents should be empowered to effectively parent their children. Blaming parents is counter-productive. It is essential that parents feel "heard, understood, and validated" before any attempts to alter their parenting techniques is attempted. Parents should see their efforts to change as part of the solution to the problem, not as necessary change because "they are the problem."
- Finding and helping to train a reliable respite care provider is essential to taking care of yourself. Getting away helps to refocus and re-energize parents. It also helps to develop a supportive ally when a consistent caretaker begins to see the same child the parent sees daily.
- Establish attachment disorder parent support groups. This will help you to heal in the context of relationships. Support groups help to heal a parent's damaged sense of self and damaged connectedness to others. An accepting, understanding, sympathetic group will help to: validate your experiences and feelings; reaffirm your worth as a person; explore and clarify your perceptions; assist with problem solving; gain a point of reference; develop alliances and strengthen your resolve. Support groups also help increase

your understanding and form a base for educating and advocating in your community.[7]

- Networking with others in your community who could be resources for you, for your child, and who could help to establish increased awareness of attachment disorder.
- Openly advocating for attachment disordered children so that resources will be available for them.
- Identifying and contacting potential funding sources will help to make appropriate resources available for others. Contacting local, state, and national legislative bodies to educate them as to the need for resources. Emphasize the savings when a child's life is turned around early vs. the expense of housing an adult in corrections who might have been helped if appropriate resources had been available.
- Get out of the victim role and take back your power as a parent. You are in control of your own home and you do not have to accept blame for your child's difficulties. Learn effective parenting strategies. Educate yourself. Take care of yourself and of your spouse. Focus on the needs of other children in the family. Learn to have fun again.
- See a therapist to help you resolve your own issues. Identify your own weak points, understand why some behaviors "drive you up the wall" and learn how to interrupt those negative interaction patterns.
- Improve your marriage. Grieve your losses. Change your expectations.

Number eight suggests seeing a therapist to help parents resolve their own issues. This is extremely important because parents of attachment disordered children sometimes fall into the trap of reworking their own childhood issues when parenting one of these children. It is known in the field that many parents who have adopted children are in a "rescuing" mode because of past, unfinished business, regarding their own childhoods -- perhaps there was abuse, neglect, etc., that has not been resolved.

But how to find a therapist? How to choose the one that is best for your life and your issues? We cite an excellent article written by Tim Bandy, a child and family therapist at the Therapy Center for Adoptive,

---

[7] An excellent national network resource is the ADPN (Attachment Disorder Parents Network) started by Gail Trenberth of Boulder, CO. The address is: P.O. Box 18475, Boulder, CO 80308.

Divorced and Step Families in Ann Arbor, MI, appeared in the July/ August, 1995, issue of Adoptive Families, (See the Appendix)

THE PLACING PARENTS ROLE IN TREATMENT AT THE ATTACHMENT CENTER AT EVERGREEN, INC.

Placing a child in a treatment facility is done with mixed feelings on the part of the parents. Usually there is relief that finally a place has been found which can provide the child with the help needed to improve his/ her functioning as a caring, loving person. There is also a sense of relief in having the child out of the family, on a temporary basis, because the child's presence has been the focal point and source of difficulty for some time. With the child gone from the immediate family environment, other members of the family can focus attention on each other and express caring, encouragement and support for one another -- which has been almost impossible with the constant disruptive influence of the child who has been placed with The Attachment Center. Relief is usually accompanied by some feelings of remorse, regret and doubt.

Questions persist as to whether the "right" thing has been done for the child. One wonders if just one more thing would have worked. It is also difficult not to become caught up in, "What did I, or we do wrong?" The "what ifs", "shoulds", "coulds" are always there. Another concern is whether the treatment at The Attachment Center can help. A closely monitored and coordinated team approach is believed to be the most beneficial treatment situation for a troubled child. Such a coordinated effort provides a child with the consistency and security necessary to create the environment needed for positive behavioral and attitudinal changes to take place.

One of the most important elements in the team approach is the family environment in which each child is placed. We believe a natural home environment with well-trained therapeutic parents provides the best situation in which a child can learn new ways of behaving. Because our therapeutic parents have received extensive training and have a great deal of experience in working with troubled children, we view them as having paraprofessional status. This means they work "along side of" the professionals in helping a child to learn better ways of functioning. A child in one of our therapeutic homes receives the needed loving care along with close monitoring and training of their behavior.

The placing parents are heavily involved during the initial two weeks of treatment in what is called a "Two Week Intensive". This Intensive is what "opens the door" to being able to work with and live with these children. It breaks through that control and resistance the children use to keep people who love them at a distance. Many children go home after the Two Week Intensive. With trained follow-up therapy and different parenting techniques the child continues to improve. The more severe children can be admitted to our long-term treatment program for as long as they need to be there. Reintegration back into the home is carefully planned as the child progresses. (See the chapter on reintegration.)

Because of the importance of the Two Week Intensive, both parents are asked to come and stay for two weeks. Placing parents are required to bring a home-town therapist with them to participate in the Two Week Intensive process. This is extremely important for a successful outcome. The home-town therapist with the placing parents are the basis for one component of the therapeutic team.

The other component consists of the therapist, secondary therapist, the therapeutic foster parents, the psychiatrist and the program manager of The Attachment Center. Each member of the therapeutic team has a very important role to play in accomplishing the healing process for everyone. (See Chapter Six) Each part of the team will have specific goals to work on to facilitate the eventual reintegration of the child back into his/her family.

Siblings are invited since they, too, have been very affected by the child being placed. They are at times actually involved in the intensive therapy process to help them understand why they have been the recipients of such rage and abuse. They, too, are helped to express their feelings about this. This time can be used by the parents to devote more attention to the other children and to themselves. Often some healing begins for the entire family during this time, which affirms their decision to place the child in long-term treatment, if necessary, so that the whole family can have the chance to heal.

During the Two Week Intensive the parents usually are involved in the therapy with the child approximately three hours daily, five days a week. This is also a time when placing parents are able to meet and spend time with the therapists and the therapeutic parents. They watch the therapeutic interventions with the child from behind a one way mirror. At strategic points in the therapy, they are invited into the treatment room to participate directly. This facilitates the placing parents' need to process and deal with their own anguish over their previous unsuccessful efforts to love and help the child (which in many cases has involved YEARS of effort). At the moments when the child is most accessible to nurturing, the parents are brought in to hold their child in order to facilitate the attachment process.

The Two Week Intensive also provides an opportunity for the placing parents to see their child express directly their deep-seated feelings of rage, fear and sadness -- often for the first time -- and to see the feelings focused on the real sources of the child's pain. This is very helpful for placing parents to finally come to understand experientially why all their efforts to love and help have been so long rejected by the child.

After the Two Week Intensive and placement of the child into the long-term treatment phase of the program, the parents return home and are encouraged to keep in close contact with the therapist. They are encouraged to work with their home-town therapist on their goals, issues and parenting strategies. This begins a period during which contact with the child is scheduled therapeutically through the therapist. Progress may seem slow. It can be a difficult time for parents. It is helpful for parents to focus their energies during this time on healing themselves, their marriages, and their families. This is a time when the focus can be on learning effective parenting strategies to assist their child. Recommended readings and videotaped trainings can supplement parent training sessions offered by The Attachment Center. The ability of placing parents to change parenting strategies is critical to the child's success in continuing his/her improvements. This time can also be utilized to select and train respite care providers or to establish a support group.

Reintegration of the child into his/her home is a carefully planned process. Visits between parents and child are coordinated by the therapist during the last three-fourths of the child's placement. The purpose of these visits is to help the child and the placing parents put into practice their new ways of interacting. The therapist helps the parents and the child deal with any problems which arise.

As a child's discharge from the program becomes imminent, parents again frequently have mixed feelings. Parents look forward to being reunited as a family, but there is genuine anxiety as well. "Has he/she really changed?" "Will it be like it was before?" "Am I really ready to parent this child?" "The therapeutic parents make it look so easy." "What if it doesn't work?" These feelings typically are shortlived as the family goes about the business of daily life. There will be some difficult times and some testing behavior, but with the different parenting techniques and appropriate therapy the significant changes that have been made will continue and the families quality of life should improve.

After a child returns to his/her home, we assume there will be a need for consultation with either the therapist or the therapeutic parents. The placing parents are encouraged to remain in contact with the therapist and the therapeutic parents as long as it appears helpful to do so. On-going therapy with the hometown therapist, access to respite care, and participation in a support group are important to successful reintegration. A year of planned follow-up support and a structured aftercare plan help to consolidate the gains made. Consultation, training, support and respite are available through the Attachment Center to help this family succeed.

TURNING POINTS

Placing parents have a very difficult role to play. They have survived incredible insults and pain to see that their children receive the help that they need. They bear the scars of battle. The struggle can take many different turns. Some parents witness a breakthrough moment when the light goes on and the child "gets it", lets go of the pain and starts to let the love into his heart. There is a strength that comes from knowing that the battle was fought and won. Some parents must come to terms with limitations that their child may continually face. An acceptance of what is and an acknowledgement that "no stone was left unturned" help to make this process easier. These parents are special individuals who offer much to the children they love and care for.

RESOURCES:

McKelvey, C. & Stevens, J (1994) Adoption Crisis: The Truth About Adoption and Foster Care, Golden, CO.: Fulcrum Publishers, pps. 12-17.

Diagnostic and Statistical Manual, (DSMIV), American Psychiatric Associations, 4th ed., 1994.

Chaterall, Don R., PhD., Back From the Brink, A Family Guide to Overcoming Traumatic Stress. New York: Bantam Books, p. 30-59.

Attachment Disorder Parents Network, P. O. Box 18475, Boulder, CO 80308.

Banty, Tim, "When Your Child Needs Special Help, Finding A Therapist," Adoptive Families, July/August 1995.

Attachment Center at Evergreen, Inc. Program Literature.

6

The Therapeutic Team

By

Paula Pickle, LCSW
Diane Meyer, LCSW
Forrest Lien, ACSW

The "team concept" has been around for years. The dynamic of a group working together toward a common goal is not only powerful but invigorating/energizing.

> *"A team is a group of people with a high degree of interdependence geared toward the achievement of a goal or completion of a task. In other words, they agree on a goal and agree that the only way to achieve the goal is to work together."*

This concept has become an integral part of our modern society. However, it has also become a catch phrase, implying simplicity of the process. The process becomes much more complicated to put into action. The Attachment Center at Evergreen, Inc. using a team approach, works toward building a firm foundation from which to treat the severely emotionally disturbed child and the family who is trying to raise the child. The team focal point is the "child" in treatment. Yet there are many other factors which need to be considered.

At the Attachment Center at Evergreen, Inc., the Treatment Team concept has been extensive and is best seen in the form of the diagram found at the end of this chapter.

In the Attachment Center model the layers of support surround each other and are dependent one upon the other, thus creating a ripple effect. The direction of the whole can be impacted by positive or negative movement of any of the layers. Each concentric circle represents another layer of support. Each concentric circle also represents a progression from intensive involvement to peripheral support. The whole team together represents layers of support which provide a "cocoon" where healing can occur.

THERAPEUTIC TEAM: ROLES

- The center of our treatment team is the CHILD. The child is the focal point of treatment, as well as the most vulnerable member of the team.

- The next focus of treatment is the child's FAMILY. Families not only need to heal from the trauma of living with and loving an emotionally disturbed child, but they also need new skills so they can effectively serve as treatment team members.

- The next team "layer" represents the THERAPEUTIC FAMILY. They are intensively involved in the daily life of the child, helping the child learn to be a loving family member. They provide education and support to the placing family. They provide essential information to the treatment team regarding the child's behavior on a daily living basis. The therapeutic family is the "heart" of the treatment team.

- The next concentric circle represents the HOME-TOWN THERA-PIST. Many of our children come from other parts of the world. Reintegration of the child back into his/her family requires that a "hometown team" be established. The "hometown therapist" is a key ingredient in this team. The therapist will assist the placing family in understanding their child, in understanding their own response to their child, in providing support and/or developing support groups, as well as communicating progress to the treatment team.

- The next concentric circle represents The Attachment Center's PRIMARY THERAPIST. The therapist provides intensive treatment to the child, and encourages the family to address their own issues. He/she consults with the therapeutic parents regarding specific behaviors the child exhibits and they determine the particular parental therapeutic interventions that are appropriate for the child and family. He/she also provides support and assistance to the family in carrying out the plan for treatment. The primary therapist serves as a consultant to the "hometown" therapist, providing education and support.

- The next concentric circle represents the referring agency or CASEWORKER, who serves an important function as a supporting team member. Frequently, the caseworker helps to advocate not only for the treatment itself, but for the funding necessary for treatment. The caseworker has access to local support mechanisms and systems which are essential for the continued success of the family's treatment.

- The next concentric circle represents additional members of the Attachment Center therapeutic team:

a). The <u>PSYCHIATRIST</u> evaluates the child. Using the medical history, direct information from the family, and reports from the treatment team, an appropriate diagnosis is made. The use of an effective medication regimen can be extremely helpful.

b) the <u>SECONDARY THERAPIST</u> adds extra therapeutic support for the primary therapist and helps the placing family and hometown therapist understand the therapeutic process. He/she provides follow-up support to the hometown team by calling periodically to assess progress. This information is then shared with the rest of the treatment team.

c) the <u>PSYCHOLOGIST</u> provides psychological testing as necessary, to gather additional information for the treatment team to utilize in developing an effective plan of treatment.

- The next concentric circle represents additional <u>COMMUNITY SUPPORT SYSTEMS</u> which may be in place or which may be developed by the hometown team. This *could* include supportive family and friends. It *should* include trained respite care providers and a support group. Efforts should be made to develop understanding supports within the educational, medical, therapeutic, legal, and social services communities.

- The next concentric circle represents The Attachment Center Program, represented by the <u>PROGRAM MANAGER</u>. The Program Manager oversees the process and facilitates the building of a working team. This includes gathering of admission information, assisting with creative funding options, and working with the team to support creative therapeutic interventions. The Program Manager helps to integrate State guidelines/regulations and program philosophy with the treatment plan that will best help the child. Additional services available through the Attachment Center program, (e.g., relief, recreational, educational, ancillary treatment options, and follow-up services) would also be represented by this concentric circle.

Each member of the treatment team plays a vital and distinct role. The success of this treatment is dependent to a large extent on each member of the team fulfilling their particular role within the context of the team. The roles are defined more specifically by the treatment plan which the team develops.

THERAPEUTIC TEAM: PROCESS

The team process begins with a family making application for treatment at The Attachment Center at Evergreen, Inc. The initial contact is between the Program Manager and the family. During this time, an understanding of the child and his family begins to develop. Efforts are made to assist the family in understanding The Attachment Center's treatment process.

The application process is extensive. It includes medical, social, psychiatric, psychological, educational and background information on the child. It explores previous treatment records. It also includes autobiographical information and personality profiles on parents, descriptions of current family functioning, descriptions of their child's behavior, and the family's response to that behavior. The family is asked to describe their hopes, expectations and fears.

The purpose of this extensive application process is to enable the treatment team to begin the treatment process with an understanding of the child in the context of his/her family. It also helps the team to know the strengths, talents, personalities and issues which the placing family will bring to the treatment team. The Program Manager selects the rest of the treatment team members -- a primary therapist and a therapeutic family as well as any additional team members deemed necessary. The application information is shared with these team members so that they can prepare.

The Program Manager also initiates contact with the hometown therapist and referring agency/caseworker. Placing families are encouraged to begin meeting with these individuals, if they have not already done so. It is important for the hometown team to be familiar with each other and to develop a good working relationship prior to treatment at The Attachment Center. Any issues or concerns which arise prior to treatment can be dealt with so that the treatment process can begin upon arrival of the hometown team at Evergreen. We ask that the entire family, as well as the hometown therapist and caseworker participate in the first two weeks of treatment. This helps to facility the team process.

It is important in helping all team members understand the process so they can effectively contribute to this team effort. During the first two weeks of treatment, each therapy session begins with a meeting of the treatment team. During this time, a clear understanding of the treatment goals is established. This is an opportunity to share information regarding the child's behavior and progress and it is an opportunity for various team members to address issues, concerns, and reactions, as well as to bring up questions that they may have. It forms the basis for that day's therapy.

During the therapy sessions, various treatment team members will alternately be in the treatment room or the observation room (which is behind a one-way mirrored window). Usually, there will be an ACE treatment team member with the family or hometown therapist during these sessions. This allows for questions to be answered as they arise. It also ensures that family emotions that arise during the course of treatment can be facilitated and worked through as they occur. Opportunities for placing family and therapeutic family to interact are provided. It is important for these families to trust and respect each other, so that exchange of information can occur. The therapeutic family's task is to support the placing family and provide information about effective parenting philosophy and techniques. This is the beginning of a relationship that may continue for a long time, as the placing family begins to develop new skills and understanding.

Opportunities for home-town therapist, caseworker, and the therapeutic team at The Attachment Center to exchange ideas and treatment strategies also are an important part of these two weeks. Educational opportunities are provided for the hometown therapist to assist the therapist in gaining specific treatment skills necessary to effectively serve the attachment disordered child and the placing family.

The Program Manager brings the full range of supportive services available through The Attachment Center to the treatment team. The manager's task is to continue to coordinate, facilitate, and assess the process as it occurs. Arrangements are made for psychiatric evaluations and other services as necessary.

Toward the end of the second week of treatment, the team begins to develop a longer range treatment plan. This plan could involve the child entering the Center's long term treatment program, or it could involve the development of a plan that will be carried out by the hometown team. In either case, the plan will include both segments of the team working closely together to achieve a common goal.

On-going assessment of the treatment plan and the team's progress toward goals is essential. This is particularly important when the child does not remain in the ACE program in Evergreen but goes home after the two-week intensive for follow-up treatment at home. This contact occurs through regular phone conference calls between treatment team members.

On-going follow-up contacts are made for one year following discharge from the treatment program. In addition to the support that this provides, it also encourages team members to identify problem areas early so that appropriate intervention strategies can be developed by the team. The team must remain intact, even after discharge from treatment at The Attachment Center.

THERAPEUTIC TEAM: TREATMENT GOALS

THE TREATMENT PLAN DRIVES THE TEAM. This plan is individualized for each child. Each team member has objectives which they work on as their contribution to the overall team goal. Monitoring this process and adjusting the plan to account for changes which occur is a task which each team member must take seriously. It is not enough for each team member to fulfill their particular role, it is also essential their efforts be integrated with those of the other team members.

It is imperative that all team members clearly understand the goal of treatment. Unspoken goals or conflicting goals can sabotage the process. It is also essential that the child contract for treatment, to the extent that child is capable of doing. Issues and conflicts among team members must be dealt with as they occur, so that the focus of treatment can be clear. Each team member must be willing to address their own issues.

Treatment objectives which support the overall goal of treatment must be clear and measurable. They must be supported by action plans which clearly state how the objectives are to be achieved and who is responsible for implementing the plans. A well developed treatment plan will keep the treatment team focused, involved, and accountable. As an example of how this treatment modality works, here is the story of "Nancy" (not her real name) and how the treatment team interacted on behalf of this one child:

A CASE HISTORY

Nancy was brought to The Attachment Center by a representative of the placing agency and her adoptive parents. At ACE the home-town team was joined by the treatment team: the primary therapist, treatment family and program manager from The Attachment Center.

The initial team meeting was held prior to treatment on the first day of the "Two-Week Intensive". Additional information was shared regarding history, basic care and treatment goals. At this meeting it was determined that Nancy would need to stay at ACE from nine to 18 months to accomplish the treatment goals. After a period of observation of the therapy in progress, the placing agency representative (caseworker) and the adoptive (placing) parents were to return to their home state.

The treatment team for Nancy was made up the adoptive parents, placing agency representative, therapeutic family, primary therapist, Attachment Center staff, psychiatrist and Nancy. In this case, since the family and placing agency were from another state, contact and involvement with them was done in a variety of ways:

a.) *PHONE CALLS:*

Contact was maintained during the course of treatment with weekly phone calls from the therapeutic family to the adoptive family and monthly phone calls to the placing agency. Also, on a monthly basis, conference calls were held; this contact was accelerated toward the end of treatment.

At the beginning of the calls the discussing parties included the primary therapist, therapeutic parent, adoptive parents and placing agency; at the end of the call Nancy was added to the conversation. Phone calls between Nancy and her parents were few at the beginning of treatment, because of her inability to reciprocate and interact positively, which was depressing to her parents. Phone calls in this situation between the adoptive parents and therapeutic family were discontinued for several months at the adoptive family's request. The parents were having issues of their own come up after the removal of such a disturbing influence from their home. The phone calls for a time were disturbing reminders of the pathology with which they had lived for so many years. This was a time for them to strive to return to normalcy for their family and the family resumed a more normal life. As this occurred, the damage done to them by Nancy became more apparent, causing resentment toward the absent child.

Soon phone calls were resumed, after the parents felt rested and better able to deal with hearing about Nancy's progress. With the help of their hometown therapist, they had worked through their own anger and feelings of being victimized. Toward the end of Nancy's treatment, calls were made at least once a week and sometimes twice a week between the therapeutic family and placing family. When special areas of concern arose the therapeutic family and placing agency also talked. Such areas included: orthodontic care for Nancy; starting public school; and involvement in an outside program dealing with Nancy's learning disabilities. The calls provided information the agency needed to secure funding for these procedures, and to report progress.

In addition, phone calls were taking place between the Attachment Center staff, the placing agency, the adoptive parents, the therapist, etc., on a monthly basis.

After Nancy returned home after treatment, the therapeutic family made phone calls twice a week at first and then once a week, finally slowing down to twice a month to do follow-up and support for the family and Nancy.

b.) VIDEO TAPES:

Because of the distance between Nancy's home state and Colorado, frequent visits were impossible. To fill the gap, video tapes were sent recording the child's progress. The therapeutic family filmed Nancy in a variety of situations, the therapist reviewed the tapes and the Center copied them to send to the placing agency and adoptive family every three months. These video tapes allowed all members of the team to remain involved and to see the child on a regular basis to assess the progress being made. On several occasions therapy sessions were also recorded and sent.

c.) WRITTEN REPORTS;

Once a month the therapist prepared a report with information from the therapeutic family, therapy sessions, the psychiatrist and any outside programs. Copies of the report were mailed to the placing agency and family. In all cases, the therapeutic family keeps a daily log and numbered behavior scale checklist (including 19 behaviors exhibited by an unattached child). Also, reports were written by the therapeutic family or therapist regarding any special services the child was receiving. In Nancy's case, such reports included information on her progress while attending a program for learning disabilities. Because of all the information coming to the agency and placing family, this component of the treatment team was kept well informed about Nancy's progress in their absence.

d.) VISITS:

Visits between Nancy and her parents and the placing agency were limited due to the expense of traveling great distances. A visit was made by Nancy to her home once during the first year of therapy. This visit was nine months into treatment. Nancy's visit was used to assess her readiness to return home and what areas still needed work in treatment. During the second year of treatment, another visit was made and the two visits compared. In between the home visits, the adoptive family came for a visit of one to *two weeks twice. The placing agency representative also visited Nancy on a quarterly basis to coincide with the adoptive family visit so that the entire treatment team could consult.*

When Nancy had successfully completed the treatment plan, the reintegration phase of treatment was implemented. Preparation for this phase was accomplished through increased phone calls between Nancy and her family. At this juncture, the adoptive family and caseworker traveled to ACE to join Nancy in her "graduation party." A treatment team meeting prepared everyone for the reintegration and a written plan was introduced at the meeting. This reintegration plan was designed to make sure Nancy and her family would have the support and resources needed to ensure a successful placement. Three months after Nancy returned to her home, her therapeutic parent traveled for a visit. With all three parents at home, they had a chance to brainstorm ideas for the home situation and Nancy. Three months after the first visit, Nancy returned to the Center for a week to maintain the relationship she had established with her therapeutic family and therapist. The next week the adoptive parents travelled to ACE to stay for two weeks and participate in another phase of the program for learning disabilities with Nancy.

As we look at the case of "Nancy" it is easy to see that each member of the treatment team played a key role in the success Nancy found during her treatment. This particular case had many challenges in maintaining a team approach, since the team members were from states so far away. In this situation, initially contact was maintained between two states, however, the adoptive parents moved during the course of treatment, meaning team members eventually ended up coordinating information between three states. The success in this case can be measured by the commitment of each member to the team approach to assure Nancy's success.

The ACE staff did the coordinating of all special services, travel arrangements, support for the therapeutic family, scheduling and participation in meetings inside and outside the treatment center. The staff made sure all team members received various forms of communication of progress during treatment and kept a comprehensive file of all services and psychological testing. As in all cases, the primary therapist provided therapy sessions at the center and in the therapeutic home; was available at any time (often at night); and was available to participate in meetings.

In such a situation, the placing agency caseworker provides stability throughout the treatment process and served as the one person who knew Nancy well before, during and after treatment. In Nancy's case, the caseworker was instrumental in securing additional funding for special services required by this child. In addition, Nancy had to stay a few months longer than originally estimated and that was an additional cost as well.

The caseworker also make arrangements for travel to the Center, participated in the therapy program by contacting Nancy's birth parents for information and maintained contact with and provided support for Nancy's adoptive parents.

The therapeutic family's role included providing daily living care for Nancy, carrying out treatment plan goals daily; scheduling appointments for Nancy and providing transportation; keeping documentation of progress, providing emotional support to Nancy and the adoptive family and maintaining contact between all team members.

Nancy's progress was followed by the psychiatrist throughout the process and he supervised trials of medications and had periodic sessions with Nancy.

In addition, a backup therapeutic family was needed to provide support for the therapeutic family in the way of respite relief and to contribute ideas in implementing treatment goals.

The most important member of this team was, of course, Nancy. Nancy went through a variety of emotional experiences and made the commitment to work hard to change her behaviors that had threatened to prevent her from living in a family and having a happy life. Nancy had the courage it took to make the necessary changes. She is now home with her adoptive family and is being successful in her family.

Certainly, each team member contributed to the success of this one child; the common factor being concern for Nancy's success and happiness in the future.

WHY THE TEAM APPROACH IS ESSENTIAL

Attachment disordered children operate from a different perspective than most people. Living with an attachment disordered child will test the mental and emotional capacity of most individuals. Effective treatment involves all aspects of the individual:

cognitive,
emotional,
social,
spiritual,
behavioral,
and physical.

To effectively reach an attachment disordered child on all these levels on a continuous basis, team members need a logical point of reference. These are children who resist any attempts to alter their way of looking at things, their way of behaving toward others, and their beliefs about themselves. They seeks others who confirm their distortions. To be able to help them consider alternatives, it is necessary to create an environment which consistently presents to them a real world, logical perspective.

The team approach does this very effectively. This approach helps team members maintain their perspective in the midst of chaos. This approach provides support when individual team members feel like giving up.

The task of helping an attachment disordered child achieve a more realistic and rewarding way of life, is too large a task for one individual. It requires group effort. Attachment disordered children are masters at splitting, triangulation, pitting one person against another, creating chaos, and destroying motivation of others trying to assist the child. A working team of individuals who understand this child, can provide a tight wall of support for each other and provide a clear picture of reality for the child.

CHARACTERISTICS OF AN EFFECTIVE TEAM

There are many different surveys identifying characteristics of effective teams, and similarities in the lists which emerge. One such list is found in The One Minute Manager Builds High Performing Teams by Blanchard, Carew, Parisi-Carew. It uses the acronym PERFORM to describe essentials of an effective team:

- *Purpose*
    1. *Members can describe and are committed to a common purpose.*
    2. *Goals are clear, challenging and relevant to purpose.*
    3. *Strategies for achieving goals are clear.*
    4. *Individual roles are clear.*
- *Empowerment*
    5. *Members feel a personal and collective sense of power.*
    6. *Members have access to necessary skills and resources.*
    7. *Policies and practices support team objectives.*
    8. *Mutual respect and willingness to help each other is evident.*
- *Relationships and Communication*
    9. *Members express themselves openly and honestly.*

10. Warmth, understanding and acceptance is expressed.
11. Members listen actively to each other.
12. Difference of opinion and perspective are valued.
• *Flexibility*
13. Members perform different roles and functions as needed.
14. Members share responsibility for team leadership and team development.
15. Members are adaptable to changing demands.
16. Various ideas and approaches are explored.
• *Optimal Productivity*
17. Output is high.
18. Quality is excellent.
19. Decision making is effective.
20. Clear problem-solving process is apparent.
• *Recognition and Appreciation*
21. Individual contributions are recognized and appreciated by leader and other team members.
22. Team accomplishments are recognized by members.
23. Group members feel respected.
24. Team contributions are valued and recognized by the organization.
• *Morale*
25. Individuals feel good about their membership on the team.
26. Individuals are confident and motivated.
27. Members have a sense of pride and satisfaction about their work.
28. There is a strong sense of cohesion and team spirit.

It is upon these principles that the treatment team of ACE is built. According to Jon R. Katzenbach and Douglas K. Smith, authors of The Wisdom of Teams, Creating the High-Performance Organization.

"Groups become teams through disciplined action. They shape a common purpose, agree on performance goals, define a common working approach, develop high levels of complementary skills, and hold themselves mutually accountable for results. And, as with any effective discipline, they never stop doing any of these things."

Putting together a team and developing that team into an effective unit is an important task. It requires planning and effort. The results can be great. An effective team can accomplish more than each of its individual members can accomplish individually.

OBSTACLES TO EFFECTIVE TEAMS

- Many people resist the team concept. According to Katzenbach and Smith, there are three primary sources for this reluctance.
- a) One of these is a lack of belief in the team concept or a belief that teams are more trouble than they are worth.
- b) Another source is an individual's personal discomfort with the team process, or a preference for working alone on tasks.
- c) A third source of resistance involves a lack of strong performance ethics on the part of an organization and the individual's reluctance to commit to such a team.
- Many individuals have had unsuccessful experiences with teams and may thus hesitate to actively participate in the team process. Building teams, itself, cannot be our goal. Teams develop through the process of creating a mutual plan of action, goal setting and mutual accountability.
- The Attachment Center at Evergreen, Inc., has additional challenges in developing an effective treatment team for each child. One such challenge is the physical separation between members of the treatment team. Each of our treatment teams involves the "hometown team" and the Attachment Center team.

Facilitating communication between team members and involving all team members in decision making requires coordination and planning. Failure to do so shifts the team member's focus to intro-team concerns, rather than goal achievement.

- Another challenge involves the differing levels of knowledge and experience in the area of attachment disorder between team members. This may lead to a reluctance on the part of some team members to actively share their thoughts, ideas, and concerns with the team. It also includes a reluctance on the part of those team members with more experience to admit vulnerability to the team or to seek assistance as needed.
- Another challenge relates to the fact that the child is the focus of the treatment. Those who work closely with the child -- the therapist, the therapeutic family, etc. -- typically have more clearly defined objectives. The home-town team has an equally important

task which must be just as clearly defined and integrated into the overall treatment plan. Failure to do so leaves an important part of the team feeling that there is nothing for them to do but wait, wasting valuable time. Ignoring this part of the team will lead to difficulties when it is time to reintegrate the child with the placing family.

SUMMARY

At the Attachment Center we have made it a priority that the treatment team needs to be very tight in communicating with each other, because of the clinical dynamics of an attachment disordered child. The collaborative treatment plan must be the path for a child's treatment while placed at The Attachment Center. The desired outcomes for a child in treatment, for example:

trusting others,
being vulnerable with others,
being respectful of others,
sharing feelings,
making mistakes and
learning with each other,

-- are all characteristics a good team requires. Attachment disordered children will challenge our teamwork because of the intensity in helping these children return successfully to their families and communities.

RESOURCES:

Parker, Glenn M. (1990), Team Players and Teamwork, The New Competitive Business Strategy, Jossey-Bass, Inc., p. 16.

Blanchard, Kenneth, Ph.D., Carew, Donald, Ed.D., and Parisi-Carew, Eunice, Ed.D., (1990)

The One Minute Manager, Builds High Performing Teams, William Morrow & Company, New York, NY. p. 22-23.

Katzenbach, Joh R., Smith, Douglas K. The Wisdom of Teams, Creating the High Performance Organization, NY, NY.

The Treatment Team

THE ACE TEAM
1. Child
3. The Therapeutic Family
5. The ACE Therapist
7. Additional ACE Team: Psychiatrist, Psychologist
9. ACE Program Support: Program Manager, Relief, Ancillary Services

THE HOME TEAM
2. The Family
4. The Hometown Therapist
6. The Referring Agency/ Caseworker
8. Community Support Systems: Groups, Respite Care, etc.

$$7$$

Two Week Intensives

Terry M. Levy, PH.D
& Michael Orlans, M.A.

CASE ILLUSTRATION: "RYAN"

The following case example demonstrates selected aspects of a two-week treatment process known as a Two Week Intensive. The clinical interventions and dialogues are authentic, but are considerably more comprehensive in the actual case:

> Ryan, age ten, was physically and sexually abused by his birth parents until age five. Protective services removed him and his two siblings from the home in 1989. Ryan was placed in a foster home and, after five months of severe acting-out (fire setting, cruelty to pets, destructive behavior), was removed from the home and hospitalized. He was then placed in another foster home, where he was adopted at age six. For the next four years he was seen by seven different psychologists and psychiatrists, and hospitalized four additional times.
> He was diagnosed with Post Traumatic Stress Disorder and Depression. The adoptive parents were told by the therapists that Ryan had no conscience and they recommended his removal from their home. Ryan's symptoms included: frequent rage reactions involving physical aggression and destruction of property; oppositional, defiant, and controlling behavior; sexual abuse of younger children; emotional detachment and lack of affection; suicidal ideation and attempts. His older brother was placed in a series of foster homes and hospitals. His younger sister was hospitalized

*with a diagnosis of Multiple Personality Disorder. Ryan's
history and background is typical of severely disturbed children seen and treated at the Attachment Center at Evergreen for attachment disorder.*

Many of the children referred to or brought to The Attachment Center
at Evergreen, Inc., for treatment initially undergo what is called a Two
Week Intensive program of therapy.

In this therapeutic approach, the child, parents, and, when appropriate,
other family members (e.g., siblings) participate in thirty hours of therapy
over a two week period (three hours per day for ten consecutive working
days). This therapy format was originally developed at The Youth Behavior
Program (the predecessor to the Attachment Center) to provide treatment
to children and families in need of services unavailable in their own geographic locale. These families traveled to Evergreen from every region of
the United States, as well as abroad, to receive specialized treatment for
attachment disorders. We realized that this short-term format provided
an array of clinical advantages for these typically highly resistant, controlling, non-trusting children. The consistency and intensity of daily therapeutic contact created a context in which defenses were reduced, motivation
increased, and a trusting therapeutic relationship was established. Although significant and dramatic changes often occur during the two-week
experience, this therapy was never intended to be a "magical cure". Intense
confrontation of emotional issues, in conjunction with strong support and
nurturance, "opens the door" for conventional therapy to be more effective. Follow-up therapy is essential.

Another advantage of this therapy format is our ability to observe and
modify family relationships and dynamics. Parent-child, marital and sibling
issues become evident in daily therapy sessions. Also, we encourage referring therapists to participate in the treatment process whenever possible.
This increases the likelihood of effective follow-up, and provides training
and supervision to mental health professionals interested in learning about
this modality.

The therapeutic setting incorporates a treatment room and observation
area separated by a one-way mirror. This provides the therapist with the
option of working with the family as a unit or having the parents observe
the child's therapy from behind the one-way mirror. The reasons for using
the one-way mirror are:

(a) It allows the parents to be a part of the treatment process
while interrupting destructive and inhibiting relationship
patterns;

(b) It provides the parents with effective role models in reference to the management of the behavioral and emotional problems of their child;

(c) Therapists can assess the affective responses and emotional availability of the parents as they observe their child in therapy. These sessions are routinely videotaped to provide feedback to family members, serve as teaching tools in the training and supervision of therapists, and provide valuable clinical information to the follow-up therapist.

A multi-disciplinary treatment team approach is used, consisting of co-therapists, therapeutic foster parents, and ancillary caseworkers, (e.g., referring social service caseworkers, follow-up therapists, psychiatric consultant). A male-female co-therapy team provides balance and flexibility, and is helpful for both individual and family intervention. For example, as one therapist works with the child, the other can provide support and guidance to the parents as they observe the therapy. Therapeutic foster parents are specifically trained to understand and work with attachment disordered children and their families. They provide a therapeutic milieu for the child during the two-week treatment. This "practice family" offers the child a valuable learning environment, and provides the parents with much needed respite, as well as role models of effective parenting skills and attitudes.

THERAPEUTIC GOALS

Successful therapy outcome depends upon the establishment of clear and concrete goals. Goals help the therapist, child and parents envision what needs to change. This creates the notion that possibilities do exist, leading to a more hopeful and optimistic attitude. Goals are framed positively, describing what is desirable rather than what is undesirable. They must be stated in specific behavioral terms, and be within the person's control, so that they are realistic and achievable in the here-and-now (e.g., "Express your anger verbally, face-to-face, starting your sentence with, 'I feel angry with you because...'"). Feeling a sense of ownership over goals motivates the individual to work hard and succeed.

General goals which govern the therapeutic process include:

- Develop a therapeutic context which facilitates a constructive working alliance with the child and parents.
- Clarify parents' (or primary custodians') level of commitment to the child.
- Encourage family members to identify their expectations and attitudes about therapy and, if pessimistic and limiting, to consider new possibilities.

- Encourage parents and child to personally invest in the treatment process which promotes a genuine desire to change (contracting).
- Increase expectation of success and facilitate a sense of hope.

General therapeutic goals for the child include:
- Contain and reduce acting-out behavior.
- Identify and express emotions verbally in face-to-face interaction.
- Address prior attachment-related trauma in a direct and honest manner with the therapist and primary caregivers.
- Experience positive (safe, genuine, nurturing) interaction and attachment with significant others (therapists, caregivers, siblings).

Specific therapeutic goals for the attachment disordered child or adolescent include the following:
- Provide a clear and honest account of past traumas: secrets are counter-productive.
- Direct anger and responsibility for maltreatment towards the perpetrators, rather than towards him or herself or current caregivers.
- Identify the source of his or her negative working model, understand the current behavioral patterns which ensue, and develop a cognitive set which includes positive self regard and a realistic perception of others.
- Interrupt the vicious circle of negative relationship patterns by experiencing trusting, supportive and nurturing interactions.
- Reduce the emotional charge of past traumatic events and memories by dealing with those traumas in new and effective ways (empowerment, mastery, desensitization).
- Acknowledge and express a range of emotions (anger, fear, sadness, pain, guilt, shame) in a direct and genuine manner with positive personal and interpersonal consequences.
- Take responsibility for one's own actions and decisions; learn to problem-solve and make healthy choices.
- Relinquish the extreme control orientation; rather than equating survival with vigilance and control, learn to allow certain safe and trusting relationships.
- Learn how to trust and whom to trust.
- Experience a constructive grieving process regarding the loss of attachment figures.
- Develop positive regard (trust, respect, caring) towards one's self; reduce self-contempt associated with the negative (internalized) self.

THERAPEUTIC METHODS

A variety of therapeutic strategies and techniques are used to promote cognitive, emotional, behavioral, and interpersonal change. These methods are based on the following principles regarding the process of change. Change occurs sequentially and developmentally. Thus, interventions are planned in stages, moving step-by-step towards desired goals.

The focus of change is multi-leveled: past, present and future. Past trauma is confronted and explored. Current patterns of thinking, behaving, coping, and relating are modified. Visions, goals, and plans for the future are emphasized so that positive possibilities become realities. Change occurs via actions. Thus, experiential methods are used extensively. Specific skills are taught (e.g., anger management, communication, conflict resolution) which reduce the anxiety associated with change, while building a sense of competency. As one relinquishes old patterns of behavior it is reassuring to have effective replacements available.

Therapists use a language of hope and communicate an expectation of success. Negative expectations can create self-fulfilling prophecies. The focus is on strengths and resources, not only on deficits and problems. Therapists acknowledge and support the positive aspects of the child and parents. Therapists are active, often serving in the role of guide or coach, and provide a balance of challenge and support. Resistance to change is expected; the child's sense of survival is correlated with maintaining the status quo and being in control. Humor is crucial. Therapists use humor to provide a balance to the seriousness and intensity of the therapy, and to send a message of perspective. The following specific therapeutic methods are used extensively.

Cognitive restructuring. Depending on the age and developmental level, the child is helped to identify and modify his or her negative internal working model. Using the first year of life attachment cycle story and other clinical techniques described later, the child learns how perceptions of self and others were developed, and is guided through a process which encourages a revision of cognitive beliefs. A two-step process is used. 1.) First, the current belief system is identified and verbalized (e.g., "I am bad and unlovable because I was abused"). 2.) Next, this cognitive frame is challenged and modified (e.g., "Your mother was abusive; you are good, worthwhile, lovable"). This process is repeated many times throughout therapy.

Psychodramatic reenactment. Treatment team members role-play individuals in the child's life to recreate prior traumatic scenarios. The child is encouraged to: (a) experience and express his or her genuine responses ("I feel frightened and helpless with my angry father") and, (b) experience and express alternative emotional, cognitive and behavioral responses, facilitating empowerment and corrective emotional experiences ("I am angry with you for abusing me and I am not powerless any more"). This experiential method reduces intellectualization, denial, and detachment, while encouraging genuine emotional expression and enhancing the child's sense of mastery and self esteem.

Inner child metaphor. The child is asked to visualize him or herself at a younger age, and to put a voice to this little boy or girl. The method of separating-out the hurt or traumatized part of the self often makes it easier to discuss painful and frightening experiences. The child is encouraged to nurture and protect his or her inner child, thereby reducing the rejection and contempt typically experienced.

Therapeutic holdings. The therapists holds the child in a special position to engender a sense of safety and security and encourage healing therapeutic work. Therapeutic holdings are done in the infant-nurturance position on a comfortable sofa. The child lies across the therapist's lap with his or her head resting on a pillow, allowing for close proximity, eye contact, and appropriate physical restriction. The child typically goes through four stages: (1) resistance and anger; (2) capitulation (allowing external control); (3) sadness and pain: (4) increased trust and attachment (see Anderson, 1990; Cline, 1992; and Welsy, 1988). This position meets the fundamental limit-setting needs of the rageful and out-of-control child, prevents the reinforcement of violent and destructive behavior, and provides external control when internal control is lacking (Bath, 1994). Children often fear the consequences of their anger and impulses, and this position allows for the expression of rage, without the possibility of hurting others or being hurt. Trust, confidence and respect towards the therapist is developed when the child feels safe, and unable to manipulate or control. This position also facilitates an interactive process, with the therapist responding to the child in empathic ways, reducing the negative consequences of power struggles and control battles, and providing a context to teach about healthy touch and closeness. A regressive experience often ensues, allowing the child to work through early life attachment issues in a safe context. Behaviors and interactions associated with secure attachment (eye contact, smile, safe proximity, movement) can be practiced and internalized. As previously explained, these children typically display strong control needs due to prior attachment trauma. The holding position is designed to penetrate rigid defenses, and is based on the premise that the relinquishment of control and the expression of rage and other emotions in a safe environment leads to the resolution of loss and separation, the development of trust, and the building of secure attachment.

Skill training. Basic social and psychological skills are taught, such as communication, problem-solving, and anger management. Role-playing situations are created which provide repeated practice with new behaviors and coping strategies. Learning such skills interrupts negative and destructive relationship patterns, encourages a sense of competency and mastery, and enhances self esteem.

TWO WEEK TREATMENT PROGRAM: SESSION ONE

Therapeutic goals for the initial session include: (a) parent interview and assessment, (b) continued assessment of child, (c) creating a therapeutic context, and (d) contracting. Every session begins with a dialogue between the parents and the treatment team. The therapeutic foster parents report on the child's behavior, mood and attitude in the home, and the child's response to specific therapeutic tasks. Therapy issues and progress are discussed with the parents, in addition to answering their questions and responding to any concerns. At the conclusion of each session, the parents and treatment team meet again to process the specific issues covered in that day's session. In the first session, the role and purpose of the therapeutic foster home is explained to the parents.

(a) The parent interview provides detailed information regarding the child's early history, current symptoms and behavior, parenting styles and family dynamics. Important issues to identify include: strengths and deficits of marital relationships; support systems of the parents; similarities and differences in the parents' perception of the child's behavior; level of functioning of the siblings; parents' level of stress, frustration and emotional availability to the child; and effectiveness of specific parenting attitudes and techniques (parents' prior attempted solutions). Parents are asked to bring historical records such as life books, family albums, court documents, diaries, social service reports, and letters and adoption records, which provide additional information and can be used therapeutically at a later time.

Parents often present as highly frustrated, desperate, wary and exhausted. For example, adoptive parents are often told by professionals, "All this child needs is love and a stable home." However, the attachment disordered child has little or no foundation to understand or accept love and, therefore, the parents typically experience rejection, feelings of inadequacy, despair, and hostility towards the child. They are often blamed for their child's inability to respond positively to the family environment. One of the primary goals of the initial session is to join with the parents and let them know that we understand the nature of their frustration. The parents are educated about the causes and consequences of attachment disorder, which enables them to be more objective and feel less responsible and guilty regarding their child's problems. The therapists provide considerable empathy, support and validation in order to build a working alliance with the parents.

Another primary goal is the development of a specific treatment contract in which parents and therapists agree on certain desired outcomes (e.g., learn parenting skills; reduce resentment towards child). It is important that parents end the initial session with a sense of hope and enhanced expectation of success, thereby increasing their investment in the treatment process. (b) Also during this initial session, the child is asked to fill out a sentence completion questionnaire which provides information about content (attitudes and feelings) and process (how the child responds to the task). Finally, the child is introduced to the therapeutic foster parents. The rules and expectations of that home are explained, including the reason why chores are emphasized. The manner in which the child accomplishes chores is diagnostic of responsibility, compliance and family involvement. The child is told, "This is a practice family where you will learn new skills, behavior, and ways of relating to parents." The child's questions are answered and he or she leaves with the foster parents.

At this time, the authors would like to revisit the case of "Ryan" whom readers met at the beginning of this chapter on Two Week Intensives:

CASE EXAMPLE: A LOOK AT "RYAN'S" TWO WEEK INTENSIVE

Case Illustration Session One. *The session began with the parent interview and the introduction of the treatment team. Mother said, "It seems he thinks he will die if he lets go of control," and, "We are desperate and at wit's end." Father shared, "We considered giving him up, because he was destroying our family." They reported that Ryan kicks,* *screams, and throws things during his rages, experiences severe guilt in reference to the prior vicious sexual abuse of his sister, and attempted suicide recently by leaping in front of a car. Mother shared her goal for Ryan: "If he is not a serial killer, I'll be happy."*

The father appeared somewhat distant, reticent and wary of the treatment process. Mother seemed more engaged and motivated, and was the spokesperson in the marriage. The therapists provided support, empathy, and a conceptual framework for understanding attachment disorder. Both parents expressed frustration about Ryan's behavior, but the father was more intolerant and the mother more accepting, even though he acted-out more consistently towards her. Although marital issues are not the focus of the first session, we observed a moderate level of stress and conflict regarding the handling of Ryan's problems.

The parents were given a general overview of treatment and agreement was reached on a specific treatment plan (contract). Ryan was then introduced to the therapeutic foster parents, was told why he was spending time at their home, and was given the opportunity to ask questions.

SESSION TWO

Therapeutic goals include: (a) continued rapport building, (b) educate and provide a cognitive frame, (c) contract with the child. Initial contact with the child includes a review of the sentence completion task and an explanation of the first year of life cycle (Figure 1, page 55).

Educating the child about his or her early attachment experiences and the resultant psychosocial difficulties gives the message, "We understand how you got to be this way and can help you." Further, this positive reframing gives the message, "This is not your fault, but rather, an appropriate and predictable response to unfortunate circumstances." This sets the stage for cognitive-affective revision; the development of positive regard for self and others, and the working through of emotional trauma.

Contracting with the child is a crucial component of treatment with children ages ten and above. The contract is typically between the therapists and parents with younger children. Contracts are agreements about specific behaviors between the therapists and child. There is a direct correlation between the strength of the treatment contract and the desire, commitment and motivation to change. The specific contract is based on the first year of life story.

The following questions are posed:
* What happened to you in the past?
* How have past experiences affected you?
* How is your life going now?
* How will you be in the future if you remain the same?
* How will you be as an adult, parent, employee, husband?
* Are you willing to do what it takes to work on your life?
* Are you willing to accept our rules?
Next, the child is informed about the ground rules of therapy.
* We will not work harder than you on your life.
* Actions are important, not just words, (You have to show us).
* Eye contact and quick answers are expected.
* 'I don't know' is not an acceptable response.
* We often will be working in the holding-nurturing position.
* When the therapist says, 'got it?', you are expected to respond with a reciprocal, 'got it!' (concrete demonstration of compliance). You are expected to work in therapy our way (learn to trust safe caregivers).

When the child agrees to adhere to the ground rules, the therapist conveys his or her commitment ("We will go the distance with you") and instills hope ("We can help you change"). The information provided and contracts created in session two sets the stage for the therapeutic interventions which follow.

> ***Case Illustration Session Two.*** *We began with a discussion of Ryan's behavior in the therapeutic foster home. He was described as slow, passive-aggressive and moderately non-compliant. He had to do his chores over several times before successful completion. Following the parent-treatment team discussion, we started our work with Ryan. A review of the sentence completion revealed that Ryan wrote, "I like to win." "I lose control when I get mad." "My parents did bad things to me when I was young." The first year of life story was now explained, with Ryan in the holding-nurturing position.*
> *The following are excerpts from the dialogue during this portion of the session:*
> *Therapist M: How do you feel in this position?*

Ryan: I don't like being here; I don't feel anything (starts to cry).
Therapist M: What did you learn in your first year of life?
Ryan: I had bad parents, learned to control, to not trust.
Therapist M: Do you want your own family someday?
Ryan: I don't like to get close to people. I have a wall around my heart.
Therapist T: How were you treated in your birth family?
Ryan: My parents did bad things to me, but it's hard to talk about.
Therapist T: How did that little boy feel about himself?
Ryan: He thought he was a bad boy.
Therapist M: Why is it hard for you to look into my eyes?
Ryan: I don't like eye contact; I had a bad life; I don't want people to see me.
Therapist M: How do you feel about your birth parents?
Ryan: I still love them. I love and hate them.

Despite being apprehensive and somewhat guarded, Ryan disclosed valuable information regarding his feelings and perceptions. The therapists offered validation and support: "You have a good heart. You learned to be controlling for survival. We will teach you safe ways of expressing your feelings. We will teach you about healthy touch. It wasn't your fault that your birth parents did bad things to you." The ground rules of therapy were discussed as part of the contract. For the final contract, Ryan was encouraged to maintain eye contact with each therapist, one at a time, and verbalize his request for help:

Ryan: I want to work on my life. Will you help me?
Therapist M: I will help you improve your life.
Therapist T: I will help you improve your life.

SESSION THREE

The goals of session three include: (a) manage resistant and controlling behavior, (b) provide validation and support, (c) re-contract, (d) initiate cognitive and affective interventions. The therapeutic holding-nurturing technique, introduced in the preceeding session, is used in this session and throughout the remainder of treatment.

The child's oppositional and controlling behaviors typically escalate now as a result of deliberate therapeutic confrontation and control. In contrast to other modalities, where the expression of the child's intense affect is discouraged, our goal is to encourage the release of these emotions and disturbing behavior as a first step towards constructive change. The therapists' messages to the child are: "We care about you and we will help you"; "We will take charge and you will be safe;" "You are not omnipotent;" "We can handle your controlling behaviors." "You are safe in this situation to express your intense anger, hurt, and fear." The child begins to learn that the therapist is not intimidated by his or her anger, cannot be manipulated, and the child will not be abandoned even at his or her worst.

The therapist is prepared for the child's resistance and responds in one of several ways: (a) acknowledgment and acceptance, "I understand it is difficult for you to look at this issue now"; (b) prescribe the behavior, "Try holding in your feelings even more"; (c) give permission, "It's all right to resist, change is scary"; (d) direct encouragement, "I know you can handle these feelings." A specific therapeutic style and response is essential for treatment to be effective. The therapist must provide a balance of confrontation and support, be nurturing but yet firm, avoid power struggles, maintain a positive focus, provide validation and encouragement, and instill hope.

The child's negative working model is now addressed. Specific perceptions and expectations are identified: "I am bad, defective, and deserve to be abandoned and abused"; "Adult caretakers can never be trusted"; "To survive I must be in control at all times"; "It was my fault that I was maltreated"; "If I get close to people I will be hurt and abandoned." We begin to challenge the child's belief system through a variety of strategies which will be explained in the next session.

> ***Case Illustration Session Three.*** *During the treatment-team discussion, the therapeutic foster father reported an interchange with Ryan from the previous evening.*
>
> *Foster Father: Why do you think you do chores so poorly?*
> *Ryan: It's hard for me to do anything well (starts to sob).*
> *The parents discussed how Ryan is unable to handle confrontation at home, as well, and described his pattern of "needing to fail". The therapist reframed Ryan's need to fail as a manifestation of his self-contempt, and described parenting techniques designed to minimize power struggles. The mother described numerous power struggles at home, and Ryan's typical violent responses. She referred to Ryan as a "potential rapist" due to his intense anger towards women.*
> *The therapeutic phase of the session with Ryan focused mostly on his resistant, controlling and defensive demeanor:*
> *Therapist M: What is your worst fear if you let your parents in your life?*
> *Ryan: (Silence).*

Therapist M: What feelings did you have when you were young?
Ryan: I don't remember.
Therapist T: Some feelings are sad, mad, glad, scared. Which ones did you have?
Ryan: I don't know.
Therapist T: You learned to be in control to survive, but in here you have to give up that control to get better. You decide if you want to work on your life. We cannot force you. You have a choice.
Ryan: (Four minutes of silence)...I guess I'll do it.
Therapist M: Great! Now show us you really mean it by kicking your legs up and down in a swimming motion.
This interchange depicts an effective therapeutic response to deliberate attempts to control and manipulate. The therapists remained emotionally neutral, gave him permission to be resistant, and empowered him by giving him the choice. The kicking technique provided a physical demonstration of his compliance and reinforced the message, "In this therapy, actions are required, not just words."

SESSION FOUR

The goals of session four include: (a) initial phase of emotional and cognitive treatment, (b) manage resistant and controlling behavior, (c) initiate positive attachment with caregiver. The session begins with a review of the child's thoughts, feelings and behavior regarding therapy and specifically, the therapeutic foster home. Foster home issues include: accomplishing chores; learning to verbally communicate needs and feelings; learning about choices and consequences. Contracting is once again emphasized.

The therapist and child agree to work on certain issues resulting from their discussion. The child is often reluctant to comply at this point in the treatment process as a function of the changes in the dynamics and structure of his or her environment. Unlike the home environment, where the child maintains control via acting-out or passive-controlling behavior, the new context (foster home and therapy) offers an entirely different experience, one in which the child is responsible for choices and the consequences of those choices. For example, the child who is unwilling to cooperate in treatment is informed of two choices and consequences: (a) work hard in therapy, change, and have the possibility of a loving and satisfying family life; or (b) do not cooperate, remain as you are, and face the consequences.

One consequence may be that the parents set limits, informing the child that his or her disruptive behavior will no longer be tolerated in the family, and, "We will always love you, but it might have to be from a distance." (The parents have been prepared for this limit-setting strategy in prior discussions with the therapists.) Choices are given in an empathic and nonpunitive fashion, and the child is free to select either option, thereby circumventing power struggles and control battles.

We now begin to focus on specific treatment issues regarding attachment and emotional trauma. The therapist and child review reports and records which provide details about significant events in the his or her early years. Some mental health professionals believe that it is contraindicated to delve into the details of child maltreatment, because it may be too threatening to the child. It is our experience, however, that honest and open discussion of abuse and neglect is crucial to the healing process, and that most children are capable of effectively dealing with these issues with proper support and guidance.

This review process sets the stage for a variety of therapeutic experiences. An array of thoughts and feelings emerge for the child as we review the records. We begin to provide the child with an effective framework to identify and express these thoughts and feelings. The child is helped to label specific emotions (sad, mad, scared, glad) and to verbalize feelings (face-to-face, eye-to-eye) in contrast to acting-out or avoiding. This skill of direct verbal communication is emphasized and encouraged throughout treatment.

When age-appropriate, the child is helped to understand the relationship between current behavior and prior traumatic experiences. This information is not provided with the premise that insight produces change, but rather, because it helps the child realize that he or she was a victim of other's maltreatment, reducing the burden of self-blame and shame. The therapists offer empathy and validation, giving the message: "It was not your fault. You were not responsible for the maltreatment, but you are responsible for your behavior and choices now and in the future."

The therapists begin to challenge the child's belief system, providing empathy for negativistic perceptions ("I understand that you don't trust adults because you were abused"), while simultaneously showing the child new possibilities and options ("Your adoptive mother didn't abuse you, and yet you are mistrustful towards her"). When clinically appropriate, the primary caregiver participates directly. For example, the adoptive mother, who has been observing the child's therapy from behind the one-way mirror, is invited into the treatment room to interact with the child, using the holding-nurturing position.

The mother has typically been the primary target of the child's hostility and rejection, and consequently, often believes that these problems are her fault. As a result of observing the child's therapy, the mother develops increased understanding and empathy, is relieved of the burden of self-blame and guilt, and becomes more emotionally available to the child. This mother-child therapeutic experience serves two purposes. First, it actuates the process of positive attachment. Second, it provides diagnostic information regarding emotional availability and capacity for change in both mother and child.

Case Illustration Session Four.

Therapeutic foster father reported that Ryan was somewhat more compliant, but still had to repeat chores and tended to "act dumb." He described to the parents effective ways of responding to the child's passive-resistant behavior. The mother shared additional information regarding details of Ryan's incestuous relationship with his birth family and reported that the birth mother told Ryan, "If you tell, we will never see you again, and it will be your fault." Consequently, Ryan refused to discuss these issues in four years of prior therapy. The birth father was characterized as a passive and submissive husband, and a participant in the incestuous relationships.

Ryan's therapy began with him demonstrating resistant and controlling behavior. The following interchange occurred with Ryan in the holding-nurturing position:

Ryan: I don't know (repeated response to therapists' inquiries).

Therapist M: Show me you want to work hard by kicking your legs (Ryan's resistance is exemplified by half-hearted kicking).

Therapist T: This is not good kicking; is this how you work hard? Maybe you want to quit?

Ryan: I'm tired.

Therapist M: I understand you are tired, but do you want to talk about being tired or about getting better?

Therapist T: (Directs comment to co-therapist). He wants to do it his way; he wants to be the boss (third party dialogue is an effective way to avoid power struggles with the child while making a point).

Therapist M: It's okay if you decide you don't want to work hard on your life. And, you need to understand the consequences of your choice. (The parents are now invited into

*the session to clarify the consequences of his choice, and
to shift the focus to the parent-child relationship).*
Mother: *If you don't want to work hard in therapy it's your
choice. But you cannot continue to live at home if you don't
get better.*
Father: *You can't continue to be this way and live at
home anymore.*
Ryan: *I will work hard (following a brief silence).*
*Ryan now discloses his fear of relinquishing control and,
with the support and encouragement of the therapists, re-
veals details of sexual abuse (All of Ryan's disclosures of
abuse had been previously documented by social services).
He expresses a range of emotions (rage, shame, guilt, fear)
regarding incestuous experiences, and talks about one inherent conflict of sexual abuse ("Sex with mother was
wrong, but it felt good"). The therapists challenge Ryan's
negative working model in reference to self-blame ("It was
not your fault"). Mother is now invited back into the treatment room. Ryan is asked to share the previously discussed
information and feelings with her while she holds him.
Mother provides reassurance and acceptance, and the therapists validate Ryan's courage and healthy choices.*
Therapist M: *You faced your memories and feelings today;
how did it work out?*
Ryan: *I feel better; I'm okay.*
Therapist T: *How do you feel about yourself?*
Ryan: *I don't hate myself now. I guess it was not my fault.*
*The session ends with mother and child gazing into each
other's eyes, in an affectionate embrace, for ten minutes.
This is the first time Ryan allows such closeness and contact.*

SESSION FIVE

Goals for session five include: (a) teach parenting skills, (b) explore
parent's family-of-origin, (c) continue child's treatment, (d) enhance child-
mother attachment. The initial focus is on the specific parenting skills
required to effectively manage the child's behavior. The parents and treatment team review the child's experiences in both the therapy sessions
and the therapeutic foster home in order to clarify the salient aspects of
child management. The parents are informed that conventional parenting
skills are often ineffective with attachment-disordered children, due to
their desperate need to control, lack of trust with and attachment to
the parents, and perception that authority figures are abusive, neglectful
and unreliable.

The parenting skills taught in this session (and reviewed and reinforced throughout therapy) stress the importance of the parents "not getting hooked" into the child's attempts to manipulate, control and compulsively replay prior dysfunctional relationship patterns. Parents are taught to stay neutral and provide logical consequences in an empathic manner, in contrast to becoming angry, hostile and punitive. The angry, punitive parent is unknowingly "playing the child's game", allowing the child to maintain control and repeating prior patterns of parental hostility and rejection. These and other parenting techniques provide concrete tools which enhance the parent's sense of competency, improves their self esteem, prevents further marital discord, and offers an alternative context in which the child's chances of changing are improved.

Often, it is necessary to help the parents identify and explore psychosocial issues from their own family-of-origin. The parents complete the Life Script in a discussion session with the therapist, in order to obtain information such as: the roles, messages and discipline techniques of their own parents; their parents as role models regarding conflict-management, communication and affect; family relationship patterns; their self perceptions as children. The therapists encourage the parents to examine the association between family-of-origin and current marital and parent-child relationships.

The second part of the session focuses on continued treatment of the child. The child is encouraged to verbalize thoughts and feelings regarding maltreatment issues which were raised in the previous session. Feelings regarding rejection, abandonment, abuse (physical, sexual, emotional), helplessness, hopelessness and fear now begin to emerge into consciousness. It is common at this point for the child to volunteer specific memories never before revealed. The child is guided through a discussion of these difficult emotions and of the concomitant defenses which arise. The therapist provides a balance of challenge and support. The supportive message is, "We understand that you needed your defenses for protection and survival in the past." The challenging message is, "Those defenses are now preventing you from learning to love and trust, and we know you can handle these issues and emotions." This work with the child is preparatory to the experiential interventions which begin in session six.

At this point in the session we invite the mother to participate. We facilitate a mother-child dialogue in which the child reiterates the information shared with the therapist. This sharing serves several purposes as the mother listens with acceptance and empathy: It reduces the child's shame about his or her role in prior traumatic events; The child's repeated airing of the heretofore "taboo" subjects reduces the negative emotional impact (desensitization); and, it enhances the closeness and trust between mother and child. The session ends with a review of the therapeutic issues from the entire week. The treatment team and parents address relevant issues and make plans for the parents to visit the therapeutic foster home over the weekend.

One purpose of the visit is for the parents to observe the way in which the therapeutic foster parents deal with rules, responsibilities, discipline, problem-solving, and communication. A second purpose is for the parents to practice their new parenting skills, giving the child the opportunity to experience them in a new light.

Third, the parents and therapeutic foster parents are encouraged to interact in a cooperative and congenial manner, thereby presenting a united front to the child.

Case Illustration Session Five.
Therapeutic foster parents reported that Ryan was more oppositional, angry and resistant after yesterday's therapy session. This is a common and predictable reaction to the initial confrontation of emotional trauma and increased intimacy. Mother reported that her experience with Ryan at the conclusion of yesterday's session was, "the first time he ever allowed genuine closeness." Father stated that this was the first time in four years of therapy that Ryan talked about his honest feelings regarding abuse in his birth family. Therapeutic foster parents reported that Ryan was more oppositional, angry and distant after yesterday's therapy session. This is a common and predictable reaction to the initial confrontation of emotional trauma. The focus now shifted to a discussion of effective parenting concepts and skills, including: providing logical, non-punitive consequences; teaching the child to be responsible, respectful and resourceful; setting limits and avoiding control battles; modeling healthy attitudes and behavior; managing anger and frustration. The treatment team provided the parents with concrete examples of child management techniques. Next, the parents' family-of-origin issues were explored using the Life Script as a tool. Mother's history: oldest of nine children, strong mother and unavailable father, often in a parental-child role, learned to be assertive, domineering and affectionate. Father's history: youngest of six children, domineering and punitive father and submissive, emotionally unavailable mother, learned to be a good provider, punitive and unaffectionate. A connection was made between these prior issues and current parenting practices.

Mother tended to rescue and over-control Ryan, while the father became angry, punitive and withdrawn. Based on the trusting therapeutic relationship established over five days, the parents were now open and responsive to the information.

Therapy with Ryan began with validation and support, followed by continued work on trauma and attachment issues.

Therapist T: You are brave and you stick to your work; you came back.

Ryan: I want to work on my life.

Therapist T: What feelings do you have when I hold you?

Ryan: I have bad memories; I wasn't touched in the right way; I'm scared.

Therapist T: (To Therapist M) He is being honest about his scared feelings.

Ryan: I'm scared, but I'll work hard anyway.

Therapist T: Start kicking and let me know when you are ready to talk about what happened; then give me a loud "Ready".

Ryan: Ready! (He then shares details of abuse.)

Therapist T: How do you feel about your birth mother for what she did to you:

Ryan: I hate her for that.

Therapist M: Did she put love or hate in your heart?

Ryan: They put hate in my heart; I am full of hate (He repeats this several times with increase intensity.)

Therapist M: (Shows Ryan a photo of birth mother) What do you want to say to her?

Ryan: I hate you for abusing me; I don't want you running my life anymore (screams).

Therapist T: You are doing a great job.

Ryan: I'm learning to get my feelings out and to trust.

Ryan is beginning to direct his rage towards the perpetrators rather than towards his adoptive parents or himself. He is breaking the "code of silence", communicating verbally rather than acting-out behaviorally, and learning to allow others to help him. He begins to examine a loyalty conflict, both hating his parents for abandonment and abuse, and desiring a positive connection with his roots.

The final portion of the session included contracting for new behaviors and positive attachment to adoptive mother. Ryan and therapeutic foster parents discussed new ways of handling non-compliance. Ryan agreed to discuss his feelings directly regarding the need for control rather than demonstrating them through oppositional actions. The session ended with Ryan hugging both therapists followed by ten minutes of close contact with Mother.

SESSIONS SIX, SEVEN, EIGHT

These sessions represent the middle phase of treatment. Therapeutic goals include: (a) utilize experiential interventions, (b) initiate process of emotional resolution and cognitive revision (c) increase positive attachment to parents. The middle phase of treatment builds on the foundation constructed during the first five sessions, shifting into a deeper and more intensive focus on direct emotional experience. A primary therapeutic method used is psychodramatic reenactment. As previously described, the child and treatment team role-play prior traumatic scenarios, giving the child the opportunity to: direct rage towards those responsible for maltreatment; experience and release the fear, pain and sadness associated with loss and helplessness; experience vulnerability in a safe and secure context.

Over the course of session six, seven and eight, the child progresses developmentally in the reenactment experiences from a posture of pain, resignation, hopelessness and victimization to a more hopeful position of emotional and interpersonal mastery, leading to improved self esteem. The specific therapeutic results are: increases the sense of personal power; reduces the self-perception of "victim"; extinguishes the negative emotional charge associated with traumatic events; revises unrealistic perceptions and fantasies about self and others (e.g., birth family); develops a positive alliance with primary caregivers.

Some health care providers fear that these experiential methods will re-traumatize children, assuming that these children are emotionally fragile and will suffer further psychological damage.

Our experience in working with hundreds of children, however, is that despite their dreadful early life experiences, most are capable of confronting these harsh realities, do benefit significantly from deep and emotionally genuine therapeutic experiences, and do demonstrate positive changes which are reported in follow-up interviews. For example, children consistently report that although the therapy is difficult and challenging, they are pleased that they participated, feel a sense of relief and increased well being, and would recommend it to others with similar problems.

Another primary therapeutic method used is the inner child metaphor. The recent popularity of "the child within" concept in current psychology self-help manuals has caused some observers to view this method as faddish and trendy. We have found, however, that when utilized in a specific therapeutic manner, this metaphoric technique is a powerful tool for positive change. The child, while in the holding-nurturing position, is gently guided back to a time in his or her life which is associated with traumatic events, and is asked to visualize him or herself as that little boy or girl. The inquiry proceeds as follow:

> *"Picture the little girl. How old is she? What is she doing? What is she thinking and feeling?* At this point the child is emotionally involved, genuinely expressing the thoughts and feelings of the "little girl". Children commonly express their sadness, pain, loneliness, and helplessness.
>
> *"What does that little girl need now?"* The child typically responds by identifying the needs of the little girl (e.g., "I need someone to hold and protect me"). Attachment disordered children have learned to discount and dissociate from their emotional needs. This portion of the therapy process enables them to acknowledge and "own" their basic needs. We now introduce a small stuffed animal (warm, fuzzy bear) to symbolically represent the little girl. This shift from a visualization paradigm to the use of an external symbol facilitates further concrete expression of thoughts and feelings in a less threatening manner.
>
> *"What does this little girl (bear) need?"* The child's ability to identify and meet the needs of the little girl (bear) is diagnostic of the extent to which her negative working model is changing. This change is from a negatively internalized self ("I am bad and do not deserve love") to a positively internalized self ("I am good and I do deserve love").
>
> *"Have you taken very good care of this little girl?"* This question discloses the child's self-contempt and the vicious circle of attachment disorder ("My caregiver mistreats me; I feel defective and unlovable; I hate myself; I treat others badly; others mistreat me"). The child is encouraged to display nurturing, supportive behaviors towards the "little girl" in order to teach self-acceptance and self-love, thereby breaking the negative cycle.
>
> *"Can she forgive you for not taking good care of her?"* This question is diagnostic of the child's capacity to mitigate self-contempt. The therapist informs the child, "You were treated badly so that you learned to treat yourself badly." This initiates the process of self-empathy and self-forgiveness.
>
> *"Who is in control of your life if you continue to treat yourself badly?"* The paradox of control is elicited via this

question: These children are motivated by a profound need to control, yet their choices and actions are driven by prior events and relationships (e.g., unresolved pain and anger about the loss of birth mother). They typically experience severe loyalty conflicts. They want to remain loyal to birth parents, regardless of any pain or abandonment suffered, due to an intrinsic need to maintain the birth connection. They often have an unrealistic reunification fantasy, hoping and expecting to one day reunite with the birth parent(s), and live "happily ever after." This loyalty to a prior attachment figure creates guilt and anxiety about attaching to a surrogate caregiver, such as a foster or adoptive parent, and results in the child distancing from that caregiver. The "anger triad" is a part of these conflicted loyalties and includes: (a) self contempt ("I am unwanted and unlovable"); (b) anger towards birth parents ("I hate you for leaving and hurting me); (c) anger towards surrogate parents ("I blame you for taking me away from my birth parents"). Most of this anger is directed towards the current caregivers and/or towards the self.

"How does life work out for her?" The therapist instructs the child to give the "little girl" (bear) a detailed accounting of her life, emphasizing the information gleaned from therapy. This exercise provides a vehicle for the child to synthesize and integrate the therapeutic experience, and is diagnostic of the child's capacity for awareness and disclosure.

"Do you know anyone else who can help you love this little girl?" Children consistently respond by identifying their current caregiver (e.g., adoptive mother) as a potential source of love and protection. This represents a shift from pushing the caregiver away to inviting the caregiver into their life. Children express this change concretely by inviting the mother into the session and asking her for help ("Mom, will you help me learn how to love my little girl?"). The mother is instructed to place the child and "little girl" into the holding-nurturing position, and to provide a healthy model of affection and comfort. This reinforces and enhances the positive mother-child bond as well as the bond between the child and her "little girl" (positive internalized self).

"Do you wish this could have been your mom from the beginning?" This question serves as a springboard for enhancing mother-child attachment. Mutual acceptance and affectionate sharing increases intimacy, trust and attachment. The mother is asked a similar question ("Do you wish you could

have been this child's mother from the beginning?"). The mother now has the opportunity to tell the child her thoughts and feelings about the child's prior trauma and how she is wanted and loved. This portion of the session ends with approximately ten minutes of positive attachment (silence, eye contact, holding) between mother and child which serves to further cement the connection.

The desired outcome of the preceding interventions is twofold: the healing of prior trauma, and the development of the social skills and the emotional capacity necessary for healthy relationships. Therapeutic interventions described above provide the child with positive attachment experiences that did not occur at earlier development stages. During these new attachment experiences the child may become threatened, sensing a loss of identity and control. To reduce this anxiety, it is crucial to provide the child with a new sense of self. We use the metaphor "letting-go of the rage and darkness in your heart, and replacing them with love and lightness."

The mother-child attachment exercises are repeated many times during treatment. The emphasis on the attachment to a mother figure is based on the primacy of the mother-infant bond. Recently, there has been an enormous increase in information pertaining to prenatal psychological research and theory (Verney, 1981). It is understood that "bonding is a continuum of physiological, psychological, and spiritual events which begins in utero and continues throughout the postnatal bonding period" (Verrier, 1993). The regressive experience provided during this therapy enables the child to simulate that original mother-infant bonding. We even use baby bottles and blankets during the attachment exercises to enhance the authenticity of the experience. It is interesting to note that although older children may initially be embarrassed by the use of these items, they rarely object and most often enjoy the experience.

The role of the father-figure therapy is important, despite the initial emphasis on mother-child attachment. The father learns parenting skills which increase the likelihood of positive family involvement at home. He is encouraged to provide support to his wife throughout the treatment process in order to strengthen and unify the parental dyad. During the mother-child attachment exercise, the father often sits next to his wife, his arm around her shoulders, giving support to her and to the mother-child bonding. Subsequently, the focus shifts to father-child attachment.

The father uses the holding-nurturing position and proceeds through the phases of the attachment exercise with the child.

Case Illustration Session Six.
The parents found the home visit helpful, as they were able to observe parenting skills in action. Ryan is informed we will now use role-playing to further resolve emotional issues. The dialogue begins with re-contracting.
Ryan: I don't like doing this.
Therapist T: I know this is hard, but will you do it anyway?
Ryan: I promised not to quit, so I'll work hard.
Therapist M: The harder it is, the more you can get out of it. What do you want to tell your birth mom (role-played by female counselor)"
Ryan: (To birth mother) I don't want to be around you; I hate what you did to me; you taught me to have a sick mind.
Therapist M: Use powerful words (Ryan becomes physically agitated).
Ryan: I want to kill you (screams).
Therapist T: Was anyone there to help or protect you?
Ryan: No, my father did not help me: he was on my mom's side (sobs).
Therapist M: Who do you have in your life now to protect you?
Ryan: My mom.
Therapist M: Call her.
Ryan: Mom, help me! (repeats several times).
Mother enters the treatment room, holds and comforts Ryan, and they both tell the "birth mother" to leave. Ryan now shifts his allegiance to his adoptive mother, allowing her to be protective and nurturing. The session ends with extended dialogue and closeness between Ryan and his Mother.

****

The following are excerpts from the psychodramatic reenactment regarding birth mother.
Birth Mother: You can't change, you will always be just like me.
Ryan: I am changing.
Therapist M: You are doing great: Now, stand up, look her in the eyes, and tell her how you are changing.

Ryan: I'm not afraid of you anymore: I'm not helpless.
Therapist T: How are you feeling now?
Ryan: I feel stronger now, but how do I get my sad feel-ings out?

****

The preceding intervention gave Ryan the opportunity to feel, think and behave in a genuinely powerful and self-confident manner in reference to his birth mother. The inner child method which follows facilitates the expression of his vulnerability, the process of grieving over losses, and the resolution of self-contempt.
Therapist M: Close your eyes. Picture yourself as a little boy. How old is he? What is he thinking and feeling?
Ryan: I'm four years old. I'm feeling alone and scared.
Therapist M: Here is a little bear. Pretend this is you when you were that little boy. Tell him what he needs.
Ryan: You need protection and someone to trust. You are sad because of what you parents did to you.
Therapist M: Tell him what happens in his life.
Ryan: You get abused, you can't trust anyone, your mother never meets your needs, you go to an orphanage, and you are adopted by a family that loves you but you can't love them back.
Therapist T: This little boy was very hurt and disappointed. How did he learn to feel about himself?
Ryan: He learned to hate himself!
Therapist T: Have you taken very good care of him?
Ryan: No, I thought he was bad.
Therapist T: Ask him if he can forgive you for not taking good care of him and if he wants to learn how to love.
Ryan: Yes, he wants to forgive me, but he is afraid.
Therapist T: Do you know anyone who can help you learn to love this little boy?
Ryan: (Calls for Mother. She comes in and holds Ryan and the bear.) Could you teach me how to love?
Mother: Of course I will help you.
Therapist T: Tell your mom you are scared, but you don't have to push her away anymore.
Ryan: I still am scared, but I won't push you away. I'm learning to love and trust.

Ryan is confronting and resolving the losses of attachment figures while simultaneously forming a positive attachment to his adoptive mother. Father is now invited to participate. He is told to sit next to his wife, place his arm around her, and provide support. Ryan agrees to drink juice from a baby bottle, while experiencing ten minutes of family bonding. He maintains eye contact with his mother while allowing closeness and comfort from both parents.

Case Illustration Session Seven.

Foster parents stated that Ryan was more controlling, bossy, and did his chores poorly last night. We told the parents that regression is common, and explained that this is a manifestation of the fear of change. We then prepared them for the technique of "firing" the child from therapy. This technique is commonly used to avoid power struggles and places the responsibility for change on the child.

Ryan was predictably resistant and controlling in treatment. The therapists dialogued with one another about his resistance, and informed him that he can only come back to therapy if he earns it by showing that he wants to work hard. Ryan left with the foster parents, obviously angry and conflicted.

Case Illustration Session Eight.

Foster parents reported that Ryan was antagonistic and belligerent after being "fired". However, they reported as the day progressed Ryan became more cooperative and "did a great job" with his chores. Ryan began the therapy by expressing his feelings, "I'm angry you fired me and I want to work hard today."

The paradoxical technique of firing the child the day before had the desired effects: It gave him the opportunity to make his own choice about participating in therapy; it prevented a therapist-child power struggle; it solidified his commitment and increased his motivation.

Session Nine

The final phase of therapy begins with this session, and includes the following goals: (a) enhance father-child bond, (b) facilitate process of grieving and forgiveness, (c) reinforce effective parenting skills. Birth father issues, such as abuse and abandonment, become the central focus. Psychodramatic reenactment is utilized to provoke and resolve traumatic issues between child and birth father. Again, the child is in the holding-nurturing position with the current father surrogate (foster, adoptive or stepfather).

The child is given the opportunity to further complete the grieving process regarding the loss of birth parents.

Grieving and mourning their losses is an essential component of the healing process. Although sad and painful, it promotes a letting-go of the past, creates the possibility of a new future, and can lead to the beginning of forgiveness. A "magic wand" technique is used, in which the child can speak directly to "birth parents" role-played by others. The child is told, "For the next ten minutes your birth parents will be healthy. They will be open, honest and available to address your comments, questions and concerns." The child can move towards closure on birth parent issues by expressing feelings of loss and asking questions about the parents' lives.

For example, the "parents" may explain what happened to them in their childhoods which influenced them to be abusive or neglectful. The child's increased understanding of the parents serves several purposes. It helps the child understand that he or she now has the tools to break the cycle of abuse. Unlike the parents, the child is receiving help and is now free to make different and better choices. Second, it promotes a more empathic and forgiving attitude. The concept of forgiveness has several meanings. Therapeutically, forgiveness involves the release of pain and anger associated with a traumatic event. The goal is for the child to acknowledge the parents' responsibility for maltreatment, but also to release him or herself from the burden of emotional pain.

Parent-child reunification occurs after session nine. Instead of going back to the therapeutic foster home, the child leaves with his or her own parents. This gives the parents an opportunity to apply the parenting skills they have learned and is diagnostic of the child's progress. The child's confidence is increased as he or she experiences a concrete demonstration of parental effectiveness.

Case Illustration session Nine.

They reported that Ryan was cooperative, animated and communicative. Therapy with Ryan began with birth father issues, again using psychodramatic reenactment.
Ryan: (Speaking to birth father) I needed you to help me. I hate you for not helping (screams).
Therapist T: Tell your birth father how you would have turned out if you did not get help.
Ryan: I worried I'd be like you.
Therapist M: You are breaking the cycle.
Ryan: Yes, I'm breaking the cycle. I'm learning to care, love and trust.

Father: (Adoptive father storms into the treatment room and forcibly evicts the "birth father".) I am here to protect you now. (Father holds Ryan and comforts him.)

Ryan: Thank you for protecting me. I love and trust you 100%.

Father: We love you 100%.

Ryan: I was afraid I'd be like my birth father, abuse kids and go to jail.

Father: You don't have to worry about that anymore. You're getting the help you need.

Ryan: (Discloses "secrets" to his father.) My parents made me watch them have sex and taught me how to do it. I'm ashamed of what I did and am afraid I would become a homosexual.

Father and son spend considerable time relating positively and discussing the prior issues. Mother then joins them and they prepare for the "magic wand" forgiveness ritual. Ryan speaks directly to his birth parents (in the role-playing format).

Therapist M: Pretend we have a magic wand. Your birth parents are healthy and can hear what you have to say. Ask them why they treated you poorly.

Birth Parents: We didn't know any better. We were also abused.

Therapist M: What do you want to say to them, Ryan?

Ryan: It was your fault and your parents' fault. You should have gotten help. Will you ever get help?

Birth Parents: No, but we are glad you are getting help.

Therapist T: Ryan, ask your birth parents how they feel about you being in a loving family now.

Birth Parents: (Responding to Ryan) We are happy you are in a good family and getting the love you deserve. Can you ever forgive us for how we treated you?

Ryan: I forgive you for what you guys did to me.

SESSION TEN

The goals of session ten include: (a) review and summarize treatment, (b) develop follow-up plans and goals, (c) closure. The final session begins with a report by the parents regarding the child's overnight visit. The treatment team, parents and child process the family interactions and issues. Positive changes in parenting style, child's coping skills and family dynamics are validated and supported.

A discussion now ensues regarding the entire ten sessions. We review the major treatment issues and the learning experiences of each family member. A specific follow-up plan is now developed collaboratively. The treatment team, parents and child provide input regarding: type and frequency of follow-up therapy; unresolved treatment issues that need further attention; medication evaluation if appropriate; availability of current treatment team for future consultations with parents, therapists, school and caseworkers.

The parents typically have many questions for the treatment team. We provide concrete answers as well as give information about what can be expected in the future. The parents are informed that children often test upon returning home. This is the child's attempt, they are told, to determine the reliability of the parents and is only transitional in nature. Parents are also informed that children commonly have a major setback, referred to as "the last hurrah," after a long period of improvement. This brief period of escalating negativity represents a "last ditch effort" to hold onto old destructive patterns. We help the parents prepare for this setback by emphasizing the importance of using their newly acquired parenting skills.

Final closure involves a group exercise in which the treatment team, parents and child respond to the following question: "What has this two-week therapy experience been like for you?" The intensity and emotionally of the two-week experience creates a sense of intimacy and connectiveness between all participants. This closure exercise gives everyone the chance to share personal reactions and, typically, feelings of appreciation.

Case Illustration Session Ten.
Ryan's mood was positive and he related in a close and comfortable way. Father stated, "He was more respectful, did what was asked, and seems to have made a 180 degree turn-around." Mother shared, "He seems more like a little boy - he's softer." Next, plans were made for the future. The therapists informed the parents and Ryan what they can expect (e.g., testing, regression), and discussed follow-up therapy. A family meeting was recommended after returning home so that Ryan could share his therapy experience with his siblings and apologize for prior negative behaviors.
Therapy ended with the closure ritual: Family members and treatment team expressed their feelings and thoughts. Mother stated, "This has given Ryan the solid foundation he never had before." Father shared, "At first I thought this was hocus-pocus, but now I realize this has done a world of good for Ryan and our family." Ryan said, "I'm doing

great! Thanks for helping me. This was hard work but I'm glad I did it."

FOLLOW-UP

Follow-up interviews were conducted at three, six, nine, and eighteen months. The parents reported continued steady progress at six and nine months. They reported Ryan's newfound ability to deal with disappointments, a complete cessation of violent outbursts, and a consistent demonstration of loving and affectionate behaviors. He also showed no signs of depression, was genuinely kind and protective of siblings, and was receiving straight A's in school. He appeared at peace with himself and had become a team player (soccer and basketball). The parents also felt overall improvement in the quality of family life, including a significant reduction in stress and increased harmony among all family members.

The eighteen month follow-up revealed similar positive results. Although Ryan's grades dropped to B's, he still responded well to rules and authority and was easily correctable. He was initiating hugs on a daily basis and was expressing anger appropriately. Ryan was maintaining friendships and a talent for art and music was beginning to emerge. The mother had stopped rescuing and the father no longer disciplined in a punitive fashion.

CONTRAINDICATIONS AND CONCERNS

The therapeutic holding-nurturing technique described in this paper is indicated only for children who are not amenable to conventional therapy approaches due to their extreme control orientations and their inability to form a constructive therapeutic rapport. Children who are accurately diagnosed with serious attachment disorders typically benefit from the safety and security of this technique when utilized correctly. Therapists must be nonpunitive, provide considerable support, empathy and validation, and be confident and personally comfortable with this technique. Therapists must also be emotionally clear and neutral, having substantial awareness of their own issues and areas of sensitivity. This technique should not be employed without a careful client screening process, and without specialized clinical training and supervision.

It is necessary to have a therapy environment conducive to the treatment process described in this paper. A treatment and observation room separated by a one-way mirror, proper sound-proofing, and videotaping equipment are important components. Further, it is crucial to have sufficient time allocated to accomplish clinical goals and resolution, both on a daily and weekly basis. Lastly, a supportive and knowledgeable treatment team is essential.

8

Long Term Therapy With Attachment Disordered Children

Neil Feinberg, LCSW

In the emerging world of managed health care and time limited treatment I have been afforded the luxury of doing long term therapy with attachment disordered children. This is fortunate because, even the most experienced therapist cannot treat or heal the psychological damage caused by early abuse, neglect and abandonment in six to twelve sessions. These emotional wounds cut deep into the psyche of children, touching the core of their beings, influencing every aspect of their emotional, behavioral, intellectual and neurological development.

When I first started my work with attachment disordered children, fifteen years ago, I had some naive goals and unrealistic expectations. Now, I formulate my treatment plan in terms of:

(1) what skills and controls can I teach this child, within the context of his motivation and capacity to learn;
(2) help him to stay out of jail and
(3) live within the laws of our society, hopefully productively.

RECIPROCITY, ACCEPTANCE, EMPATHY

Reciprocity, acceptance and empathy provide the guidelines for the ongoing and overall goals of treatment in working with attachment disordered children.

Whatever techniques and interventions are being utilized therapeutically, the therapist must impart and impact the learning of reciprocity, acceptance and empathy in working with this severely disturbed client population.

Reciprocity is essentially the Golden Rule "Do onto others as you would have others do onto you." In a very real, albeit negative manner, this is exactly what an attachment disordered child is doing in organizing his relationship to the rest of the world. He is doing to others what has been done to him. He is rejecting, destroying, abusing and lying. His internalized model for how the world works and how he must operate, in order to get his needs met is essentially based on "negative reciprocity." He needs to learn "positive reciprocity" if the psychological damage is to be healed. Only by learning "positive reciprocity" does the attachment disordered child mature beyond the infantile narcissism in which so many are behaviorally and emotionally stuck.

Initially, this positive reciprocity needs to be learned within the context of the mother-child relationship and then expanded or generalized to other family members and then to peer relations. Teaching an "attitude of cooperation" can be accomplished through mother-child interactive play activities, doing chores together or cooking and baking together. In the spirit of teaching the child "reciprocal responses" it is very useful to have the child respond to all parental directives with "Yes, Mom" -- stated with an appropriate attitude and tonal quality. Cuddle time, holding time and time-in (as opposed to time out) are also effective methods for enhancing reciprocity in the parent-child relationship. (For a detailed description of this technique the reader is referred to Holding Time by Martha Welch, M.D.)

Eye contact, on parental terms, is another very important component of learning reciprocity. Eye contact between a mother and her infant is a natural and primary bonding mechanism rooted in reciprocal behavior. In therapy, I stress eye contact with the attachment disordered child, fluctuating between game-like staring contests and intrusive and confrontive physical management.

Compliant behavior is the measure of reciprocity in the parent/child relationship. Obedience and compliance are the result of nurturing discipline.

Discipline, enforced with consequences and carried out in a loving non-angry, non-punitive fashion, help the attachment disordered child to reestablish trust and hence to relinquish control. The ability to trust and relinquish control are essential for the development of reciprocal behavior.

Mutual respect is the foundation for compliance and it blossoms into "seeking parental approval" as the child matures. Reciprocal behavior is fundamental for developing healthy relationships in adult life based on mutual respect, cooperation and give and take. In raising attachment disordered children, it is useful to look toward the future in terms of "what kind of an adult is this child becoming?" Remembering that the "child is father/mother to the man/woman."

Acceptance encompasses three components: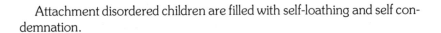
(1) acceptance of self,
(2) acceptance of others and
(3) acceptance of responsibility.

Attachment disordered children are filled with self-loathing and self condemnation.

-- Todd expresses this when he says, "I wish I was never born."
-- Debra screams, "I'm the devil's child."

They feel like they were born bad and are directly responsible for the mistreatment, abuse and abandonment they have suffered. They have been robbed of "the spirit of initiative" and feel hopeless regarding their capacity to change. They frequently exhibit self-abusive behaviors, doing to themselves what caregivers have done to them in the past and they are masters at goading their present caretakers into familiar abusive mistreatment.

The self-hatred, which becomes an integral part of their identity, grows like a weed around their personality, suffocating their sensitivity, compassion and humanity. Therapy requires nothing less than psychological surgery to separate the hate and rage from their infantile innocence.

Inner child work is a useful tool for creating a nurturing environment in which the attachment disordered child can begin to learn self-acceptance. By having the child close his eyes and imagine himself as an infant, hungry, wet, cold and in need of attention, he can begin to learn to nurture the child within, providing the comfort and reassurance which was not available to him at the time.

The child can rediscover innocence and basic goodness, counteracting his internalized sense of badness. He can begin to dispute the irrational belief that he somehow deserved the abuse and abandonment he received and that his mother was smart and wise to leave such a bad baby.

In working with attachment disordered children, I differentiate between accepting others and using others. These children are adept at using people for what they can get out of them and then throwing them away like a disposable diaper. For them it is a "use or be used" world and they usually choose to be the user, avoiding the foolishness and stupidity of the "usee". The concepts of trust and be trusted, love and be loved, are foreign to attachment disordered children and do not translate into their frame of reference. Only a long term and repetitive corrective emotional experience with their adult caregivers can begin to transform this internalized belief.

The work of "accepting others" with attachment disordered children begins with accepting what's been done to them by their adult caregivers. Statements like, "the most loving thing your mother could do was to give you away, with the hope that you would be adopted by a good family who could love you and care for you" or "you're lucky protective services removed you from your home, otherwise you might have been killed" generally fall on deaf ears. Attachment disordered children, like all children, don't feel loved by being abandoned and they don't feel fortunate about being separated from their parents. In fact, the abuse and neglect they suffer is secondary to the depth of the pain they defend themselves against in response to abandonment.

The only way to accept what has happened to them, what has been done to them, is to delicately and gently teach them how to grieve their losses. These are children who have suffered extensive losses. They have lost mother, father, siblings, safety, protection, innocence, genealogy and the ability to experience gratification, to name but a few. Grieving for attachment disordered children begins with releasing the rage that protects them from their pain and fear. A highly structured, closely supervised environment, balancing discipline and nurturance, provides the safety net which gives the child the necessary reassurance that the adult caregivers can handle his rage.

Only by going through the rage and emptiness can the child begin to grieve in a way that allows him to be comforted by his adult caregivers and to bond and attach in a healthy and positive relationship.

Grieving the early losses requires saying goodbye to one's birth parents, even for those children who were abandoned at birth. This can be accomplished utilizing role play and psychodrama techniques. Frequently, the child starts out saying goodbye in an angry way, however, by repeating the role play a number of times they can move emotionally into an attitude of acceptance and sometimes even forgiveness. The timing of this intervention is important and it cannot be forced upon the child until the child has worked through the fear of and resistance to confronting this difficult emotional task.

Attachment disordered children need guidance to choose to "get over it" and "get on with it." They can spend the rest of their lives living in the trauma of the past, defending themselves from the pain of abandonment, never taking the risk of caring and connecting or they can "get over it." Getting over it means releasing the rage, confronting the fear and experiencing the sadness. "You have the rest of your life in front of you, what do you want to do with it?"

This leads into the last aspect of acceptance -- accepting responsibility. Children with this disorder are notorious for projecting blame onto others. They live in a world of denial, rarely accepting responsibility for their choices and actions or for the consequences of their actions.

-- Like David said, in his most sincere and genuine tone of voice, "It's not my fault that I hit Ryan. He shouldn't have called me a wimp."

-- Eight-year-old Billy stated, "It's not my fault that I stole the money. My dad shouldn't have left it out on his dresser like that."

Learning to accept responsibility for their emotional reactions and behavioral responses is an arduous and painstaking task for therapists working with attachment disordered children, yet an essential part of the healing journey. By constantly reflecting back to the child, his choices and the consequences, the therapist can slowly, over time, assist the child in developing cause and effect thinking. By creating a controlled and structured environment with consistently enforced predictable consequences the child's behavior can be impacted and directed to learn to accept responsibility. By rehearsing behavioral situations, the child can be made more aware of his choices and their consequences and learn the cognitive structure of "If I do this, then 'that' will happen."

In therapy, I frequently focus on "accepting responsibility for being a member of this family." Membership requires cooperative living and being considerate of others. The Attachment Center at Evergreen litany:

"learning to be respectful, responsible and fun to be around," and *"doing things fast and snappy, right the first time, Mom and Dad's way"*

prepares attachment disordered children for family life. Learning how to do chores efficiently with a proper attitude and good effort is also a very useful tool for teaching responsible behavior.

Learning empathy is the final stage of therapy. Once an attachment disordered child develops empathy, defined as "the ability to care for others and respond to others" anger, fear and sadness in a sensitive manner, they are no longer attachment disordered. Once the child has learned to respond empathically, relinquishing control becomes far less of a problem.

-- Lisa, at age twelve, after observing her younger foster sister obnoxiously pushing her way to the front of the line to take her third turn on the slide said, "I used to do that."

-- Tom, age 11, reported in therapy that he chose to discontinue playing a board game with his seven-year-old foster brother, who kept cheating and changing the rules so he could win, and he just wasn't much fun to be around.

Tom then asked, "Was I that bad?" and I told him smiling, "You were much worse. At least Ed didn't pitch an hour long fit after you stopped playing with him, and then sneak into your room and either break or steal your favorite toy."

Reciprocity and acceptance are the building blocks of empathy. Empathy begins with compassion for the inner child, who wants desperately to be loved but instead gets abused, neglected and abandoned. Empathy is not self-pity. Frequently, attachment disordered children play a convincing and sophisticated game of "poor me," sucking in the ignorant and the innocent. The victim role comes easily to them and is a major stumbling block and obstacle on their journey to recovery. "Poor me" is just another manipulation for control and should not be confused with genuine sadness or budding empathy.

To develop empathy, attachment disordered children must first learn to have clear and unobstructed access to their own feelings. They must learn how to verbalize their feelings, as opposed to acting them out behaviorally, which they are generally very good at. In therapy, I spend a lot of time decoding their behaviors, helping them to understand what this behavior means and what message it sends to their caregivers about how they are feeling.

Through behavioral decoding I can begin to access whatever genuine feelings lurk beneath the surface of their superficially charming veneer.

In a therapy session with seven-year-old Ed and his therapeutic foster father, I asked him about the poop in the corner of his closet. After three or four lies, "I don't know how it got there, maybe David did it." "That was from a long time ago." and "The dog was in my room." Ed accepted responsibility, taking ownership of his behavior. Next we reviewed the details of the experience -- when it happened, what was going on, whether he dropped his pants and pooped in the corner or pooped in his pants and hand carried it to the closet, and of course, what about wiping. Next I asked Ed how he felt. After a couple of "I don't knows" he admitted he was mad. He was angry at Dad for not allowing him to play with his truck which had previously been confiscated for a rule violation (playing with his truck in an unauthorized play area when he was supposed to be doing a chore). After discussing how he wanted Dad to feel about him and confronting his desire to "get even" I had him tell Dad. "I was mad at you. I wanted to get even with you for not letting me do what I wanted." I had Ed repeat this until his affect matched his words, his feeling mirrored his behavior. We went on to explore who it was Ed really wanted to "get even" with and how he had been victimized (birth mother neglected him, failed to protect him from a sexually abusive boyfriend and abandoned him). Ed expressed some genuine feelings of anger and sadness and then Dad lovingly explained that it was his job to teach Ed the art of responsible behavior and make decisions regarding what is good for Ed and what is not ("It's not good for you to be sneaking and playing when you're supposed to be working and I care too much about you to let you do that.")

I then asked Ed how long it took him to clean up his mess and how that time might have been spent more productively. We rehearsed verbalizing his feelings, I shared my thoughts and feelings about "getting even" and I ended the session telling Ed I hoped he would make a better choice for himself next time he felt mad.

It is difficult to teach empathy to a child who experiences intense gratification when he inflicts pain on others and revels in the delight of sweet revenge. Yet, this is the long term goal of treatment with children who are attachment disordered. They must first develop the courage and have the support to confront their own pain. They must be taught nurturing protocol and practice it frequently, even if at first it lacks spontaneity and genuineness.

After two years of therapy, coupled with intensive therapeutic foster care, Carl was given three fish to care for. One of the fish died, not by Carl's hand, and after three more months of daily feeding and cleaning the fish tank, Carl was given a rabbit to care for. Carl bonded to the rabbit and the rabbit to him. Carl demonstrated genuine concern for the rabbit's well being, most of the time, and the relationship gave birth to empathy. In therapy and at home there were lots of rabbit metaphor stories and questions like, "How would you feel if your rabbit was cold?" and "How would you like it if your room was filled with feces?"

RE-DISCOVERING GRATIFICATION

The attachment disordered child's capacity to experience gratification has been damaged as a result of the abuse, neglect and abandonment he has suffered during the first two years of life. During the first year of life he has learned to not need what he needs most -- touch, love, food, movement and comfort. He has learned not to need his mother and in cases of abuse, had learned to fear his primary caregivers. An infant growing up in a trauma-filled environment quickly learns to lie to himself about what he needs. Survival becomes the primary focus of his adaptive mechanisms and rage helps to keep him alive. It is no wonder that in later years the desire for revenge, the calculated "getting even" behaviors, play such a prominent role in his behavioral repertoire. He feels entitled to get even for having had to sacrifice his basic needs. His exaggerated sense of entitlement grows out of his deprivation, giving him the right to compensation.

In the second year of life the child with attachment disordered learns not to want what he wants. He has learned that his caregivers and his environment do not place a high priority on responding to his desires, he is not likely to get what he wants so why ask for it? Far better to take control himself, than to rely on others. Far better to steal what he wants than be turned down and rejected. He has learned to seek control, not gratification. Due to developmental circumstances, he has lost the capacity to accurately identify what he needs, wants and desires. He has become separated from the "self", thereby losing the ability to experience gratification. Once an individual is separated from human needs and wants, gratification is an impossibility.

The attachment disordered child has effectively learned to lie to himself regarding what he needs and wants and how he feels. Learning how to accurately identify feelings, while expanding his emotional life beyond rage and anger, is an important aspect of long-term therapy. Working within the context of "mad, sad, glad and scared" the child can slowly learn the process of feeling identification. Teaching the child to "speak the emotional truth" begins with identifying what he needs and wants, how he feels and sharing this with the therapist and primary caregivers. Once he learns to stop lying to himself he can begin to learn how to stop lying to others. The lies he tells to himself about needing, wanting and feeling generally make it very easy for him to lie to others about his behavior. He must learn to stop lying to himself if he is to become a more honest and trustworthy person.

Gratification takes on perverse qualities when linked with a lack of conscience development. Attachment disordered children feel gratified when they have successfully: gotten even (revenge); not been held accountable for some sneaky behavior (stealing, lying, property destruction); or, in its most sadistic form, when they have inflicted pain and hurt on others.

Attachment disordered children must learn to rediscover gratification, if they are to abide by the laws of society and become productive citizens. They must learn how to use their feelings to guide their behavior in the direction of positive choices.

They need to be exposed to a variety of interests and activities emphasizing the ones in which they do well and derive enjoyment. They need to develop hobbies, cultivating the ability to experience joy and pleasure. They need appropriate physical outlets for their aggression, harnessing their angry energy productively and positively. They must learn to take pride in themselves and experience the satisfaction of a job "well done".

Attachment disordered children must be given the opportunity to help others and serve others in the spirit of charity (giving without expecting something in return). Helping people who are in need, alleviating suffering and assisting those who are less fortunate are higher forms of gratification rooted in compassion. As these children accumulate these experiences, they cultivate self-esteem and rediscover the gratification inherent in caring human relationships. Developing altruism, selflessness and benevolence can give meaning and purpose to their empty, narcissistic lives, guiding them toward the healthy fulfillment gratification offers.

LOW SELF-ESTEEM

Low self-esteem is a universal symptom in children suffering from Reactive Attachment Disorder (RAD). It afflicts them like an addiction, spreading contagiously into every aspect of their lives, infecting all of their relationships. David's foster father was instructing him on how to dig post holes.

-- David's self-esteem was so low he could not tolerate receiving instruction. It made him feel stupid and inadequate not to know how to do something. A child's learning is seriously compromised if he is threatened by instruction. He got even later that day, by breaking his dad's table saw.

-- Todd was so sensitive to criticism that he would fly into uncontrollable rages whenever his adoptive mother corrected him about anything. He had to believe that he was perfect, to assure that he would not be abandoned again.

Abuse, neglect and abandonment form the foundation of the attachment disordered child's self image. They see themselves as worthless and manipulate their caregivers to treat them accordingly. They treat their possessions and caregivers with an "I don't care" attitude. They don't feel special or important. They feel like garbage or trash, throw away children who deserve to be disposed of. They trash their toys and their families, constantly reaffirming their underlying sense of worthlessness, undeservedness, and inherent badness.

The experience of literally being abandoned, followed by the fear and certainty of future abandonment, fuels the attachment disordered child's feelings of low self-esteem.

Roger, age eight, proclaimed in therapy, "My birth mother was smart to get rid of me. I'm nothing but trouble."

These are children who feel anxious when they perform well or have an excellent day, due to the internal incongruity this creates with their poor self-image. Frequently, I'll instruct parents to structure a "blow it day" to help to decrease the child's anxiety when he is doing well.

When treating attachment disordered children in long-term therapy, their poor self-image and low self-esteem must be addressed. I work with the child and parents -- to develop mastery from a physical, emotional, social and intellectual perspective. Physically, I'll have the child perform exercises on a daily basis, so he can master his body and be in control of it. Later on, when the child demonstrates an increased capacity to handle responsibility I'll encourage participation in team sports, such as soccer and basketball.

Emotional mastery revolves around "speaking the emotional truth" and learning anger management. In therapy, I have the child practice the technique of emotional shuttling -- going into a feeling and learning how to pull out of it, like an experienced surfer on a wave that doesn't feel quite right. So often attachment disordered children get overwhelmed, flooded by their feelings, especially anger. They are emotionally immature due to limited practice, problems with trust and feeling unsafe. I teach them how to install an emotional thermostat to regulate the expression and intensity of their feelings. I teach them breathing exercises and other relaxation techniques. We thoroughly explore what activities have a calming effect on them, like drawing, exercise, listening to music, playing with Legos, or watching the fish tank. I frequently have them practice verbalizing their feelings in session and we rehearse emotional responses in role play situations to develop emotional mastery.

Social mastery requires respect and reciprocity. Participating in groups at school, therapy groups and activity groups, all foster social mastery. Initially, highly structured groups with close and competent adult supervision are required, boxing the child into appropriate behavior and positive feedback.

Parenting the low self-esteem of an attachment disordered child calls for the five to one ratio - five positives to every negative. Parents need to become adept at asking themselves "What's good about this..." (situation, behavior, expression of affect, etc.) and finding the silver lining.

Intellectually, children with attachment disorder frequently require special education and patient attention to master reading, writing and math. They are often educationally handicapped, with learning disabilities and attention deficit disorder. Their ability to learn is compromised by their need for control and their lack of desire to seek approval. Their underlying feeling of inadequacy constantly threaten their fragile self-image. They are so afraid of failing or appearing stupid that they would rather "give up" and not put forth the effort. It is important to find out how they learn and maximize their learning potentials utilizing all available resources and a variety of sensory modalities. With structure, repetition and support they can optimize their intellectual functioning and learn to feel good about themselves.

COGNITIVE RE-STRUCTURING

The children we are working with internalize fundamental belief systems which reinforce their poor self-image and prohibit the development of conscience. Beliefs like, "love hurts," "trust no one" and "nobody cares about me" are common. They are trapped in the abuse, neglect and abandonment of their own past, due to their internal working model. These dysfunctional beliefs must be exposed, challenged and restructed -- if they are to make progress in therapy.

Attachment disordered children relive the pain and trauma of their past on a daily basis. They behave, in the present, in such a way that they inevitably reinforce feeling lousy about themselves. They are masters at manipulating their current caregivers to treat them like they have been treated by caregivers in the past -- abusively and neglectfully, often resulting in re-abandonment.

They feel helpless and hopeless. Having been robbed of their spirit, they don't believe in their ability to change or grow. They are on a collision course with what they believe to be their destiny, plummeting narcissistically toward survival, driven by their need for control while the desire for immediate gratification of their primitive impulses guides them through the darkness.

The end result is the empty shell of a human being.

In therapy, they have to discover their personal power, if they are to effect change in their lives. Establishing and accomplishing small, sometimes insignificant goals, from week to week, helps to empower them.

Attachment disordered children must feel safe if they are to practice self-revealing behavior with their caregivers. To feel safe, they must recognize that they are no longer with the people who hurt them. The transference of the feelings of hurt, fear and anger from their inept and abusive caregivers onto their present caregivers needs to be addressed through the process of emotional release. These children end up hating and fearing their adoptive parents when it is their birth parents who have hurt them. I frequently tell them, "You have been hating the wrong person all these years. This Mom isn't the one who hurt you," confronting their belief that all Moms are the same.

These are children who need to understand the longing inside of them to be reunited with their birth parents and to share the fantasy they carry, which perpetuates their magical thinking. Birthdays and holidays provide opportunities for the therapist to confront their belief systems and re-learn a more functional model of who they are and how the world works.

For four years I have been working with David to internalize the attitudes and behaviors of his foster parents by constantly asking him in therapy, "What would Mom and Dad do in that situation?" and "How do you think

Mom and Dad felt about how you chose to handle that?" It has been a slow and arduous process, however, some new ways of thinking are beginning to take root.

Attachment disordered children need to learn and practice repeating "positive affirmations," challenging their "I don't care" and "I can't" belief systems. They must learn how to accurately identify the belief systems which guide their behaviors and utilize their awareness to recognize alternative choices which promote reciprocity, acceptance and empathy.

IN CONCLUSION

Children with attachment disorders require intermittent long-term therapy to heal from the psychological damage they have suffered. Therapy must address the rage which protects them from their feelings of worthlessness, and fuels their dangerous sociopathic and narcissistic behavior.

Treatment must help them to develop the courage to confront the terror which has been cellularly imprinted by the abuse, neglect and abandonment they have suffered. Parents and therapists must provide a nurturing and supportive environment in which these very challenged children can develop the ego strengths and confidence to face their pain and sorrow, effectively grieving their losses, discovering compassion and empathy for self and others.

Attachment disordered children must learn to love and be loved, if they are to recover from their early trauma. A corrective emotional experience helps to facilitate their journey from victim to survivor. It allows them to develop the confidence to risk being vulnerable once again, returning to the innocence and promise of infancy to learn how to trust.

Over the course of time, attachment disordered children can learn to rediscover their self-worth and become empathic and productive. Caregivers need to recognize and understand that the commitment is not time limited and that the potential for growth and change exists at every step along the path. They must find a way to sustain hope.

Therapists, foster parents, adoptive parents, and social service agencies must commit their time, energy, love and financial resources to help these damaged, love starved children to rekindle their light so they can find their way in the world.

9

Therapeutic Parenting (Part I)

A Personal Journey by Deborah Hage, ACE Therapeutic Parent

David, A Love Story

David was adopted at six months of age. As the years passed it became evident to us and a procession of therapists and psychologists that, while I took for granted that David was my son, David felt very strongly that I was not his mother. He appeared so angry at his birth mother for relinquishing him that any other mother figure was to be totally rejected. In his view, if even his birth mother could not be trusted to love him, how could I be trusted to love him?

The clinical diagnosis for his particular emotional disturbance was "Reactive Attachment Disorder."[1] What that meant in terms of day-to-day living was that he neither wanted me as a mother, nor trusted me to take care of him.

His nights were interrupted by terrorizing nightmares from which we could not awaken him. His days were filled with trying to prove me incapable of being his mother and testing the extent of my love for him. If I said it was Monday, he disagreed. If I gave him potatoes, he wanted rice. If I said 2 plus 2 are 4, he said it was 5. If I said it was raining, he

---

[1] Diagnostic and Statistical Manual, 4th Ed., American Psychiatric Association, 1994.

insisted it was snowing. If I praised his work, he tore it up. If I helped him build blocks, he kicked them down. If I hugged him close, he kicked me away. No matter how carefully I counted out peanuts or poured juice or dished out ice cream, he screamed that everyone always got more than he did.

And what did I do? I loved him. He was my son and his behavior towards me only served to convince me how much he needed to have proved to him that he was loved and wanted unequivocally, no strings attached. It was difficult, if not impossible at times, to not return the constant barrage of anger he hurled at me or to give in to his constantly changing demands.

My husband was enormously supportive through it all. At night, though, when he came home he saw a completely different child than I did during the day. At times he found it difficult not to think there was nothing wrong with David, but a great deal wrong with me. Our other five children, three of whom were also adopted, were doing so well, though, that I knew, despite the innuendos of others, it was not me, but David who was suffering the most. That knowledge of his suffering forced me to continue loving him even after our pediatrician counseled us to relinquish him because he was too emotionally disturbed to live in a normal home and his behavior caused more tension than was healthy for a family to endure.

I have loved David through running away, through public displays of uncontrollable anger, through countless times of being shoved aside, spat at, bit, hit, and punched. He has remained my son despite his need to sneak and hide food in his room until it rots and his inability or unwillingness to control where he puts his body wastes. Why? Because he is my son. He doesn't have to earn the privilege of being my son. He is not my son because he is a good boy. He is not my son because he loves me. He is my son, because he is my son.

The miracle is that love is winning. He started receiving holding therapy when he was eight and has since gone on to Outward Bound, a two week wilderness experience. David is now 15 years old and time is showing me that my love is finally prevailing over the hurt he suffered over his birth mom's rejection. David talks to me, often nicely. He lets me help him. We tickle and touch, he even hugs me sometimes. Nothing dramatic, no overnight cures, just the second by second unrelentless love that I have for him is giving him a window on life as it can be.

Therapeutic Parenting

Therapeutic Treatment Parenting is a professional approach to treating children and training parents of children with severe emotional disorders. The therapeutic parent is a highly skilled and trained individual who works in conjunction with a treatment team to treat the child in the therapeutic milieu of a family. The expertise and involvement of the therapeutic parent is the foundation of this unique approach.

The therapeutic parent creates a therapeutic environment in which the team treatment plan is implemented on a 24 hour basis. In consideration of expertise, specialized training, intense involvement, and high risk factors, the therapeutic parent should be compensated on a scale commensurate with other highly trained professionals.

"A therapeutic parent is committed to children, committed to remaining emotionally stable and healthy, committed to remaining open to consideration of all therapeutic tools, committed to continuing education, and committed to a team approach." Parents of ACE Handbook[2]

Effective Parenting

Successful parenting involves high structure, effective environmental controls, and helping the child develop appropriate responses to authority and the development of internal controls. Further, it concerns the use of logical and natural consequences, the reinforcement of reciprocity and nurturing/reparenting. Goals of this parenting are: to prepare the child for the real world and to help the child learn to be respectful, responsible and fun to be around.[3]

Writing about the parenting of emotionally and behaviorally problematic children is not so much to teach parents how to mold their children into responsible and cooperative human beings, as it is to enable them to have the tools, desire and energy to stay their children's parents over the long haul.

Going into any relationship with the aim of changing the other person into someone more easily loved has always been of dubious value. It is far more valuable to find ways to make the relationship work within the constraints of already developed personalities.

"The therapeutic parent realizes the abuse (emotional, sexual and physical) cannot be erased or forgotten, but the effects can be decreased"[4] This is the foundation of the techniques developed by therapeutic parents at The Attachment Center at Evergreen. Stopping a child from engaging in negative behavior is always nice, but many parents will be disappointed, discouraged and defeated if that is their primary goal.

---

[2] The Attachment Center at Evergreen, Inc. Parents of ACE Handbook, 1995.

[3] The Attachment Center at Evergreen, Inc., Attachment Center Brochure, 1995.

[4] Op.Cit., 1995.

So, the question is not, "How do we make our children more lovable?" Rather it is, "How do we love unlovable children?"

Learning how to love children who have learned in the past that love hurts, who are afraid of love and who actively seek to rebuff love and the human contact it engenders is the essence of therapeutic parenting.

Oddly enough, the first requirement of learning to love unlovable children is to love ourselves. What hope does a child have to learn how to love himself or others if the adults who are most present in his life don't demonstrate that they love themselves? The message to the child is, "Look at the abuse and neglect you have suffered. Your experience has taught you that you are not entitled to be the recipient of loving concern when you are a child. By observing me you can tell that when you grow up you are not entitled to it either."

Step One in therapeutic parenting is to take very good care of yourself and your significant relationships. It is important that parents take time out for themselves. Children need to see that their negative behavior does not imprison their parents and prevent them from having a good time together. Parents need to demonstrate they are not going to be punished for their child's choices by allowing fear of the child's ability to misbehave be the focus of their lives. They need to actively seek, train and pay well for alternative care for their children several times a month for evenings out and at least once a year for extended vacations. This is not a luxury. This time together is essential; parents of these children need to be filled up by the one-on-one time involved in eye contact, touch, smiles, food, and movement, before we can pass these essential ingredients of feeling loved on to our children. We cannot give our children what we do not possess ourselves.

Parents also need to have each other's disciplinary efforts validated in the presence of the child. Questioning the use of an intervention is often appropriate, however, it needs to be discussed in private. Parents who communicate to a disturbed child they are in disagreement about what to do increases that child's commitment to splitting and manipulation to the detriment of the marital relationship. The child will continue to use any behavior as long as he can get one parent to endorse it. Many therapeutic parents follow the dictum, "When parents are in disagreement the stricter parent decides."

By taking good care of ourselves and our children, there is an optimum chance for everyone to enjoy life and living together.

A natural extension of parents who treat themselves and their children with a high degree of respect and loving care is having the children treat them that way as well. Let there be no mistake, however. Children do not need to treat their parents respectfully because parents need the boost to their egos. Children need to treat their parents with respect because that is how children learn self-respect.

Parents, teachers, and other adults who tolerate disrespect are saying to children, "I am not worthy of respect." The children then say to themselves, "If I can treat others with disrespect and get away with it then people can treat me with disrespect and get away with it. None of us are worth anything at all, not even me." The damage done to a child's self-esteem when he or she is allowed to whine, curse, swear and, in numerous other forms of speech and behavior, be disrespectful of the loving authorities in their life is incalculable.

How do parents manage this two faceted task of care-giving and care-taking? The answer lies in therapeutic parenting. Therapeutic parenting is implementing those techniques which encourage us to take care of ourselves and our children and which put in place the reciprocal nature of being truly loving so children respond by taking good care of themselves and of their relationship with us. It is not taking the power to change children too seriously, but taking the power to love in constructive ways very seriously.

Pro-active and Re-Active Approaches

Being a therapeutic parent is approached from two directions simultaneously - pro-active and re-active.

- Being "proactive" means setting up a home and environment which is fun for the children to be in. Creating a place for children that is warm, welcoming, respectful and fun encourages children to practice behaviors which allow them to stay there. If home is not a safe haven for children it will seem pointless for them to change their behavior to live there. In fact the opposite may occur. Certainly, children who do not perceive they are in a caring environment will deliberately choose negative behaviors which will cause them to be moved. Consciously designing an inviting family setting is pivotal to both the well being of the child and the well being of the parents.
- Setting family tone, however, is not enough. "Re-active" parenting techniques ensure that when negative behavior does occur it is met with firm kindness and respect while placing the child in the position of having to take responsibility for his or her behavior.

During both proactive and reactive parenting, therapeutic parents make sure they demonstrate to the children that they take good care of themselves first. When they choose to participate in something fun for the child they make sure it is fun for them also. Likewise, when a child's negative behavior requires a response, the parents ensure that regardless of how the child reacts to the consequences of his behavior, the parents feel good about themselves and the child so they are able to continue to care for the child. When parents are firm about what they are going to do, not what they are going to make their child do, win-win situations are created and ego-crunching defeat is avoided for everyone. To accomplish this end:

1.) The pro-active approach is used to avoid problems and encourage positive behavior.

2.) The re-active approach is used as a response to negative behavior.

Both work simultaneously and involve touch, eye contact, food and smiles. In neither is communication done principally with words. Both approaches are based on actions.

1.) Pro-active Therapeutic Parenting:

Setting Family Tone

Proactive techniques involve creating a home environment and relationship with the children so being "respectful, responsible and fun to be around" is a desirable goal to the child. To that end it is important to set a tone that is positive and makes valued behaviors worthwhile. A high level of joy and enthusiasm is achieved by planning family activities, minimizing negatives and maximizing positives, knowing that behavior will be repeated which gets the most attention.

Many aspects of maintaining a welcome family atmosphere are detailed in Delores Curran's book Traits of a Healthy Family.

Curran details fifteen qualities commonly found in healthy families. While the families studied did not have the stressor of an emotionally and behaviorally problematic child, it is still an excellent tool in helping families assess themselves and find ways to capitalize on their strengths and minimize their weaknesses. The perfect family doesn't exist, but with effort, parents can improve their family setting so it is healthy for their children.

Tone of Voice

Part of creating a positive tone is speaking in loving ways and avoiding sarcasm and anger. After all, why would a child want to bond to someone who is irritable and belittling? While there is a place for parental anger, for the most part, words spoken in anger or frustration push children deeper into themselves and away from their parents. When a parent is confronting a child on his lost coat in a biting tone, for example, the child is not thinking about where the coat is. The child is wondering how to get his parent out of his face, how long the harangue will last, and often, how to avoid the imminent blow. The parent is communicating, "I love you so much I don't want you to get cold." The child is hearing, "Mom hates me. The stupid coat is worth more to her than I am."

In such a situation it is far better to use an appropriate reactive technique, than to confuse the child by phrasing deep love and concern in harsh tones of criticism.

Eye Contact, Smiles, Touch, Nurturing Take Time

A great deal of time spent one-on-one with each child is important to the development of a parent-child relationship. Most therapeutic parents act on the belief there must be at least five positive interactions with a child for every negative interaction, for bonding to occur. It can be helpful to keep track of the time it takes after a bonding contact involving eye contact, touch, movement or food for the child to misbehave. Knowing how long a child can maintain good behavior allows the parent to intentionally interact with the child in a bonding way in the minutes, or seconds, prior to when an incident could be reasonably expected to occur.

Game playing, cuddling, rocking, and occasionally feeding a bottle to an unattached child is part of the life of the therapeutic parent. Specific methods for holding and snuggling with a child are dealt with in the book Holding Time by Dr. Martha Welch.[6] The author goes into great detail on one technique, which, when used in concert with others, is helpful in creating a close, nurturing relationship:

> Time spent cooking for or with a child is never wasted. Filling a home with the good smells of home-cooked meals is one of the best gifts a parent can give a child. "Nothin' says lovin' like somethin' from the oven" is an old advertising jingle which captures the essence of this principle.

Time is a critical factor when it comes to volunteer activities as well. It is no accident that those people who make the best parents for their own children also make excellent volunteers in the lives of other people's children. Being a den leader, Sunday School teacher, classroom aide, soccer coach, etc., are all admirable, worthy endeavors. Parents must guard, however, that they do not get so involved in working with other children they neglect their own. Activities must be prioritized so the responsibilities which fall closest to home are taken care of first.

---

[6] Martha Welch, M.D., Holding Time New York: Simon and Schuster, 1988.

When several of our sons were in elementary school I became involved in Cub Scouts in order to join with them in the fun activities. As our program grew I became more and more active in the leadership, until I was responsible for 110 little boys and their den leaders, plus remaining the den leader for my children. One night as I was running out the door for yet another meeting one of my sons said to me, "Mom, if you are doing all of this stuff for me, don't." His words stopped me dead in my tracks.

Other forms of nurturing are important as well. Children need to look attractive to see a high regard reflected back to them from others. Unless someone close to the family is an excellent barber haircuts need to be professionally done. It is unfair for a child who needs to feel good about himself to look at his reflection in the mirror and see a chopped up embarrassment. Children also need nice clothes. Hand-me-downs and thrift store purchases can be used as part of a child's wardrobe, when they are in good condition, but nothing makes a child feel smarter and sharper than walking out of a store with brand-new, purchased-just-for-him by a parent investing the time and energy to shop just with him, new clothes. That does not mean a child can trash new clothes without the application of natural consequences, it just means there are times when new clothes are the best thing that could happen to a troubled child. The clear message the child gives to himself as he walks through life is, "I am worth looking this good."

Television

Another proactive trait is tight parental control of the television. Even good TV is bad for kids, particularly those with problematic behavior. Television is geared to the selling of products. The goal of the script writer is to gain viewers attention so they remain in their seats through the commercials. Whatever is going to keep people watching is what will be shown -- regardless of the moral or violent tone of the images required. Yet, it is not merely the content of television programming that is the problem. It is the process of watching. The rapid fire images accustom children's eyes to stare intently at the same spot with the colors and shapes chosen for them by the camera. However, in order for children to learn to read, their eyes must tract from image to image. Rather than the information being shot effortlessly into the children's brains, reading requires the slow accumulation of skills and the application of imagination. Watching television is counter-productive to the development of both those skills.

To the child whose behavior is problematic, watching television creates yet another layer of distance between their parents and themselves. The TV does not relate. It does not answer questions or teach problem solving.

Problems are presented and solved within thirty minutes, often with some-one getting hurt in the process -- definitely not reflective of real life.

The bottom line is, children who are watching television are not relating to anyone. They are not engaging in reciprocal smiles, eye contact, move-ment or touch. None of the interactions essential to bonding and the development of healthy relationships are present. It does not need to be cut out of life altogether, however. Using the TV sparingly, as an occasional reward when earned, gives children an incentive to work on their behavior. Even then, well-chosen movies tend to be better for children than commer-cial television programming.

We have a TV. The children could be baking in the kitchen, playing basketball outside, assembling a puzzle, reading or otherwise engaged in a variety of worthwhile pursuits. Somehow, the indiscernible click of the TV being turned on resounds through the house and, one by one, the children stop what they were doing and gravitate to the family room, to sit entranced. When it became clear the TV was causing more problems than it was solving we decided to lock it up. An inexpensive money box was purchased and a metal fabricator punched a hole in one end which was big enough for the cord to fit through but too small for the plug. The plug was then locked into the box with the understanding that the T.V. would be available more selectively in the future. After several months, the children figured out how to pry open the box without unlocking it. When I discovered it I told them the lockbox was just a reminder of the house rule, they were still responsible for its enforcement. I then unplugged the TV and cut off the plug. The kids were speechless with surprise. It took them several days to figure out how to rewire it, but I never had to use the lockbox again as they policed each other's use of the TV. They knew that if I cut the plug off again, the cord would then be too short to reach from the set to the wall.

Music

Through the ages people have been aware of how mood is affected by music. While therapeutic parents would not get into any control battles over what music children quietly listen to in their rooms, they often pre-empt the air space in the home with classical and harmonious sounds. In homes where children may attempt to take control, by keeping the family in a high level of tension, calming music helps set a more desirable fam-ily tone.

Encouragement

Proactive parents get excited whenever children are caught doing some-thing right. Massive amounts of attention are not given to bad behavior.

It is dealt with matter-of-factly, while the pizazz is saved for good behavior. For example, squealing with delight when children brush their teeth and ignoring it when they don't, focuses on the positives of their personality. Grabbing them up in a hug and swinging them around when they walk by other children without hitting them is worth an exclamation of joy and delight.

Parents may exclaim, "Wow, did you see what you just did?" You walked by Jim without punching him!" or "Charlotte left her candy bar on the counter and it is still here! It is wonderful to know you are learning to respect her property."

School Issues

The separation of home and school is invaluable when building a bonded relationship with a child. Children who have experienced a fairly normal development benefit from having parents who are present in school and, depending on what is developmentally appropriate, actively involved in the child's education.

This is not necessarily true for children whose relationship with their parents is problematic and who could actively work to cause a split between the parents and the teachers. When parents are stretched to the limit trying to maintain a child in their home it is not realistic for them to additionally monitor homework and be continually called to the school to discuss discipline problems. It is far better for the parents to directly say to the child and the school, "Good luck, hope you can work it out. If you can't, fourth grade will also be available again next year." School performance is a child's issue and to make it the parent's issue can confuse the bonding work.

> As we told one son, "As long as you are stealing it is OK for you to choose to flunk school. The world does not need smart thieves."

The child's potential behaviors must be shared with the school in advance and parents can help the school by discussing what consequences will be endorsed and what won't, and what tends to work and what doesn't. Letting the school know the parents can be called in as a resource is different than allowing the school to have the expectation that problems which arise at school regarding behaviors, homework or grades, will be automatically consequenced by the already struggling parents.

In exasperation I once sweetly said to my son's teacher, "I tell you what, when you are having difficulty coping with my son's behavior at school or getting him to stay on task I will be glad to come over and help out as long as when I am having trouble coping with his behavior at home because he is fighting with his brother or won't do his chores I can call you and you will come over and help out."

A parent can be a valuable resource to the school by supporting any consequence the school decides is appropriate. Generally the parents are supportive of more severe consequences than the school would consider, but there are times when a consequence can be negotiated and, even a few rare times when the parents can volunteer to enforce the consequence.

During a particularly difficult week with one of our children -- after running away, foul language, refusal to do work and other angry behaviors not typical of second graders -- his teacher called home to ask for suggestions. We agreed to "fire him" from school. We explained to him, "Everybody has a job. Daddy has a job earning the money to pay for our food and home. I have a job keeping everything at home running smoothly. The teacher has a job educating the children in her classroom. Your job is to learn to read and write. There are times, however, when people just don't seem to be capable of doing their job and when that happens they can be fired. If Daddy doesn't do what he needs to do for his company than his company can say, 'We don't need you anymore' and so can fire him. People who do not learn to read and write can be fired from jobs which require reading and writing and then taught to do jobs which they can do with their hands. So, next time you decide you do not want to do the work of reading and writing, your teacher is going to fire you and send you home where I will teach you how to clean the stove, wash the refrigerator and learn other jobs which do not require reading and writing."

The next time he acted out in school and was clearly not contributing to his own or anyone else's learning the teacher "fired him" and I came and got him. He worked the rest of the day on chores at home. The next week he needed to try the behaviors again and was then "fired" for three days. That was the last time the consequence needed to be used.

This consequence worked, with the parent enforcing it because the parent had already established a relationship with the child. When that is not present, then the child needs to be fired to a foster home or day care where the foster or day care mother is present to teach the chores and enforce the consequence. At the end of the school day the child would then go home, regardless of the state of the required chores, to return the next day and the next until compliance had been demonstrated.

Working with schools on discipline and performance issues is easier when the school sees the parents as allies. Volunteering to help with fundraisers and aiding in the library are ways for parents to support the school, while not interacting directly with their own child. The more school staff sees the parent as an asset to the school the more willing they are to work with them to problem solve issues regarding the child.

Community Issues

While parents can legitimately leave school issues to the school to handle, that is not the case with community issues. Parents need to demonstrate to their children and to the police they are on the front line with law enforcement officials and will fully cooperate with them. Sometimes that means parents must be the first to call police when their children commit an illegal act. The family and child will get more fair and respectful treatment from the police and the courts when they know the family is doing all it can to establish a sense of law and order in the child. To protect a child from legal consequences of their behavior is to set the child up to behave illegally again and the family up to be disrespected in the community for adopting children who prey on their neighbors and drain the communities resources.

An acquaintance called and said, "I think I just saw your son climb out the window of the house next door." The police were immediately called and they were at our home within minutes of the time our son walked in the door, allowing them to confront him and catch him with the stolen items still on him. Another time, a son came home with a bleeding arm and an unusual story of how it happened. After we went to the emergency room for stitches I called the police and said, "My son has just gotten stitches in his arm. It looks like he gashed it on broken glass. If anyone calls to report an incident of breaking and entering let me know." The next day an officer called and said the school had been broken into and there was blood on the floor.

The boys learned from these incidents, if they get involved in illegal behavior we will cooperate totally with law enforcement. The police and community residents learned we can be depended on to support them in their efforts and they may call us any time they see our children act suspiciously or they have reason to believe any of our children were involved in a delinquent or illegal act. We will not rescue or make excuses for them.

The down side is the ire we arouse in other parents whose children are with ours when an illegal act is committed. We have been heatedly told, "You turn your children into the police, but don't you dare turn in ours!" Our stance has also angered our children, as they have had to do community service hours, pay restitution and even go to a juvenile lock-up while their compatriots experienced no consequence as a result of their actions, because their parents hired a lawyer and got them off.

Nonetheless, we remain committed to the belief that our children and society will benefit from our totally cooperative stance with the police and a little "confinement therapy" may be just what a child needs to give thought to the direction of their life.

Home Hygiene

Sometimes you don't need to be a better parent, you need to be a better housekeeper.

Children whose lives have been disrupted by the lack of structure inherent in moving from place-to-place and caretaker-to-caretaker are affected by disorganization. It is unrealistic to expect children who are emotionally and behaviorally chaotic to internalize a sense of order, when they get up in the morning to a kitchen filled with the previous night's dirty dishes or come home after school to a living room cluttered with unsorted laundry. Working with a child, as opposed to continually leaving it to the child to do alone, to restore order in a home is as valuable a therapeutic technique as it is a concrete way for children to symbolically address their psychological need for internal structure. When done with a loving parent it also provides an opportunity for bonding contact.

Chores

Chores make a child capable of taking care of himself. They build a sense of being needed and accomplishment. They teach the importance of reciprocity in relationships and help make the child appreciative of the work that parents put into running a home. In short, they are essential teaching tools for children to feel good about themselves and others. Children who don't do chores grow up believing someone else will always take care of their needs and life does not involve work. The problem with chores, however, is that teaching children how to do them requires a greater investment in time and energy on the part of the parent than will be immediately realized. Difficult children oftentimes need to be placed in the position of having to do something, and do it right, in order to give parents the opportunity to congratulate them on a job well-done. In the long run the parental positives given after the task will transfer to a willingness to do tasks for others, e.g., teachers and employers. Initially, however, the results will not be worthwhile, so long term commitment to the realization of future goals must be kept in mind. Teaching children how to do chores requires three elements:

- One is the understanding on the part of the parents that the issue in doing chores is not just in getting a task done or achieving compliance. The issue is about trust, connectedness and where the child fits in life. Therefore the bonding elements of eye contact, touch, movement and food need to be present and pizzazzy for the child to connect doing chores to loving and being loved.
- The second element of teaching chores requires a foundation in consequencing skills. There is no point in asking a child to do

something if there is no plan of what is going to happen when the child doesn't do it.

- The third element involves planning. Initially doing chores must be fun for the child and fun for the parent. As the child gets older the parent gradually is removed and more and more of the chore is done by the child, there is less and less an expectation of fun and more an expectation of taking personal responsibility to do one's share of the work involved in running a home.

Teaching my daughter to do the dishes by herself after a meal took five years to accomplish. When we adopted her at four she occasionally helped by standing on a stool in front of the kitchen sink, playing in the soapy water while rinsing the dishes prior to being loaded in the dishwasher. As she got older we did not leave it to her to volunteer to rinse the dishes but assigned her one evening a week when it was her turn to help. By the time she was five she did not play so much, rather she took is as a matter of course that one night a week she needed to rinse the dishes. She could play if she wanted, as it didn't matter how it was done or how long it took as long as the results met expectations. The foundation of expectation had been laid.

By the time she was six she was helping to clear the table and rinse. Later, loading the dishwasher was added. There was a gradual introduction of new tasks. At eight she was helping to clear the table, put items away, rinse the dishes, load and unload the dishwasher, wiping the counters, cleaning the sinks and sweeping the kitchen. She was not working alone yet, there was still a family member helping. Sometime during her ninth year she was asked to do it alone intermittently. Doing it by herself, one evening a week, became the norm several months later.

This process can be shortened considerably, and possibly even eliminated, with older children but the elements remains the same. In some way there needs to be some form of pleasure or reward injected into the chore. Parents must model doing chores themselves, occasionally working alongside the child. Consequences need to be available to ensure the task is completed so the child can earn approval for a job well done. Parents must keep in mind the chore is a means to an end, not the end.

The goal is not chore completion but growth in the child's ability to love himself and others and to demonstrate that love with reciprocity.

When having a child do chores the distinction between compliance and cooperation is helpful to understand. Cooperation comes from a deep willingness of the heart, compliance just means getting the unwanted task done. It is wonderful when children cooperate with doing chores out of sense of joy and fulfillment. However, since cooperation is a higher level concept for many children we settle for compliance, hoping the sense of cooperation will develop as the child matures and learns to trust and love.

Compliance is indicated by the attitude, "I don't want to do it and I'm going to do it anyway." Having the child verbalize that sentiment when asked to do a chore can help to break down the resistance and allows the parent to acknowledge how hard it is for the child to do what is being asked and to express appreciation for the child's efforts. "I know how hard it is to help out when you don't want to. Mopping the floor is a dirty job. I want you to know I really appreciate your help and am glad you are learning to do things you don't want to do. That is a tough skill even for adults."

Work does not have to be done with a good attitude. By doing chores, even when they don't want to, in an acceptable frame of mind, parents model for their children that chores are simply a part of life. It gives them an excellent opportunity to demonstrate it is possible to have negative feelings and handle them well.

This also teaches children to look past the unpleasant parts of the task, to the joy of completion and the rewards which follow -- play time, ice cream, picnic, money. No one works for free, even volunteers get some form of reward for their efforts. Adults hold jobs to get the pay at the end of the month. Children are no different.

They must have an expectation of something good happening when their work is all done if they are to buy into the concept that doing chores well will ultimately work out well for them.

Changing Family Tone

Despite a parent's best efforts there will be times when everyone in the house is tense and ill-tempered. Those times can be minimized by a parent determined to not let a negative mood infect the entire day and pervade the atmosphere.

Rather than homing in on the child causing the most disturbance it is often helpful to gather everyone together in an activity consciously designed to lighten the mood. For some reason, ordering pizza is a guaranteed mood lifter. Parents may be perfectly capable of making an excellent pizza from scratch, at home, for half the price. However, there is something magical and mystical about having pizza delivered to the door which says, "Let's party!"

Making cookie dough is another sure-fire way to lift spirits. Note, the point is not to bake cookies, the point is to make cookie dough. Any dough which is not eaten with the fingers and actually makes it into the oven to be baked does not count. The concern for the therapeutic parent is not cavities in their children's teeth, which any good dentist can fix, but holes in their children's hearts, which only they can fix.

Fingerpainting with catsup on the refrigerator, taking a long walk, reading out loud, playing a non-competitive board game or game of cards are all good ways to change tone.

Creativity and the willingness to be unorthodox are essential to turning frowns into smiles. It is important that parents not always get caught up in techniques which consequence, force a sense of responsibility, and cause thoughtfulness in the children. Sometimes it is appropriate to just lighten up and have a good time. After all, children spend more time in relationship with their parents as adults than they do as children. They need to have a memory bank full of good times, which will glue them together as a family long after they have left home.

<u>Rituals</u>

That memory bank is often filled with the rituals in which a family engages. It doesn't take much to create a family ritual:

- Baking cookies once at Christmas causes children to say at every Christmas thereafter, "We always bake cookies at Christmas." Such is the importance to children of predictability and stability.

Children who have come from previous family experiences which left them looking at the world as an unfriendly, dangerous place need help seeing the world as predictably positive. Rituals, by fixing in the child's memory that a certain positive event will occur at the same time each day, week, month or year, enable children to look forward to the future with pleasure, instead of hopelessness.

- Reading to a child every night before bedtime, brushing a child's hair each morning, attending worship every Sabbath, singing a certain song when a child is blue; all these enable a child to feel hopeful for the future.
- Knowing that the first day of school will be greeted with new pencils and new clothes gives a child a new outlook that this year will be better.

Due to the previous abuse issues of most of our children and the understanding that for some of them the abuse occurred primarily at night or was somehow connected to the dark, we consciously strove to surround bedtime with a sense of warmth and safety. We made it a predictable calm routine of baths, teeth brushing, getting into pajamas, bringing a stuffed animal or blanket into the living room and reading aloud.

The first books read were generally funny and entertaining. Sometimes, we would read a little poetry. <u>Jabberwocky</u> by Jewis Carroll and illustrated by Graeme Base was a favorite. It and the book we tended to finish with, <u>Goodnight Moon</u>, by Margaret Brown, were both memorized by most of the children. From the day after Thanksgiving, to when the children went back to school after Christmas, our large collection of Christmas books were shared each evening.

Following reading time the children went to their rooms to get into bed. We would then go from room to room, bed to bed, sitting on the edge, talking quietly for a few minutes, hearing concerns of the day, plans for tomorrow, blessing, hugging and kissing each other in the quiet ritual of love. Lights were turned out as we left, however bedroom doors were always left open so light would shine in and the children could hear us continue to talk or move quietly through the house as they relaxed their vigil and nodded off to sleep.

Holidays are known by their rituals and there is a reason why adult children come home for them. They come home because there are certain events during the year which have become surrounded with massive amounts of rituals and they want to recreate the enjoyable times of their childhood and share those times with their spouse and children. They want to link the joys of the past to the joys of the present and establish a foundation of joy for the future.

Family rituals fill that need. Parents do their families a disservice when they get so caught up in the negative behavior of their children they neglect the creation of family rituals.

Reciprocal Relationships

Because unattached children are, by definition, self-centered and self-dependent for everything, developing reciprocal relationships is part of the therapeutic parenting process. Therepeutic parents must provide many opportunities for disturbed children to interact in a reciprocal way.

Learning to trust others to take care of them, take comfort in being cared for, and to take care of others in return, is essential to success. Participating in joint activities, doing chores and paying back those they injure through their thoughtlessness are all learning tasks of the unattached child.

Particularly important is making sure siblings are taken care of when a child hurts them or destroys their property. This allows the children to maintain a good working relationship between them. To allow the build up of a wall of resentment to occur between the children who injure and the children who are in some way injured destroys morale in a family. Children need to know they will be taken care of when their brother or sister misbehaves at their expense so they can forgive and move on with the relationship.

The bottom line is, "The victim decides". It is not up to the child who wreaked havoc to determine the value to the victim of the destroyed property or the amount of pain experienced. It is up to the child who has been hurt to decide what needs to be done to make up for or counteract the ill will generated by the misdeed. The victim can request: a toy be handed over in exchange for the destroyed one; a victim's chore be done by the perpetrator to make up for the hurt; a dessert handed over to compensate for the embarrassment to friends, etc. The victim needs to be counseled, however, that to extract too great a penalty will cause resentment and the need to seek further vegerance. Responsibility for the behavior will be enhanced, while escalation of the behavior will be avoided, if there is a sense of equity between what was done and what needs to happen to make up for it.

One child continually made demeaning comments to his sister regarding her race, her size, her sexuality and anything else he could to arouse her ire. Finally, she had enough and decided a pay-back was required for the humiliation he caused her in front of her friends and when she was alone. It was negotiated that he would do her dishes for her the next time it occurred. That was all it took. It stopped immediately as our daughter would walk up to him and say, "I don't want to do the dishes tonight because I have made plans with friends. Could you please say something ugly to me right now so I can leave after dinner?"

Reactive Parenting Techniques

Despite the best efforts of the best parents children will continue to act in negative, inappropriate ways.

When children do not take advantage of the enjoyment life and the family have to offer and make poor behavior choices, then it is necessary to react and find various ways of demonstrating "sad for" the child, rather than "mad at" the child, in a manner that is not punitive; this interaction should allow both the parent and child to have a "win-win" experience.

There are a variety of techniques to accomplish this. Deciding which one to use is one of experimentation. One thought to keep in mind when choosing, is to reason with the child when he is being reasonable and take action with the child when the child is being governed by emotions.

In the next chapter I will discuss, specifically, some of these techniques.

10

Therapeutic Parenting (Part II)

The Ace Philosophy Of Parenting
By Deborah Hage
ACE Therapeutic Parent

The therapeutic foster parents at The Attachment Center at Evergreen believe:

"You can do the wrong thing over and over, or, you can do the right thing once!"

When a technique has been tried several times and has not achieved a desired behavior change, the parent modifies it. Because techniques are continually being changed, the parents have developed a wide repertoire of responses to negative behavior. Positive behaviors forced upon children are not internalized as well as those they choose to adopt with therapeutic parental nudging, so the goal is to create thoughtfulness in the child so the child chooses to change. Most people do not change their behavior until the price gets to be too high to continue it. Really, the goal is to create situations where the price for maintaining a behavior is high, and the reward for changing the behavior is equally high.

The reactive techniques, used to interrupt, redirect, and/or correct poor behavior, can be seen as a continuum, ranging from non-intrusive (ignoring behavior) to extremely intrusive (one-minute scolding), with the least intrusive form of intervention always being the first choice. The techniques are generally used without warning in order to avoid a build up of resistance. Underpinning all reactive discipline is a firm foundation of consequencing, which is to have children experience either a real-world or similar to a real-world consequence to their behavior. Consequencing as a parenting technique is dealt with further in Parenting With Love and Logic and Parenting Teens With Love and Logic, both by Foster Cline and Jim Fay.[7]

Pivotal to understanding consequencing is differentiating between which behaviors are worth controlling and which ones are not. The child's unspoken job is to get the parents, the parents job is to not get got. Avoiding control battles, especially those which cannot be won, is essential if children are going to be raised who listen to and respect parental authority.

Therapeutic parents, therefore, do not attempt to control:
- food intake,
- hygiene issues,
- choice of friends,
- hairstyle, etc.

They believe that you "take it all, you lose it all", so they willingly give away the control they don't need and they don't have anyway.

Rule Number One of avoiding control battles is to pick the issue very carefully, because Rule Number Two is that, once it is picked, it must be won. Being relentlessly persistent in the face of relentless provocation, while maintaining a sense of lightness, grace and humor is the mark of a great parent.

Ignoring Behavior

Naturally, the least intrusive reactive parenting technique is to simply ignore all behavior which can be ignored, such as sloppy dressing and careless schoolwork. Unkempt kids simply aren't invited on family outings and poor schoolwork has its own, built-in consequences. Children who have no sense of their own worth do not tend to take care of themselves in healthy ways. Poor hygiene is common. Other symptoms of attachment issues which can often be safely ignored at home are abnormal eating patterns, abnormal speech patterns and persistent nonsense questions and incessant chatter.

There are much more dangerous and important behaviors to be addressed than these. These behaviors are not the problem, they are symptoms of the problem and attempting to control them will ultimately be fruitless and may be counterproductive. Removing them prematurely may only drive the child to find other ways to demonstrate their lack of attach-

---

[7] Love and Logic Press, Golden, Colorado, Jim Fay and Dr. Foster Cline, 2207 Jackson St., Golden, CO. 80401.

ment. The chances that replacement behaviors will be as benign as baby talk and silly questions are slim.

Many behaviors which are better ignored during the course of the day, however, may be addressed by the therapist and/or parent as a therapeutic (not a parenting) issue as they are usually indicative of a larger problem in the child's life.

> Keep in mind there are two ways in which the technique of ignoring behaviors can be used:
> 1.) Behaviors are ignored by the parent and possibly referred to a therapist.
> 2.) Behaviors are ignored for the moment, but consequenced later. Ignoring a behavior, if it is safe to, when it occurs allows the parent to give thought to an appropriate consequence and implement it when both the child and the parent are not emotionally involved.

Joining In

The opposite of ignoring is joining the child in the behavior. When the child tantrums, throw yourself on the floor right next to them and scream and pound. It is helpful if every minute or so you look over at the child and ask them if you are doing it right. Or, when the child complains petulantly about what someone did, respond in kind and tell them in the same manner and similar choice of words about a time someone did the same thing to you. Or, come screaming out of your room that you haven't a thing to wear and you're going to flunk the spelling test. The possibilities are endless.

Touch

The next least intrusive technique is a simple touch to remind children you are present and aware of their behavior. A hand rested lightly on the shoulder often is all that is necessary to help children become more thoughtful.

Bringing children in close with a gentle touch when they misbehave catches them off guard. Their defenses are up to ward off a physical or verbal blow. When a hug, accompanied by a sympathetic, "My, my. You must be feeling pretty bad inside in order for you to do that." comes instead, there is a lapse of their defenses which allows for a brief opportunity for parental acceptance to enter. This is a particularly effective response when children call their parents foul names or refer to them in vulgar terms. Language is very difficult to control and it is sometimes best to not get in an overt control battle over it. Disarming the child's need to lash out in this way is often more effective than confronting it. "I am sorry you feel that way, as I love you very much" is one response. Another might be, "I wonder if someone has said such things to you and hurt you very badly. You must want to hurt me the way you were hurt. Well, I don't want to hurt you. Here's a hug. Hope you get over the need to say such things."

Attachment is created through a myriad of small, reassuring occasions such as these. Consequencing is essential, and is useful in keeping children from falling into disrespectful patterns, but it does not need to occur as a response to every negative behavior, every time it happens. Don't underestimate the power of a smile accompanied by raised eyebrows, or a widely mouthed "I love you" to stop some unacceptable behaviors in their tracks.

Mom Time

"Mom time" is slightly more intrusive than touching as the child is brought in close after misbehavior and held or cuddled on the lap. Making a child feel loved and valued while giving him a chance to regroup and choose a different behavior is the goal. This can be for a few minutes or long enough to read him a couple of short storybooks. Afterwards the child can be given a consequence or sent off with a hug to try again.

"Mom time", when it is extended, becomes "line-of-vision-supervision". The child is kept within sight at all times. There are three rationales for what can be called the "umbilical cord":

- One is that the child needs to observe another person making good decisions concerning what to say, where to go to the bathroom, how to handle objects, etc.
- Another is that the child can be confronted with his behavior and told, until he learns to make good decisions, he needs to be close to someone who can make good decisions for him.
- The third task of the child is to practice asking permission.

Children who have a negative world view have learned in order to survive they must be in control. Asking someone else for help or permission to do something is a relinquishment of their need to control and is psychologically very difficult. Being placed in a position where they need to ask permission to play with a toy, speak, go to the bathroom, or eat gives the child practice in asking permission and gives the parent opportunities to establish trust by saying "yes" to the requests as often as possible. The child learns he will not die if he allows someone else into his life.

Clearly, unless the supervisor can relax with it, line-of-vision-supervision can be very tiring for the supervisor, especially if it goes on for days or weeks, which is possible with unattached children.

Practice Sessions

Having "practice sessions" is another technique which is only minimally intrusive. Because the goal is to get the child to enjoy cooperating, the person conducting the session can be silly and pizazzy. Practice sessions are conducted at the parent's convenience, not necessarily when a behavior infraction occurs. A child who does something once for the parent is in a better position to comply twice. Having the child do something appealing or funny is an easier prelude to compliance than having them do something unwelcome.

"Please get a piece of candy from the dish for everyone" is an excellent way to initiate cooperation. "Run to the door and put your nose to the doorknob" can be incorporated into a game situation similar to 'Simon Says'.

After the child is cooperating he can be asked to do what he needs to practice, "Please go flush the toilet." "Please get in the car and buckle your seat belt." When the child replies that they didn't use the toilet, they are not going anywhere in the car, the parent says, "I know. This is just a practice session, so when you need to do it you know how." If the child won't do it, it is ignored for the moment. However, the next time he asks for something, the command is repeated. Dinnertime is often the next opportunity as the child almost invaiably asks, "Please pass the milk," and with a gentle smile the parent can say, "Please, go flush the toilet."

Sometimes a child will get mad and react in a negative way. If that occurs the parent needs to keep in mind if there is going to be anger over a child's behavior, it needs to be the child getting angry, not the parent. Often enough to make the technique worthwhile, however, the child will smile and comply. If not, quietly stick to your intent without contributing to an escalation and then weigh whether or not it is something worth trying again with that particular child. The point of therapeutic parenting is not to do what doesn't work harder, but to do something different in hopes of finding something that will work.

A balance must be achieved between consistency, and unpredictability. Consistency is the child knowing there will be a consequence in response to a negative behavior. Unpredictability is not knowing what that consequence is going to be.

Practice sessions can also be conducted around negative behaviors which have become habitual. A parent can say delightedly to a child who has just spit, "I didn't know you liked to spit. This plant needs watering. Just start spitting right here until you are done." Though this has the potential to make an initial mess of the plant, the child will soon tire of the "game" and will ask to quit. The parent then checks with the child, "Are you quite sure you are done spitting? I don't want you to stop until you have no more left in you." The goal is to get the child to state in a believable manner, "I am sure I am done."

Anytime the parent engages in a technique such as this, however, it is critical to be aware of their tone of voice. These conversations must take place in a congenial manner. This is not the time for cruel wit or sarcasm.

A similar activity can be done around stealing and lying. Hiding in obvious places identifiable items for the child to steal and then having them practice "stealing" them is a way to get a covert activity out into the open where it can be dealt with. When the child is seen with the "stolen" item in his hand then he is gleefully chased through the house in a wild game which ends in wrestling and laughing and giggling on the part of both parent and child. When the child is successful in "stealing" the object when no one is watching, nothing occurs and the child gets no reinforcement.

Similarly a game can be devised where the goal is to tell the most outlandish lies. The better the lie the more guffawing and laughing. Lies told in the course of normal conversation get no reinforcement, negative or positive.

Having a child practice hearing the word "no" can be a fun activity while diffusing the need for control on the part of the child and helping the child realize that being told "no" and not having total control over a situation does not threaten their survival.

> *"Let's play a new game. It is called the "No Game." I will tell you to do anything I want to and you need to tell me "No". Then you tell me to do anything you want to tell me to do and I am going to say "No." We'll take turns back and forth. I will start. Spell your name backwards. Stand on your head. Waddle like a duck. Say, 'I love you, mom'. (Each time the child responds with a negative.)"*
>
> *The child then makes silly requests with the parent responding in the negative. The game then goes to asking for something with the parent beginning. "Please do the dishes." "May I have a hug." "Have you brushed your teeth." "Get yourself a piece of candy." No matter what the parent requests the rule dictates the child must answer "No". The child then asks the parent for something. "May I have more ice cream?" "May I please go ride my bike?" "It is all right if I go do my homework now?", etc. The parent must say "No", even if is something it would be wonderful for the child to do.*

Sometimes it is the parent who needs to practice. Practicing dealing with those behaviors which they have found to be the most annoying can be very beneficial to removing the emotional content of the child's behavior. It is important for parents to know which of their children's behaviors have the most negative impact on them and so actively work to diffuse their reaction. This can be done in front of a mirror. Chewing with the mouth open while watching themselves in the mirror until the sight no longer bothers them is one way of getting to the point where a child cannot push a button with the parents over bad table manners. Screaming at the mirror, "You F---, A---, B---!" is a way of getting used to the sounds of foul language, so the reaction when a child says it is impassive rather than emotional.

The Double Bind

Another technique that can be fun for parents is the "double bind". It is a paradoxical technique that allows for, and sometimes encourages, oppositional behavior in a way that keeps the parents in charge. This can be used in concert with several other techniques. The point is to tell the child to do what he is going to do anyway. If he does it, the parent is in control. If he doesn't he has made a right choice.

For example, "Go clean up your toys, but first, whine and cry." If the child righteously declares that he can pick up his toys without whining and crying, the parent has won. If he whines and cries, the parent has still won. "It's your turn to do the dishes, but don't worry, take your time, there's no rush. They'll still be there tomorrow, and the great thing is that there will probably be more then, so you'll be able to help out even more than if you do them tonight." "Feel free to not study for tomorrow's spelling test. Your dad and I are perfectly capable of loving a child who doesn't know how to spell." "Keep practicing flipping the bird. If you are going to do something, do it until you are the absolute best at it!"

Try pizazz for good behavior plus a double-bind: "Wow, did you see what you just did? You walked by Jim without pinching him!!! I bet that was an accident. You meant to pinch him and forgot. Walk by and try it again to see if I saw what I think I saw!"

One of the beauties of the double-bind is the parent gives the child permission to make a bad choice. Then, when the child does make a bad choice, the parent is ready for it and does not get sucked into an angry response. It doesn't make sense to get angry at a child for doing what he has been told to do. Additionally, since many negative behaviors are done to enrage the parent, having the parent give permission often robs the child of the reason for doing it.

This is particularly useful when a child has had a very good day. Some children are so unaccustomed to good behavior they need to sabotage their success to get back to their more comfortable role of behaving badly.

To diffuse the child's need to succeed again it is helpful to say, "It must feel pretty weird to not have people yelling at you all day. Don't push this being good thing too far. One day is enough. Tomorrow, relax, take it easy, try something sneaky just to keep in practice. See how often you can make people angry."

The child can then think, "I'll show Dad. He can't tell me what to do. I can too, be good two days in a row."

Or, he can think, "Dad's right. That was hard today. No point in setting everyone up to think I've changed when I really don't want to."

Either way, everyone hopes for the best but is prepared for the worst, so whatever happens can be greeted with equanimity, rather than a sense of failure that one good day wasn't extended to two good days.

Repayment

Sometimes the best response to continued bad behavior is to declare, "You are draining my energy," or, "You're hassling me. Which chore do you want to do to fill me back up?"

Then, list some of the things that need to be done and have the child choose one. Having a child perform a necessary task creates a win-win, reciprocal situation because the parent is taken care of, so can continue loving the child without being blocked by anger, and the child feels good for doing something right, so feels entitled to the parent's love. However, a firm foundation in consequencing skills is a must. Assigning a chore and having no way to make sure it is done properly is signing a death warrant to winning control and subsequent trust.

A reactive technique used to deal with lying and stealing is to impose a consequence on the basis of who is probably responsible. This gets parents out of the "proving it" game, which they almost are guaranteed to lose. Faced with either behavior a therapeutic parent is likely to impose a consequence on the probable violator and when the child protests he didn't do it say evenly, "What do you think I believe?"

When the child says, usually petulantly, "You believe I did it!" The parent calmly says, "That's right," then imposes a consequence, while assuring the child that if the wrong person has been held responsible then, as soon as the parent is aware of their mistake they will repay the wronged child. This is a fairly safe technique with unattached children as they usually, despite their protestations, are responsible. Rarely have therapeutic parents had to repay a child wrongly consequenced!

An additional verbal message can be given if the child continues to protest his innocence. The parent can ask, "Have you ever stolen (or lied) and not gotten caught?" The answer is invariably in the affirmative. "Well, then this just makes up for all the times you did it and didn't get caught. In the end it will all work out evenly." Generally children are silenced by this reasoning as it makes perfectly good sense to them and they can see the truth in it.

Contracting

When it is clear what level of behavior a child can achieve parents can contract to ensure that behavior will predictably occur when it is most needed. One way to get a child to buy into good behavior is to arrange for the behavior in advance. Verbal or written agreement on a contract, which outlines expected behavior and the consequence for poor behavior allows children to buy into the process of participating. It often becomes clear that a child is not behaving appropriately because he does not want to be involved in the activity in the first place. Getting that out in the open before you go to the store, leave on a trip, attend a school activity helps you decide what to do next.

Sometimes getting a baby sitter, which the child pays for, or changing/ postponing plans is in order. If plans cannot be changed a trade may be offered in exchange for good behavior. "You pull off spending one hour at the dentist's while I get my teeth cleaned and when we get home I will read to you."

Forcing children to be where they do not want to be, doing what they don't want to be doing, seeing people they don't want to see is a sure way to make sure no one has a good time. Being an effective parent requires taking care of yourself first and foremost. It's not good for children to sabotage parents' plans. Therefore, it's important that parents arrange events in such a way that they are taken care of, regardless of what the child chooses to do. What that means in extreme cases is that the parent is deprived of participating in a desired activity. The natural consequence for the child is doing something for the parent to make it up. In therapeutic homes that translates into chores, big-time. Hopefully, when a child gets involved with a contract first, it will help him choose to participate and he will understand what behavior norms are acceptable. Buying into that process in advance often is enough to ensure appropriate behavior, which is, after all, the goal!

Think-it over Spot

Another reactive technique involves having the child who has made a poor behavior choice go to a "think-it-over spot". This is a technique common to many classrooms. Instead of confronting a child with bad behavior, the child confronts himself. Whenever a child's behavior requires attention, he is told to sit in a designated spot (on a chair or the floor, back to the wall, facing the wall, whatever), until he can state, either out loud or in writing:

- what happened, how he felt, how he behaved, and how he will handle the same situation in the future.

Having the child simply sit, when behavior is problematic or non-complaint, with no directive on what to think, is another tool. Usually the child sits with his back to the wall, crossed legs, hands in his lap, back straight, head erect, eyes straight forward. That is for good sitting.

Rather than make a control battle out of it, however, it is not uncommon for a therapeutic parent to say, "You can either sit right for 10 minutes or sit sloppy for half an hour." That way the child can choose how long he wants to sit and how long he wants to think. Whichever he chooses, at the end of the allotted time, let him get up, give him a hug, get a reciprocal smile (or back to sitting), give him a "good luck" message and set him back to the task he was attempting before interventions.

Generally, if attachment is the goal of the therapeutic parenting, children who are not compliant are not sent to their room. Isolation may be exactly what the attachment disordered child prefers and it is counterproductive to reinforce it.

Rather, sitting is implemented within sight, sound and touch of the parent who is available to intermittently intrude on the child with a hug or hair tousle and:

> *"I sure am glad to know you are right where I can hug you whenever I want. I can hug you for half an hour when you sit sloppy. If you were sitting correctly you would be outside playing and then how would I hug you? Thanks for staying right where you are!"*

Tickling and Touching

Since touch is a critical element of attachment work, it becomes an integral part of any therapeutic technique. Grabbing a child up into a big bear hug and lightly tickling him while encouraging him to get a task done gets him laughing and into a compliant frame of mind. The tickler laughingly says in accompaniment, something like, "Who's the best bed maker in the world?" or, "Who can empty the dishwasher all by himself?" until the child giggles, "Me!"

A pre-teen child will then often skip off and do what is required with just a light tousling of the hair and quick, giggle inspiring tickles in the ribs. If this is not fun for both the parent and the child it must not be used.

Another time this is useful is for older children or when the child has behaved badly. Mock-wrestle and tickle the child as you laugh and say,

"Do you think I'm the kind of mom who can only love good kids?" The goal is for the child to laughingly respond, "No." However, since unattached kids are extremely resistant, the first thing he will usually say is, "Yes." As long as you both are having fun, the tickling can go another 60 seconds or until the child says, "No." Otherwise, in order for the child to not take control of the interaction by persisting in a negative answer, stop the interaction with, "Sorry you believe that." End with a quick hug and, if the behavior needs a consequence, tell it lightly to the child.

Deposits and Withdrawals

One of the benefits of avoiding control battles is that parents build up a bank account filled with all the times they have said "yes" to their child. Then when the occasion arises and it is necessary to say "no" it can be put in the context of a larger picture in which permission is given more than it is denied. This only works when parents do, indeed, say "yes" more than they say "no".

One of our sons got some new pants for school and asked if he could wear them to soccer practice. Since they were his pants and we didn't want to hassle him over it we agreed. Once there he was asked to play goalie and he asked if he could wear them in the goal box, a very hard arena on clothes. They ripped, so he came home and patched them on the outside, loving them just as much. He continued to wear them to practice. The patches ripped and he held them together with safety pins. He then asked if he could wear the pants to church. I gave it some thought and then denied the request. He became upset. I replied, "Am I usually pretty reasonable? Have I been letting you wear your new pants everywhere you wanted to wear them? Do I usually let you decide what you wear? Sorry, this time I'm deciding."

DISCIPLINE VS. PUNISHMENT
IN USING REACTIVE TECHNIQUES

As parenting techniques become more intrusive, in response to the child's escalation of negative behavior, it is critical to remember that any technique can quickly become abusive.

Professional therapeutic parents spend a great deal of time discussing when a technique constitutes thought-provoking discipline -- used to bring a child's behavior into line -- and when it becomes punishment, used to satisfy the anger needs of the parent. One common understanding is that when the parent becomes angry, discipline is no longer therapeutic and should not be attempted, until the parent is no longer emotionally over-involved. Another point of agreement - techniques which are not effective must be changed, not continually increased in intensity.

When reading this chapter it must further be kept in mind that professional therapeutic parents have children in their homes for therapeutic care. The children are generally seen at least weekly by their therapist. An ideal session begins with the parents and therapist discussing the intervening days, what behaviors need immediate attention by the therapist, how the long-term goals were being reached, and, of great importance, what parenting techniques were used with what behaviors and with what results. These techniques are added to and modified until both the parent and therapist are comfortable with the direction the parent will take next.

Note that intrusive techniques are used only when both parent and therapist have specific behavior modification goals in mind and agree that going forward with it are in the best interests of the child. Therapeutic foster parents do not operate in a vacuum and it is hoped that other parents will also be in consultation with an attachment therapist before using any intrusive therapeutic parenting technique.

Intrusive Reactive Parenting Techniques

With this in mind a few of the more intrusive techniques can be briefly explained. It is not expected that a parent would use these techniques without consultation with an attachment therapist. Additional techniques are outlined by Richard Delaney and Frank Kunstal in Troubled Transplants, a book detailing unconventional strategies for helping disturbed foster and adopted children.[8]

Increasing Blood Flow

A helpful way to create thoughtfulness and diffuse anger in children is to have them do something which requires a high degree of energy. Say to a child who is not completing a task well or has made a bad behavior choice, "In my experience a lot of kids find it easier to get their brain in gear when they have a higher blood flow. Do 25 jumping jacks and see if that is true for you as well." Getting compliance on one level often generalizes to another level.

Since it is sometimes easier to get compliance with a jazzy activity, rather than a chore, therapeutic parents may start with that. After the child has done the push-ups, sit-ups, run around the block, waddled like a duck, whatever, let him return to his activity or chore and see if his behavior improves. If it hasn't, there are two options:

---

[8] Richard J. Delaney, Ph.D., & Frank Kunstal, Troubled Transplants, Fort Collins, CO.: Corbett Publishing, 1991.

- One is to assign it again, in a larger quantity, saying, "I'm sorry, I didn't know that your brain was so hard to engage. This time do 35 jumping jacks and see if that helps you think more clearly."
- The other possibility is to switch tracks. "I see you aren't ready to even do sit-ups the way I know you can. Just sit by me until I'm ready to give you another opportunity to do what you need to do."

While the child sits it is all right for him to express his displeasure about the unfairness of life, as long as he realizes that his negative verbalizations mark his sitting as poor sitting, not good sitting, so he must sit longer. When the child is able, with enthusiasm, to say, "I'm ready to do my sit-ups and then the dishes!", then they get the opportunity to do the simple activity and if done well, then the more complex activity.

This can be repeated with some escalation, however, if it still doesn't move a child into thoughtfulness and compliance than it is back to the beginning premise, "You can do the wrong thing over and over or the right thing once."

Don't keep at a child with the same discipline technique if it isn't getting the desired results. Try something else, otherwise the child will end up digging himself deeper and deeper into a morass of consequences and he will not be able to get himself out.

A lose-lose situation has been created. In response the child may get discouraged and quit.

Correct Scolding

Shocking a child into compliance can occasionally be done with a one-minute scolding. This is definitely one of the more intrusive techniques. It also requires a good sense of timing on the part of the scolder. The goal is for the scolder to recreate in the child, in the space of one minute, the bonding cycle while modeling for the child that people can and do get angry, yet no one gets hurt.

The child needs to be aroused, then comforted by the parent in order for the child to develop a sense of trust. A whole book, Who's the Boss?, by Gerald Nelson & Richard Lewak has been written on this technique.[9]

Basically, the parent looks the child in the eye, places his hands on the child's shoulders and scolds the child severely, using rapid, fairly loud speech, until the child tears up or shows some sign of emotion.

The parent focuses in sharply on what the child did and why the parent is angry. The hard part is next. After the child tears up, the parent must have a marked drop in intensity and make a clear transition to being

---

[9] Nelson, Gerald & Richard Lewak, Who's The Boss?

nurturing by bringing the child in close, telling him how much he is loved, and letting him know how much you want a better life for him. It is also important that the child sees how his behavior affects his life. The scolder needs to end with a hug, hopefully gain a reciprocal smile, and a short question and answer session on what the child did wrong. The whole process needs to take between sixty and ninety seconds. If it takes too long than the child's thoughts wander, his brain disengages, even though he is physically present. This technique is most effective when used sparingly. One-minute scoldings administered weekly lose their effectiveness. An example:

> *One of the girls was using a can of spray paint in the laundry room, where the gas furnace is, and had closed the door to keep from getting caught. I walked in, caught her closely in my arms, and scolded her loudly with clipped sentences. "Stop that at once. That is a terribly dangerous thing to do and you knew it. Otherwise you would not have closed the door. That was very sneaky. You could have caught yourself on fire or created an explosion. You could have started the whole house on fire. I am very angry. (Having aroused her to tears I dropped in intensity and began to engage her face with eye contact.) Besides I love you. What would I have done if you had hurt yourself? You are my precious little girl. You scared me very badly. (Smiling, gentle tone, searching her face for a reciprocal smile.) Do you know what you did that was so dangerous? Will you promise not to do that again? Good girl. I love you."*

Unblocking Rage

Oftentimes a child who is misbehaving or non-compliant is so blocked with rage that he cannot function. Unlocking that rage, and thereby freeing the child to do the right thing, can sometimes be accomplished by getting the child to yell what you believe he is feeling or thinking. Goals are two-fold:

- One is for the child to experience love and acceptance, even at the height of his rage.
- The second goal is to enable the child to release his rage at a time and place and in a way that it can be controlled.

If rage is not released in a safe way it can explode in a potentially dangerous manner. Not only is that not good for others in the child's environment, but the child then must deal with all the damage and hurt he caused while he was enraged. Leaving a child in the situation where he continually has to deal with what he has done in the past leaves him with less energy to deal with present and future behavior. He becomes overwhelmed with defeat and a sense of hopelessness.

The first step in this technique is to face the child and gently place your hands on his shoulders. Very calmly suggest to him what you believe he is thinking and have him repeat it. "I won't do it your way"; "You can't make me vacuum the floor"; "I hate doing the dishes"; "You're not my boss"; "You bitch."

Or, a more accurate reflection of an unattached child's thoughts, "You fuckin' asshole bitch. I want to kill you." In a louder tone of voice tell him to say it louder. Every time you tell him to repeat it, you do it in a louder tone and gradually work the child up to yelling. All this time bring your face closer and closer to his until you are almost nose to nose, until the child is yelling into the parent's face.

While the child is yelling it's important for the adult to empathetically focus on how hard the child is working to release his rage; rather than focusing on the anger directed at the parent. Otherwise the adult could get sucked into the child's rage.

When the child has reached a peak, usually within one and a half to two minutes, drop in intensity and bring him close in a hug. As in the one-minute scolding, closeness, hugs, gentle words and reciprocal smiles are essential to lock in the sense of relief and trust that tends to flood a child once he stops venting. This release is critical to a child's future ability to be trusting enough to be compliant. After a feeling of closeness is established, with a reciprocal smile and eye contact, have the child say, "I don't want to _____, and I'll do it anyway." Then, with one last hug, gently direct the child back to the unfinished, interrupted task.

Crisis Intervention

The most intrusive technique is reserved for when the child is physically lashing out in a rage and there are no alternatives to regain control. The point is to keep the child, other people or things, safe. The touch, therefore, is controlling to the point of being confining. Therapeutic parents at The Attachment Center at Evergreen are required to take a 12-hour course entitled "Non-Violent Crisis Intervention", which teaches approved, safe holds.

It is sponsored by the National Crisis Prevention Institute, 3315-K North 124th Street, Brookfield, Wisconsin, 53005. If there is a chance that a child's behavior will escalate to the point where a forced restraint is required, then the caretakers need to be trained to do that safely. This class is highly recommended.

The Attachment Center at Evergreen, Inc. also requires training in what is called the "Cornell Method." This nationally recognized program was developed by Cornell University. The training is extensive and information is available through Cornell University. We particularly like their emphasis on de-escalation techniques as well as de-briefing strategies following any physical restraint.

It is important to end any discussion on intrusive techniques with the reminder that they should be used only under the direction, supervision and training of an attachment therapist.

CONSISTENCY AND UNPREDICTABILITY

In most parenting patterns consistency in a wide range of parent-child interactions is important for them to be effective. In contrast, when parenting unattached children, the strength of the techniques presented here often lies in their unpredictable use. Eye contact, touch, and the safety of the child need to be consistently present. However, with unattached children, it is necessary to "disturb the disturbed" and unpredictability becomes a crucial ingredient. When a child is acting the most unlovable, the parent needs to act the most unpredictable. It being predictable only that the parent is in charge and will handle all behavior in a good way.

A SENSE OF SELF-WORTH IS THE
NATURAL RESULT OF THERAPEUTIC PARENTING:

The building of self-esteem in a child has many components, which therapeutic parenting techniques incorporate as fundamental to the success of forming a bonded parent-child relationship. They build self-esteem by:

1. setting up a home environment in which the child is safe, nurtured and respected.
2. taking care of the child in warm, stimulating ways through the provision of good food, generous time, hugs and touching, frequent smiles, and hopeful rituals.
3. modeling for the child that adults take good care of themselves, giving them the hope that when they grow up they will take good care of themselves as well.
4. modeling for the child that feelings are a wonderful part of being human and they can be expressed in safe ways.
5. modeling for the child that all people are worthy of respect, and demonstrating intolerance for any words or behavior which are disrespectful to themselves or others.

6. teaching the child the importance of reciprocity in relationships.

7. holding the child accountable for unacceptable behaviors until they believe they, too, are capable of making excellent choices for themselves and others.

8. teaching the child to do chores so they acquire the ability to competently take care of themselves and others as adults.

In short, people feel good about themselves when they feel they are worth taking care of and they know they are competent to take care of themselves and others. Being given a responsibility and successfully following through on it can be euphoric. Children who are being given the responsibility to behave appropriately and taught the skills with which to do it feel good about themselves, others, and the world. They have a rightful place in the universe, they fit in and it feels very, very good.

IN CLOSING

Take good care of yourself and understand there is an uncertainty principle operating in parenting. Just because you do it right does not mean it will work and just because you do it wrong does not mean it will fail. The determination for success or failure, whatever that means, is not in the hands of parents to decide. For some children, staying out of jail is success. For others, not abusing their spouse or children will be the measure of success. Regardless, no act of love is ever wasted and all acts of love transform the lives of children, often in ways parents cannot discern or comprehend. Being the child of a parent who can love in therapeutic ways is the best thing that can happen to a reactive attachment disordered child. Few will affirm that for these special parents, often not even the child or society, but it is the truth nonetheless. It is important to keep this truth close to the heart when the pain of loving an unlovable child becomes too great to bear.

So...

Hug a child when he acts unlovable, not just when his behavior is good.

Pop a piece of candy in the child's mouth when he does well, and sometimes when he doesn't.

Ignore a behavior when it occurs and impose a consequence when the child doesn't expect it. Laughingly help a child complete a task he has angrily stared at for hours.

Understand you may not be where you wanted to go, but you are where you are supposed to be.

On the refrigerator put the sign, "I'm not Supermom. Adjust!" These techniques, undergirded with a high regard for the child, a sense of humor and balance, a projection of strength even when it might be illusory, and a well trained support system, will go far to making an unattached child livable, and hopefully, ultimately, so lovable the parents are willing, eager and able to make a lifelong commitment.

PART THREE

❦ ❦ ❦

The Implications of Attachment Therapy

Give Them Roots, Then Let Them Fly

11

Reintegration Of A Child

After Completion Of Attachment Therapy

By Margaret Meinecke, M.S.W.
& Paula Cyd Seigal, M.S.W.

Jolynn, a ten-year-old Native American girl, was adopted after being placed in numerous foster homes. Her adoptive family reported her pervasive anger, inability to trust others and inordinate need for control. This negatively impacted her parents' ability to manage Jolynn's behavior and similarly influenced her siblings. She had hurt animals, destroyed property, stolen knives and threatened to kill her entire family. She demonstrated no conscience or remorse for her actions; her oppositional attitude and behaviors and her defiance toward authority caused her family to seek beyond traditional therapies.

Upon arriving for the Two Week Intensive at the Attachment Center of Evergreen, Inc., Jolynn was placed in a highly structured treatment home and began daily therapy with the treatment team. The primary goal of the two-week intensive was to gain a clearer resolution of early childhood issues that were preventing her from bonding, in a positive way, to her adoptive parents.

The ultimate goal of treatment at The Attachment Center at Evergreen, however, is *successful reintegration* of the child with the placing family. This is made more complicated by the fact that both the child and family make numerous changes during treatment and the environment and personalities remain dynamic. In short, the child returns to a different family and arrives with new skills and expectations.

The decision to place a child in treatment impacts every member of the family and can dramatically influence the relationship patterns involved. When children have left a home in which they have been successful at maintaining a chaotic lifestyle, the relative calm experienced by the parents often causes them to reevaluate their energy level and commitment to parenting a special needs child. Perhaps they have slept soundly and safely for the first time in a long time, or have enjoyed a meal without the disruption of defiant behaviors. They may notice that their strength as a couple deteriorated in the face of almost constant emotional turmoil. Their relationship with one another and with friends and family members may have been strained by the parenting demands for a very long time.

During an out-of-home-placement the absence of the attachment disordered child may illuminate the parents' competence, personal resolve and sense of fun. When the parents seek therapy and begin the process of the Two Week Intensive, they are often desperate and exhausted. They may experience relief and ambivalence about wanting their child to return to their home. So much time was invested in trying to control the child and manage the emotional chaos, they felt spent and empty by the time help is received. Sometimes marriages have become strained, as there is little time or energy for nurturing or enjoying one another. Unless the parents are able to revive their commitment to each other and their parenting goals, the internal conflict will certainly impact the success of treatment.

There is evidence that ambivalence is a dangerous ingredient in the family of a attachment disordered child. Ambivalence is represented in inconsistent parenting techniques, emotionally laden power struggles and deterioration of personal self-esteem for everyone involved. Frequently parents of attachment disordered children are viewed as deficient and angry. This is a result of years of misunderstanding, system abuse, and other professionals not adequately recognizing diagnostic cues and special family needs.

Siblings of children in treatment for attachment disorders are often reluctant during the reintegration process. They may have tolerated numerous terrorist acts at the hands of their brother or sister and forfeited parental attention to the "high maintenance" sibling.

While the attachment disordered child is out of the home, siblings may find that they enjoy the relaxed environment so much they hope there will be no reintegration. Their ambivalence or outright disapproval of their sibling is understandable in light of the constant strain and emotional stress the family endured when trying to deal with an attachment disordered child. Siblings who have finally won their parents and home back, due to an out-of-home-placement are reluctant to welcome the offender's return.

In addition, the child who has undergone specialized and successful treatment for attachment disordered behavioral and relationship problems may also have ambivalent feelings about reintegration into their home. In the therapy process, the child being treated has experienced more control and strict limits, which feels very consistent and safe at last. Some children express a fear their parents will not be able to control their behavior as well as the therapeutic foster parents. Following treatment they now know they need structure and control, but seem to create chaos at every turn. In understanding this dichotomy, it is important to note that their attachment-disorder-caused rage was the means of the disordered child's control and survival. Upon surrendering the rage, the child often feels unsafe and vulnerable.

In reintegrating a child to their placing home, it is important to maintain a place for continued rage release -- the hometown therapist and on-going therapy sessions are believed to be the best vehicle to help the child express difficult emotions in a safe manner, without negative behavioral manifestations.

Problems with reintegration of a child back into the placing family after a Two Week Intensive at ACE or following a long-term placement are inevitable. The truth is that it is traumative whenever a child has to leave home for treatment. It is also traumatic when a child is ready to return home.

Dr. Foster Cline, in his book Hope for High Risk and Rage-Filled Children (ED Publications, 1992) puts it this way:

> "Metaphorically speaking, treating a child in out-of-home placement is the same as if I had trouble forming a lasting and loving relationship with my wife.
>
> "I am sent to be treated in out-of-home placement by my therapeutic foster wife. My therapeutic foster wife's job is to help me learn to love (her) and to get me back home to live happily with my first wife.
>
> "Sound like a great game plan? The difficulties of this approach leads all therapists to first attempt in-home treatment, but with extremely difficult children, in-home treatment may not be possible."

There are several ways to help smooth out reintegration problems. Dr. Cline, in the previous cited work notes:

> *"The following guidelines ensure a less traumatic reintegra-*
> *tion, a transition period that is almost guaranteed to have*
> *its ups and downs, even under the best of circumstances:"*
> * *"Rule One: Plan the reintegration prior to the child's*
> *admission to placement."*
> * *"Placing parents must understand that reintegration is*
> *the most difficult part of the work."*

During an out-of-home placement, the child develops new relationships and skills that help foster a sense of trust and well-being within the therapeutic foster home. It is often difficult for these positive feelings to accompany the child who is returning to the parents who sent them away in the first place. There is frequently a sense of sadness when a child leaves a therapeutic home in which he or she has accomplished some success and developed better self-esteem. Sometimes a child will maneuver in an attempt to triangulate the placing and therapeutic parents.

Once the Two Week Intensive is completed, the work actually begins. The child has gained structured guidelines for behavior and has experienced specific exercises to foster trust and reciprocity within relationships. They have been emotionally open to the possibility of warmth and love, but therapy must be maintained and follow-up services provided or there is little chance of lasting success. The dysfunctional patterns of behavior of the past will naturally return, as they were initially developed as coping mechanisms and will be tried over and over again within the "new" family setting. In effect, the child can be expected to rely on old patterns of behavior. The child and family often find themselves in a fierce battle following the reintegration process. This is a time that tests the resolve, commitment and creativity of every one. It is a dangerous time in the relationship.

Important to the success of the reintegration endeavor is the personal and marital strength of the placing parents. They undergo initial psychological testing to assess their talents and challenges. They are encouraged to improve communication styles and develop ways to minimize stress while learning to reparent and nurture their child. Attachment therapists instruct placing parents that the number one rule in effective parenting is to take care of themselves. On-going therapy to resolve personal issues that impact parenting is often recommended for the parents. During the treatment sessions, parents learn to reinforce reciprocity, foster compliant behavior and maintain structure and control with their children. Several publications are considered helpful in this process and are listed in the Appendix of this book.

Reciprocity, as taught in a clinical setting, must be practiced in the family, school and social environment, in order for lasting relationship changes to be maintained. The true test of the ideal of reciprocal behaviors and regard for others is out in the "real world" of challenges and choices. If parents are able to employ tools learned in treatment, the child's chances of trusting others enough to apply reciprocal behaviors and attitudes are dramatically improved.

Returning to the case of Jolynn, whom this chapter started with:

> *A significant component in the case of Jolynn was her inability to trust others and engage in reciprocal behaviors and relationships. This likely developed due to the abuse and neglect in early childhood, the lack of trust generating from inconsistent and inadequate care. Representative of the lack of reciprocity in relationships was the poor eye contact demonstrated by Jolynn and most other children with attachment issues.*

Some placing parents are secretly conflicted about the involvement of the therapeutic family. While hoping that the family will be able to help their child, they may fear that success in a therapeutic home means they have been inferior parents. Sometimes they feel they are being criticized as ineffective or deficient in parenting their child and are reluctant to accept the success of the therapeutic parents. This fosters feelings of inadequacy that are usually present when the parents first experience difficulty in parenting an attachment disordered child.

It is crucial that the placing parents and therapeutic foster parents maintain the mutual goals beyond treatment. Frequently the disturbed child will attempt to triangulate the parties involved, in order to regain the dysfunctional control that once prevailed. Therefore, it is important that placing parents rely on the professional therapeutic family as support for the ongoing changes.

It is a requirement that placing families contract with follow-up therapists who will work with the child and family throughout the reintegration process. Therapists who are knowledgeable about issues of attachment disorders and bonding are sought to ensure the continuity of care of the child and family. They are an integral part of the treatment team, often attending the Two Week Intensive with the child and placing family. A list of therapists used as resources through the United States is published in the Appendix of this book.

Following the Two Week Intensive therapy, communication between the ACE clinical team and the hometown therapist, the therapeutic family and the placing family is imperative. The team effort allows for the exchange of a variety of ideas. It also provides for the continuity of care with the follow-up therapist regarding techniques that are relatively new and sometimes misunderstood by local professionals. It is important to transfer the role of primary therapist from the ACE clinician to the follow-up therapist so the child will continue to utilize the therapeutic relationship and the inevitable and effective transference. The power of the therapeutic relationship is an especially important aspect of any treatment and in attachment and bonding work, maintaining the control and trust is essential as other factors vary when a child returns to their home environment.

Empowerment is the focus of the team approach. Issues of resentment, conflict or uncertainty are openly discussed so team members feel united regarding the goal of therapy and the techniques used. The focus is on providing support and techniques for the placing parents and child.

It is easy to see how this focus is necessary when one considers the prospective of a hometown therapist, who has been working with a family for a period of time, before the referral to The Attachment Center. That hometown therapist occasionally can feel inadequate regarding their previous work and intimidated about the ACE therapist "taking over" their client. It is important to recognize these feelings and openly discuss the hope for successful treatment. Different techniques and settings allow for the attachment and bonding process to begin when numerous other efforts by highly competent professionals may have failed.

Taking this into consideration, on the last day of the Two Week Intensive therapy, a follow-up treatment contract is written and signed by all team members, contributing to the future plans for the continued care of the child. It includes specific time frames, goals and measurements as well as contingency plans.

This follow-up treatment plan is the springboard for the child who is beginning a new life. Most of the time the departing placing family leaves with a sense of enthusiasm...accompanied by feelings of inadequacy and fear of failure. Parenting skills learned in treatment seem rough and unnatural at first, and it takes some time and practice for the parents to incorporate these new techniques into the family lifestyle with a sense of ease.

The follow-up contract lists major areas of work, professionals who are available to offer support, and resources for further information.

A member of the treatment team, keeps weekly contact with the family during the first month of reintegration. This communication further enhances the feeling of support for a family that is employing new tools. It also affords a quick check-up on the child's progress and connects the family with the ACE treatment team for any needed restructuring. As the parents become more familiar with techniques and add their own style to the skills learned, they become confident and secure in their ability to parent their special needs child.

As the child's time at home increases, further progress is maintained through bi-monthly documentation and contact with the family, for at least a year following treatment at ACE. During this time, checklists regarding the child's improvement are filled out and reviewed. As these checklists and the progress is reviewed, members of the original treatment team offer suggestions for enhancing opportunities for growth of the child within the family setting. There are several reasons for the follow-up services:

1.) They are designed to empower the family, rather than blame. Every effort is made to reconnect rather than isolate families who are returning to environments that contain social stressors of misunderstanding.

2.) By the time parents contact ACE, they have often been through a great number of conflicts with their extended family, friends and professionals whom they believe have overtly or subtly blamed them for ineffective parental control. The ACE team responds to these feelings of anger and inadequacy with continued support for the parents.

3.) The parents have returned to their community with new information and can, when appropriate, educate members of their support network about their special needs child and what has proven helpful in the therapy they have experienced. Providing specific information about attachment issues frequently helps family members and friends more positively support with the parents.

During treatment, the team has carefully adhered to the goals of treatment, include:

* reciprocity,
* internal behavioral controls,
* resolution of early losses and rage,
* verbal processing of feelings,
* development of trust,
* and compliance with adult directives.

The children are taught the three tenets of attachment therapy, that is, to be:

RESPECTFUL,
RESPONSIBLE
AND FUN TO BE AROUND

These goals are virtually unattainable without follow-up services which link the family with other supports, offers respite care for tired parents, educates school personnel regarding love and logic skills and natural consequences for behaviors and medications management for children who are on prescribed drugs. The ACE team supports the family's needs. We offer "tune-ups" for children who return to placing families -- but demonstrate a need for review work sessions or long-term placement. Ideally, the decision for long-term care is made before or during the two-week intensive therapy process. It requires a comprehensive evaluation of the child's and family's needs, as well as goals and resources available. The case we began this chapter with, that of Jolynn, proved to be one in which the option of long-term therapy and placement in a therapeutic home was required:

> *During the course of treatment, it became apparent that Jolynn would require long term care to further explore her feelings of victimization and rage that had developed during infancy. At the conclusion of the Two Week Intensive, it was felt that her premature return to the placing family's home could result in a return of violent and inappropriate behaviors. Following completion of long-term treatment, it was noted that Jolynn displayed more reciprocal behaviors, better internalized behavioral controls and the ability to establish a trusting relationship with her adoptive parents.*

Internalization of appropriate behavioral values is an important long-term goal of attachment therapy. Children with sufficient bonds to parental figures want to please their parents and others. Attachment disordered children, by comparison, do not trust the values of others and resist compliance with standards. Follow-up treatment frequently involves confrontive and supportive techniques.

It is important to have an equal balance when utilizing these techniques so that the child will learn to trust the therapeutic process. Initially the child will display anger and rage toward the therapist. It is important for the therapist to remain tolerant and caring, allowing the child to feel safe, knowing that the expression of rage is not larger than the therapist's ability to control the child in a safe and loving environment. During this process, the child feels safer and a sense of trust can develop.

Within the follow-up therapy, the trust between the child and therapist and placing parents continues to progress and the child begins to have a more natural human attachment to others. As a result of holding therapy and this balance of support and confrontation, the child's behavior develops in a more positive functioning way in their interaction with others.

SUMMARY

In sum, reintegration is said to be successful when the child demonstrates the ability to trust caregivers, and to manage behavior in an age-appropriate manner in a variety of settings.

In this process, the child has begun to open up to the genuine love and warmth of the parent-child bond.

The goal of the therapy and successful reintegration is met when a child returns home and does well in the family.

12

Developing A Community Approach Supporting Attachment Therapy

Lloyd A. Boggs, LCSW
Susan A. Taylor

To successfully raise or treat an attachment disordered child, it takes the support of an entire community. Understanding the issues surrounding these children is critical, and so education is an important part of attachment work. An attachment disordered child can have an effect on everyone, both directly and indirectly.

The community involved with an attachment disordered child may include:

* school systems,
* health care systems,
* legal and judicial systems,
* social service agencies,
* child protective services,
* churches,
* day cares,
* mental health professionals,
* neighborhoods,
* peers,
* extended families and other groups.

All of these systems need to be part of the effort to help a child learn to trust, learn to give and receive affection, develop a conscience, internalize values, develop a healthy sense of self-worth, and live responsibly within a community.

Such a coordinated effort to help an attachment disordered child is a tremendous task, because such a child will sabotage most efforts to help him. Often it is difficult for people to understand how an "innocent" child can be so deeply damaged that they are capable of manipulating, controlling, destroying, and hurting others. On the surface they appear to be so bright, charming and agreeable. In environments such as families or peer groups which require cooperative behavior, reciprocity and emotional closeness, another picture of the child emerges.

It is no wonder that misunderstandings frequently occur between people who are trying to help these children. Parents are often discredited and blamed, because other people don't see the same behaviors that occur in the home. Attachment disordered children use triangulation to create chaos among adults. This puts a dysfunctional child in control of the situation. It is sometimes difficult for the adults involved to realize what is happening.

What is needed is for individuals to work together to understand the "whole" child and to coordinate their efforts in helping the child. This will only happen when people understand Attachment disorder -- the causes, the symptoms, the implications, effective treatment strategies, effective parenting strategies, and effective community responses.

IMPLICATIONS FOR YOUR COMMUNITY

Reports of violent acts committed by youths are ever increasing. Prison inmates whose backgrounds closely match those of attachment disordered children are over-represented in the criminal justice system. It stands to reason that children who have difficulty with excessive rage, who have no conscience, who have difficulty with cause and effect thinking, who are destructive, who respond in oppositional ways to reasonable limits will also have difficulty obeying society's laws. Every member of society pays the price for the violent acts these children and adults commit, either directly or indirectly.

Attachment disordered children do not have the capacity to give and receive affection. They cannot place themselves in another's "shoes" and understand the other person's feelings. Their need to be in control at all times and their fear of intimacy prevents them from maintaining friendships or any meaningful long term relationships. Their difficulty in handling frustration or limitsetting, frequently leads to violent acts committed against those people who might care for them. Initially seen as charming, they may attract many loving but naive individuals who may become their victims.

Their lack of self control, need for immediate gratification, and indiscriminate sexual behavior can have disastrous results. The potential is great for sexually transmitted diseases, unplanned pregnancy, sexual assault or victimization. An attachment disordered individual would typically have unsatisfying relationships with anyone, including employers, spouses, peers, and co-workers. Many lives can be traumatized by such interactions.

Many attachment disordered individuals do not have the job skills or people skills necessary to be gainfully employed. If they do have the skills, they may lack the ability to accept supervision. They may also choose not to work because it interferes with their freedom. A strong sense of entitlement on their part, leads these individuals to believe that society "owes" them something. The result may be an individual who relies on government assistance or is involved in illegal activities or scams.

The financial cost to the community is enormous. We pay to protect ourselves from them; subsidize them; treat, support, imprison, and otherwise take care of them; as well as to assist their victims.

Many of these children have been victims of abuse in previous settings. Some, in dealing with the resultant anger and pain, make false allegations of abuse. It is an extremely difficult task for child protective services to sort this out for several reasons.

On one hand, the child has specific knowledge of abuse and demonstrates behaviorally that abuse has occurred.

On the other hand, the child can lie convincingly with no remorse, and the child's mode of operation is power, control and revenge. This is a confusing combination. Many respected, loving individual's lives and reputations have been ruined by such false allegations. Even when the allegations are unfounded, the emotional trauma associated with such an investigation has life-long effects.

The need for available, effective treatment opportunities in each community is great. Local resources typically utilize more traditional models of therapy which have proven to be ineffective in dealing with attachment disordered children.

What is needed is a comprehensive treatment approach, by highly skilled therapists who will be able to treat the child on a long term basis. Since these children have deficits on all levels, the treatment approach must focus on cognitive, affective, relational, behavioral, motivational levels. There needs to be a great deal of skills training, since these children have never developed effective coping skills. This becomes extremely difficult when one considers that effective therapy occurs within the context of a trusting relationship and Attachment Disordered children do not trust or have honest relationships with anyone. A comprehensive treatment approach also involves empowering the family to effectively parent these extremely difficult children. Trained, available respite care to provide backup support for the parents is essential to helping parents maintain a fresh and healthy perspective. Comprehensive services include a team approach with service providers on a case-by-case basis. It is important that school settings and others that work closely with a child, are actively involved in the planning and provision of services. All members of the team must work cooperatively so that the child cannot triangulate members of the team and thus thwart a therapeutic plan.

To accomplish this task, various community groups need to understand attachment disorder and effective treatment strategies.

THE NUMBERS GROW DAILY IN THE UNITED STATES

The numbers of attachment disordered children in this country grows daily. This was recognized by U.S. Representative Patricia Schoreder, who writes in the forward to the book High Risk: Children Without a Conscience, (Bantam, 1989):

> *"The unattached children or 'trust bandits' described by the authors are heartbreaking examples of what our lack of adequate attention to the needs of children and families has brought about.*
> *"We must all face reality. What we are doing now has caused irreversible damage to some of our children. Response must come from many places including the home, workplace, schools and the government."*[10]

EDUCATING YOUR COMMUNITY

Participation in the community involves the conscious attempt to share ideas to bring about changes in knowledge, attitudes and actions of the individuals in these settings. Sharing is the significant word. Sharing implies there is an interaction between parties.

It is our job as professionals and parents to involve the community in a way in which we elicit a respectful response. It is important that we involve individuals in the community who can make use of the information

---

[10] Magid, K., & McKelvey, C.A. (1988) High Risk Children Without a Conscience, Bantam Books, New York.

they receive in various ways -- media, programming changes, sharing with others.

PARENT GROUPS

It is extremely important for parent groups to have information in this area. Adoption support groups, foster parent groups, etc., are valuable resources for the early identification of children with attachment disorder.

It is important to realize that in American in 1995 more than one million children were in out-of-home care, thus contributing to their problems in forming secure attachments.[11]

These resources can be much more effective in providing effective parenting if they understand the problems.

> *When Sue's daughter, Mandy, broke her dishes rather than wash them, Sue was extremely upset. She sent Mandy to her "think-it-over" spot, while she called a member of her support group, Alice. Alice helped Sue sort things out and come up with a plan. Sue was then able to effectively deal with the situation. The group had been very helpful in many situations.*

SOCIAL SERVICES

Helping Social Services recognize the etiology and symptoms of attachment disorder will assist them in their difficult task of protecting our nation's most vulnerable children. They can then develop effective strategies for preparing foster parents, in-home family preservation specialists and respite care providers.

They will be more effective in their recommendations for foster care and permanency plans for children.

> *Sue's support group decided to sponsor a seminar on attachment disorder. Many members of the group were adoptive/ foster parents who had close ties with Social Services. They worked closely with Social Services to make sure that the seminar was scheduled at a time and place when most of the caseworkers could attend. The presentation followed*

---

[11] McKelvey, C.A. & Stevens, JE (1994) Adoption Crisis: The Truth Behind Adoption and Foster Care, Fulcrum Publishing, Golden, Colorado.

with a panel discussion addressing particular issues in that community.

EDUCATORS

All in the education field, from day care to university settings must be aware of attachment disorder. We must train our future educators, therapists, medical staff, etc. to be able to identify these children early, as well as to understand the most effective approaches for a therapeutic outcome.

> *Professor Boyd was very interested in the subject of attachment disorder. She incorporated training on this topic into her psychology and child development classes at the university level. Many times she invited the parent of an attachment disordered child to present a class on effective parenting. Professor Boyd's close friend, Edith, taught high school students. She taught the importance of parent/child attachment to high school students in her life skills curriculum.*

HEALTH CARE PROVIDERS

Public health staff, hospital staff, clinic staff, etc. need to be aware of attachment disorder as well. Physicians are sometimes the first resource parents turn to in order to seek help for their child. Many children with attachment disorder have additional problems that can be effectively helped with medication.

Young children with serious medical problems are at increased risk for the development of attachment disorder. Health care staff can assist parents in overcoming obstacles to attachment if they are aware of this problem.

> *Diane worked as a nurse in the local health department's pre-natal and well-child clinics. Diane had attended a workshop on attachment disorder and began to explore ways that this new knowledge could be used to help parents and prospective parents establish loving, nurturing environments for their children. She began educating parents about the importance of this for their child's normal development. She developed rapport with these parents who then felt*

comfortable asking questions and describing their own concerns. Diane encouraged, supported, and helped these parents develop plans and goals for parenting their children.

A foster parent recently related how she had been able to inform the nurses in the hospital to the importance of being with the baby who had bonded with her:

> *"In the beginning, the nurses wanted me out of the way. I got the feeling that they felt I was interfering with their job. Since the child was a foster child, they couldn't understand why I would want to be there whenever they had to perform a procedure. They didn't understand that the baby had the right to be comforted by the person he was bonded to, whether that was the biological mother or a foster mother. I feel sorry for mothers and babies who are not aware of the bonding cycle and do not insist on informing the nurses about the importance. Parents need support in feeling empowered enough to stand up for what they know is true and right.*
>
> *By the end of my baby's stay, I really feel that those nurses had better insight into bonding and were placing my baby's emotional welfare beside his physical welfare."[2]*

JUDICIAL SYSTEM

Those making important decisions in a child's life, ie., custody battles, termination of parental rights, permanency plans, adoptions, etc. must be aware of the problems associated with attachment disorder and the impact of their decisions on the child. This will assist them in making better decisions in the child's best interest.

> *Frank was a therapist specializing in working with children and youth. He served on many multi-disciplinary teams within his county. Frank was concerned about some of the issues related to children as they interfaced with the court system. For example, many youth who broke the law were receiving little more than a "slap on the hand" and they went on to more dangerous activities. In other situations, custody decisions were contrary to a child's need for stability and consistency. When the opportunity came for Frank*

to assist in planning a joint conference for many local ser-
vice providers, Frank insisted that one of the presenters
focus on attachment disorder.

LAWMAKERS

Those individuals responsible for establishing policies related to children and families at all levels of government must be keenly aware of this problem. Failure to be farsighted in their approach to this problem will inevitably have serious consequences for all of us.

FUNDING SOURCES

Decisions related to the funding of appropriate services for our children must also take attachment disorder into consideration. Projecting the costs of failing to intervene early in a child's life must be a key factor in these decisions.

Unless these sources fully understand the ramifications of attachment disorder, they will be unable to effectively develop a funding plan.

CORPORATIONS

Corporations and businesses need to be aware of attachment disorder as well. Health Insurance benefits for their employees should include coverage for effective treatment for this disorder. Employees who struggle to provide effective treatment for their children without assistance will be less effective as employees. Corporations also can consider funding resources and solutions for this problem that affects all of America. An important bill which helps birth and adoptive parents bond with their new children was sponsored by Rep. Schoreder, the Family Leave Act.

The law allows parents to take off a reasonable amount of time without pay to spend essential time with their new children. The importance of this time and the need for this bonding time should not be lost on corporate leaders.

SERVICE ORGANIZATIONS

There is also a great need for volunteer efforts in addressing the problems associated with attachment disorder. Many local resources work with these young people.

Understanding the importance of teaching our children to respect others, to be responsible for behavior, and to be cognizant of their effect on others will enhance their volunteer efforts.

INVOLVING YOUR COMMUNITY

CASE SPECIFIC ACTIVITIES

The best way to involve your community is on a case by case basis. Team efforts to help a particular child and family might involve social services, the local school, a local physician, the therapist, perhaps the court system, etc.

All involved can not only develop effective ways to help. They can also feel good about making the difference in a child's life. The chances of turning a child's life around are so much greater if all work together.

COMMUNITY PLANNING TEAMS

Another way to involve your community is through community planning teams that meet to address particular problems. The effects of attachment disorder are so far reaching to all in the community, this would be an excellent issue for communities to addresses as a group.

PREVENTION ACTIVITIES

Attachment disorder is a preventable problem. We understand how it develops. We understand what factors place a child at risk. We know the importance of good prenatal care. We know that a prospective mother who feels good about herself and her child is already establishing an important relationship with that child. We know the damage that alcohol and drugs can cause a fetus.

We must begin to focus our efforts on preventing attachment disorder. A little common sense, a little planning, a little education, a little advocacy will go a long way in this important task. All of us can participate in prevention activities.

FUND-RAISING ACTIVITIES

The costs associated with providing appropriate care and services for attachment disordered children are great. Efforts to assist groups raise necessary funds for services, scholarships, research, etc. will go a long way to developing important local resources.

DEVELOPING LOCAL RESOURCES

There may be a lack of local resources to effectively treat attachment disorder. Find out what is available in your own area. Help to establish groups, trained respite care, community education services. Volunteer to care for an Attachment Disordered child for a weary parent. Take the time to support a parent -- don't automatically judge them by appearances.

RESEARCH ACTIVITIES

Encourage the development of collaborative research projects with local universities and hospitals. These projects could target effective treatment methods, high risk factors, and other important issues that will help your community identify needs and develop plans.

PROMOTING YOUR MESSAGE

Information is shared in many different ways. Word of mouth is one prime vehicle for transmitting information. Unfortunately, much accuracy is lost in the transmission of the message.

Anyone who has ever played the game "Rumor" is well aware of the distortions that can occur. It is surprising then that we are so quick to believe much of what we hear or read.

Most people aware of attachment therapy have been introduced to it by means of television reports, or dialogue with people who have never observed or experienced the complete therapy.

Elements, taken out of context, added to an individual's own perceptions, are passed on as the truth. There is a recent, tragic, case example of how this can occur. A very unfortunate incident occurred in Utah in which a child was allegedly smothered during a "holding session". The local and national press leapt upon this incident as a means of proving the attachment therapy and holding therapy are dangerous.

Several individuals without direct knowledge or training in the field seized on this incident to back up this misconception.

The truth of the matter was not printed in the media. No child being treated by a trained and experienced professional attachment therapist has ever been subjected to a situation where the child might be seriously injured. No child involved in the therapy or a holding session should ever be placed in such an unsafe situation.

It is totally against the theory and motivation behind the therapy, which is of providing a loving safe, supportive environment for the healing of children. This therapy is done in a loving, supportive way, with many present during the session. Young children are never subjected to holdings in which they are physically restrained in such a manner as to be abused.

It is within the context of misinformation that the community at large could accept as fact, such an incident, and its proported cause. This was a situation in 1995 which left the entire attachment disorder therapeutic community in a state of shock and disbelief. No child has ever been injured in such a way in a structured, therapeutic setting, and no child should ever be put at risk through this therapy. It is unthinkable.

This incident is an excellent example of how a lack of grounding in attachment therapy can lead to the most ludicrous of misrepresentations.

The entire attachment therapy community grieves the fact that one child was hurt, with the blame being falsely placed on this very effective and supportive therapy. Clearly, another reason is responsible for the death of this little girl.

Foster Cline writes that "there are times that 'part of the truth' results in a greater misconception than outright untruth." He notes that when confrontive/intrustive techniques are used and they work, there may be grudging acceptance from the professional community.

This can be truthfully said of many accepted therapy methods, including: electroshock therapy, radical surgery, and experimental use of drugs in the medical field."[3]

It is important for those in the field of attachment therapy to meet with the professional community to exchange ideas and solutions. One placing parent recently said:

> "Previous to observing a therapeutic session, I was told about how cruel this therapy was. I was told the therapist makes the kids yell and cry and they put words in their mouths for them.
> "Putting words in his mouth? What abuse happened to my foster child, happened at an age before he was talking. He didn't know the words to use. The therapist made it possible for him to verbalize his anger. It was something no other therapist was able to do.
> "I don't think that other therapists really understand that a lot of what they are doing comes from the therapeutic parenting taught in attachment therapy. Natural consequences are a big part.
> "This child had already killed two Dobermans, he was threatening to kill his parents and he had set numerous fires. Knowing the whole story is important. I understand that it is necessary to intervene in any way possible for everybody's safety. I think most people have no idea what these kids do. They've never really experienced an unattached child."[4]

Attachment therapists can contribute to the growing public knowledge about this therapy by letting people really know and understand the therapy. Or, we can continue to let those who misrepresent themselves as being knowledgeable inform the public.

It is imperative those in the know participate actively by familiarizing the community with the therapy ourselves.

Paula Pickle, Executive Director of The Attachment Center at Evergreen, states:

> *"The field of attachment therapy is constantly evolving. Those dedicated individuals who reach into the world of a attachment disordered child to bring order out of chaos, and love out of suffering continually search for more effective ways to heal these children. We must continue to support their efforts to accomplish this extremely difficult task. Public education is essential to this work in order to increase understanding, develop resources, share knowledge, complete necessary research, and collaborate on effective methods.*
> *Public education is often a two-edged sword. While it is essential, it can lead to misunderstanding as well. Attachment therapy is not easily described briefly, as it is so easy to focus on technique rather than all of the subtle nuances that make up this transforming therapy. Many individuals think that they understand what is meant by attachment therapy, but their understanding may be based on secondhand information, on out-dated information, or on their own interpretation of information."*[5]

"The field of attachment therapy is a new and exciting venue. There are many areas of focus that need to be addressed:
- prevention activities that increase understanding of the critical importance of nurturing attachments for a child's normal development
- treatment activities that help children overcome difficult and traumatic beginnings and enable them to lead fulfilling and productive lives
- educational activities that assist families of attachment disordered children understand and effectively parent these difficult children
- training activities that equip therapists, social service workers, respite parents, etc. with the knowledge and skills to effectively work with attachment disordered children and families
- advocacy activities that focus on making resources available at the local, state, and national level
- community education that focuses on making the general public aware of the serious consequences of ignoring this important issue -- not only for the individual child, but for society as a whole

- research activities that substantiate the effectiveness of the work being accomplished through attachment therapy
- success stories that put the face and the heart to the statistics, that make it impossible for society to ignore the reality of what is happening to our nation's children
- national emphasis on the more than 1 million children in this nation who are in out-of-home care, and the reality that our national resources are inadequate to effectively heal the hearts of so many of our children.

The Attachment Center at Evergreen, Inc. is actively working in many of these areas to bring about change. Your efforts in this important task are important."[6]

Together, a community can create a safer, more nurturing, healing environment for children. The future of our children and of our nation depends upon our commitment to this task.

RESOURCES:

[1] McKelvey, Carole and Ken Magid. High Risk: Children Without A Conscience, Bantam, Books, New York. 1989.

[2] Foster mother, personal communication, June, 1994, Denver, CO.

[3] Cline, Foster, Hope for High Risk and Rage Filled Children, (1992) Evergreen, CO: EC Publications, p. 124.

[4] Foster mother, personal communication, June, 1995, Evergreen, CO.

[5] Pickle, Paula, "Director's Letter", ATTACHMENTS, Summer Issue, 1995.

[6] Pickle, Paula, "Director's Letter", ATTACHMENTS, Winter Issue, 1995.

13

Prologue

Throughout <u>Give</u> <u>Them</u> <u>Roots</u>, <u>Then</u> <u>Let</u> <u>Them</u> <u>Fly</u>, the reader has become acquainted with the mission of The Attachment Center, Inc., the philosophy, the treatment and the therapy.

The implications for American society of thousands of children growing up with attachment disorder are staggering. Each day, in American, the situation is getting worse. Children are being born now, this minute, who are destined to be abused and neglected to the extent they will never trust anyone. Never trust anyone, that is, unless they get help. The earlier in their life they are diagnosed, the easier it is to help them regain their childhood.

These children are being born into dysfunctional, abusive families in numbers that increase exponentially.

Say, for example, you have a young girl about to become a mother:

This young girl was abused and neglected in her own childhood, by a mother who did not know how to parent. Perhaps her mothering was impaired by a lack of adequate adults to model upon, or by drugs and alcohol, or by post-partum depression, or by circumstances beyond her control.

This abused/neglected child then has her own children, two daughters. She abuses and neglects them.

And the cycle continues.

They, in turn, have more children. In this case example, three more, two girls and a boy. They have more children, and so on and so on. Not one of these children, from the mother through the grandchildren and great-grandchildren has a connection to society. Some of them will end up killing and wind up in prison, others will be destined to go through life as con artists, manipulating as they go along, living a parasitic lifestyle. Not one of these children will ever be able to have a secure, loving relationship with any-

*one. None of them will contribute to the community good
of society; they will be parasites.*

*This is the face of attachment disorder in this country.
It isn't an easy face to look into. It is the disaster the Attachment Center at Evergreen and everyone else committed to
working with such children are attempting to avert.*

Without the loving treatment, safety and support of the family at ACE,
children with attachment disorders are destined to vent their rage and fury
on the society they feel has hurt them.

This rage and hurt is based on reality -- the reality that life, for them,
has meant only hurt and pain.

In this book the reader has heard the stories of numerous children. But
it is the success stories of which the Center is so very proud that is the
mettle by which this therapy and this treatment modality will be measured
in the future. It is stories such as Angie's, and Beth's, and Levi's. It is the
stories of children who came to the Center so challenged, so damaged,
so hurting that few could imagine how they could be helped or even, lead
happy, useful lives. Few, that is, except for the people who are the back-
bone of an exceptional place called The Attachment Center at Evergreen, Inc.

The numbers of children with attachment disorders are now growing,
as we said, exponentially in America and around the world. Among the
world-wide circumstances that cause children not to love or attach are:

- Early neglect and abuse in birth homes or foster or adoptive homes.
- War or the disruption of familial bonds. Consider all the children
  in the world who grow up in refugee camps.
- Punitive institutions around the world. Remember the intuitions in
  formerly Communist Romania and the tragedy it has sown.
- The disintegration of the American family and the impact this has
  on small children caught in the web of dysfunction.
- Divorce and ill conceived visitation plans that throw small children
  into chaos, not understanding where mommy and daddy have
  gone or for how long.
- Drugs and alcohol abuse that leave small children disabled and
  uncared for.

It is estimated that in American today (1995), more than one million
children are in some type of out-of-home placement. This is either foster
care, institutions, on the street or in detention centers.[1]

Truly, a society that does not take care of its children when they are
small, will learn to fear those children when they are adults. The small
expense of saving these children now will be more than offset by the

savings of a reduced prison population. The implications for society are staggering. As Dr. Foster Clind has said:

> *"The hundreds of children and adults who have been helped by this therapy appreciate these authors straightforward candor and explicit sharing of their techniques so that everyone can better understand this controversial work."*

In these chapters, the reader has discovered the intricacies of a therapy that has a proven track record of helping children who are destined to have few or no connections as adults. Through the words and expertise of those contributing to this volume, the reader has been shown how this unique therapy based on loving, connecting and protecting children is the answer to the paradox of attachment disorder that plagues our cities, streets and world.

The Attachment Center at Evergreen is proud of its efforts on behalf of all children who suffer from attachment disorder.

We welcome your support, either through networking, educating others or by donating funds to help our cause. For more information about the Center and its works or to contribute to the Attachment Center at Evergreen Scholarship Fund, please write to:

The Attachment Center at Evergreen, Inc.
P.O. Box 2764
Evergreen, Colorado, 80437-2764

--Carole A. McKelvey, Editor

Appendix I

Research Review

Elizabeth Randolph, RN, PhD

This paper deals with an examination of some of the research that has been conducted on attachment in normal, middle-class children, lower-class children, and abused/neglected children.

An understanding of basic concepts about attachment in normal, healthy children may make it easier to understand disorders of attachment in disturbed children. To accomplish these goals, we first discuss some early theories about attachment, followed by a discussion of attachment research with normal, high-risk, and abused/neglected children. It should be noted that this discussion of the results of previous attachment research is a rather conservative one. Several other writers who have discussed the results of attachment research have used a rather liberal interpretation of findings (particularly Karen's 1994 book "Becoming Attached" that tends to report findings that are not supported by the statistics the researchers report).

To prevent overinterpretation of research findings, only those results that are clearly supported by good research designs and statistical procedures should be reported. Such will be the focus of this work.

There are two people whose names are almost synonymous with attachment; John Bowlby, MD and Mary Ainsworth, PhD. Other major figures in attachment work include William Goldfarb, Alan Sroufe, Mary Main, Jay Belsky, Inge Bretherton, Jude Cassidy, Byron Egeland, and Everett Waters.

We begin this discussion with John Bowlby's concept of attachment, and of some of the early research that was conducted on delinquent and institutionalized children.

GENERAL ATTACHMENT THEORY

Attachment is a term that is generally understood to indicate the relationship that develops between an infant and the primary caregiver (usually the mother, and referred to hereafter as the mother) during the first year of life. For attachment to take place, the infant must develop an affectional tie with the mother and prefer the mother's presence and support over that of other people (Ainsworth, 1984). "Attachment behavior is any form of behavior that results in a person attaining or maintaining proximity to some other clearly identified individual, who is conceived as better able to cope with the world. It is most obvious whenever the person is frightened, fatigued, or sick, and is assuaged by comforting and caregiving" states John Bowlby (1982, p. 668). The ability to freely engage in such behavior is an attribute of an attached person. In addition, a person's level of attachment is a persisting trait that can only change slowly over time, not something that easily changes from moment to moment. While children and adults may show attachment behavior toward a variety of people, enduring attachment (also called an attachment bond) is limited to only a very few close people, usually family members. Children who are unable to show a clear discrimination between enduring attachments and transient ones are likely to be severely emotionally disturbed. Only extensive and intensive efforts by others can change disturbed attachment patterns once a child is more than three years of age (Bowlby, 1982). Attachment takes place over a process of phases (Ainsworth, 1969):

- Phase 1 occurs during the first few weeks of life and is referred to as "orientation and signals without discrimination of figure".
- In Phase 2, "orientation and signals directed toward one or more discriminated figures," the infant begins to discriminate her mother from people and responds more to her than to others.
- In Phase 3, "maintenance of proximity to a discriminated figure by means of locomotion as well as by signals," the infant is able to follow, approach, and seek out her mother as a safe base from which to explore the world.
- In Phase 4, "formation of a reciprocal relationship", the infant begins to infer motives behind her mother's actions.

Infants develop a number of attachment behaviors during the first year of life, and the presence of attachment behaviors should not be confused with the presence of attachment to a specific person. It is only when the child begins to use attachment behaviors to seek proximity with a specific person repeatedly, in preference to approaching other people in his life, that attachment can be said to be present. Thus, one of the hallmarks of children with impaired attachments is that they use attachment behaviors

√√ indiscriminately with a variety of adults, showing no clear preference for one person over another (Ainsworth & Bell, 1970).

Bowlby believes that each infant develops an "internal working model" about attachment figures, primarily the mother and father. By this term he means that, at around 12 months of age, the infant decides that most people will treat her the same way she was treated by her mother and interacts with others in ways that are designed to elicit the same type of care she received from her mother. The beliefs about others that make up the internal working model are subject to change and modification as the child develops. Fortunately, humans are a fairly flexible species and most children are easily able to modify their internal working models to include experiences with close relatives, child care providers, teachers, ministers, athletic coaches, and youth group leaders. However, when children experience early abuse and neglect, or separations from the mother, the mechanisms by which the child can normally modify the model are seriously compromised. For children with these early life experiences, modifications in early internal models do not work well and most of these children arrive at preschool (4 or 5 years old) with their infant working models intact. It is this factor that leads Bowlby to believe that it is very difficult, if not impossible, to modify the internal working models of abused/neglected and separated children without intensive and extensive psychotherapy (Bowlby, 1982).

As Main, Kaplan, and Cassidy (1985) note, "The working models of the relationship to the attachment figure will reflect not an objective picture of "the parent" but rather the history of the caregiver's responses to the infant's actions or intended actions with/toward the attachment figure. If this is true, then from the moment at which an animate or inanimate object can be represented there will be individual differences among infants in their internal working models of relationship to the attachment figure" (p. 75). What the infant's brain encodes is not the result of specific interac-
✳ tions with the mother, but of the entire sequence of experiences throughout the first year of life.

In addition, because the internal working model is encoded into the brain in a way that is outside the conscious awareness of each person, a wide variety of behaviors even remotely related to security and attachment will be triggered when the working model is in use. In this way, adult interactions with others are strongly related to the internal working model developed between birth and age three.

The internal working models that children develop provide rules for how they feel and behave in similar situations later in life, as well as directing attention and memory. Most of these rules are subconscious or unconscious so that the person is completely unaware that they are behaving on the basis of these rules. Once children reach adolescence, these rules have been solidified to such a degree that they are very difficult, if not impossible, to modify. Adolescents and adults then begin to screen out experiences and emotions that do not fit with the internal working model, with the result that emotions and experiences become more and more limited.

Early child development specialists believed that infants developed a close relationship (attachment) with their mother because they were fed by her. The need to eat was seen as a drive that caused the infant to seek out contact with the mother. As enough contact was obtained during the course of the first year of life, the infant became attached to the mother. Bowlby (1940) was among the first to dispute this drive theory, noting that a child would go to anyone for food (an attachment behavior), but usually only went to the mother for nurturance and support (an indication of attachment to the mother). Thus, Bowlby disagreed with other theorists and focused instead on the mother's ability to provide support, love, nurturance, and stability for the child as being the basis of the child's attachment to the mother. Bowlby's theory was based primarily upon his observations of children who had experienced poor mothering, who had been reared in institutions, and who were juvenile delinquents (1944). However, his theory was also heavily influenced by the work of Konrad Lorenz with birds, and that of Harry Harlow with primates.

Prior to reading the findings of these animal studies, Bowlby had been studying certain types of child behavior, particularly delinquent behavior; his results were eventually published in 1944. In this study, Bowlby discusses earlier work by Burt (1925), who found that 24% of delinquent girls and 37% of delinquent boys had experienced prolonged absences from their parents during the first three years of life. In fact, Bowlby noted that there was a great deal of research that indicated that there was a strong link between delinquent behavior and early parental separation, but that this data had been largely overlooked by child development experts and child therapists (as it remains to this day). Bowlby diagnosed 14 of the 44 delinquent subjects in his research as being "affectionless characters" (although he acknowledges that there were probably 4 additional children placed in other diagnostic categories who were affectionless characters, making a total of 18). These subjects were "distinguished from the remainder by their remarkable lack of affection to anyone and were, consequently, conspicuously solitary, undemonstrative and unresponsive. Many of their parents and foster parents remarked how nothing you said or did to them made any difference. They responded to neither kindness nor to punishment" (p. 38).

These 18 children were all persistent thieves. Most had begun stealing before age six. Most were inveterate liars, wandered the streets, had few or no friends lasting for more than a week, lied in ways that made little sense to their parents and other adults, were superficially charming, often appeared to be quite normal on initial encounter, were aggressive and bullying toward other children, and were incapable of attachment, affection, or loyalty. Some affectionless children were noted to be isolated loners, often appearing to be severely depressed. Most had unusual ways of viewing the world around them, and some had symptoms of frankly distorted perceptions of reality suggesting schizophrenia. The most striking characteristic, though, was the very high frequency of early separations from the mother (16 of 18 subjects, as compared to 2 of 44 control group subjects with no history of delinquent behavior). In the two affectionless children who had no history of early separation, there were some questions as to whether the history was accurate because of a tendency for both mothers to gloss over problems in these children. In addition, in a group of 28 delinquent children with other diagnoses, only three had histories of early separation from the mother.

As a result of these striking differences, Bowlby concluded that early separation from, or loss of the mother during the first two years of life had a significant negative impact on the vast majority of children (16 of 19 children with histories of early separation or loss of the mother were affectionless) who experienced it. He noted that the affectionless children were swamped by rage, experiencing tremendous amounts of hatred toward adults, especially female adults, and were unwilling to learn how to love others. He concluded that, "Love is impossible if hate is entrenched" (p. 123), and that, because the child sees others as being bad, he comes to believe that he is bad as well, creating and interpreting situations around him as supportive of this belief. The child then develops fantasies about the behavior and intentions of others, most of which involve beliefs that others will treat her the same way the mother did. As a result, both the child and those around her appear unlovable, suspicious, and secretive.

Those familiar with the characteristic behaviors of attachment disordered children can hardly fail t recognize the similarities between Bowlby's affectionless children and attachment disordered children. As described by Cline (1972), children who have attachment disorders lack the ability to give and receive affection, are self-destructive, are cruel to other children and animals, are superficially charming and phony in interactions with others, steal, hoard and gorge on food, get into extreme control battles with adults (especially women), have oddities in their speech, lack long-term friends, have great difficulty making eye contact except when they are lying, are preoccupied with fire and gore, are overly friendly with strangers, often have learning problems, and engage in a type of lying that flies in the face of all reality. In addition, the parents of these children often appear to be unreasonably angry with, or hostile toward them. Sounds a lot like Bowlby's affectionless delinquents, doesn't it?

While Bowlby was investigating the effects of early separation from the mother on British children, William Goldfarb was doing something similar work in the United States. Goldfarb (1942) studied the effects on children's behavior of being raised in an institution versus a foster home. In this article, Goldfarb quotes from Lowrey (1940), "The conclusion seems inescapable that infants reared in institutions undergo a type of isolation experience with resulting isolation type of personality, characterized by unsocial behavior, hostile aggression, lack of patterns for giving and receiving affection, inability to understand and accept limitations, (and) much insecurity in adapting to the environment. These children present delays in development and intensification as well as prolongation of behavior manifestation at these levels. At the time of transfer, the children are at a stage when they can form only partial love attachments; hostility and aggression are at a peak; egocentricity is marked, and they do not recognize the individuality and needs of others. They are unprepared for and unequal to the demands and limitations of a family setting" (pgs. 249-250). This description also bears a remarkable similarity to Bowlby's affectionless children and to Cline's attachment disordered children.

In addition, Goldfarb stated that, "Case workers have for a long time noted the hyperactivity, destructiveness and aggressive patterns which seemed to be especially characteristic of foster children whose babyhood had been spent in institutions" (p. 250). However, no controlled studies of this phenomenon had been conducted, so Goldfarb set out to do so. The group of institutionalized children he studied (N=20) had lived in an orphanage setting for the first three years of their lives before being placed in foster care. The foster care group (N=20) had always lived in family settings. A second set of older subjects meeting these same criteria (N= 20) was later selected and studied as well. The focus in these groups was to select children who had been admitted to out-of-home care prior to six months of age to be certain that very early infancy was spent in either an institution or in a foster home. Both groups of institutionalized children showed significantly more problem behaviors than both groups of foster home children. Institutionalized children had significantly more sleep problems, temper tantrums, were more impervious and evasive, lied, stole, talked back to adults, were destructive, grabbed and took things from other children, were mean to other children for no apparent reason, were easily over-stimulated and upset by trifles, were distractible, and had speech oddities. By contract, children in foster care were significantly more withdrawn and timid. Thus, although children in both groups showed problems, the institutionalized children's behavior consistently showed attacking, aggressive features, while the foster home children were more likely to be overly passive and withdrawn.

Following the results of the above study, which used six- and seven-year-old children, Goldfarb (1943) studied similar behavior problems in older children (10-14 years old). He noted that other researchers had found that institutionalized children had more difficulty adjusting to later foster home placement than did children who had always lived in family settings via foster care. In fact, the most common reason that previously institutionalized children failed foster home placements was because of aggressive, hyperactive, bizarre, disorganized, and unreflective behavior, as well as emotional unresponsiveness. These children also showed greater difficulties with speaking clearly, and often had problems learning in school. Goldfarb hypothesized that these traits were the result of fixation at an early stage of development that led these children to have primitive levels of abstract reasoning, conceptual activity, and emotional organization.

To explore this hypothesis, Goldfarb studied 15 children raised in institutions for their first three years of life before being transferred to foster homes for at least five years, and 15 children who had lived in foster homes for at least nine years. The results showed that institutionalized children had significantly lower IQs (the mean score for institutionalized children was in the borderline range of functioning, while for the foster home children it was in the average range). In face, the institutionalized children scored lower on IQ than a comparison group of children placed in special education because of known intellectual deficits. All of the institutionalized children scored below the average range of intellectual functioning, while only 40% of the foster home children were in the below average range. Thus, there was a highly clear relationship between retarded intellectual performance and early institutionalization. Further analysis of the data also indicated that institutionalized children were far more impulsive in their responses to test items, and had difficulty organizing and planning out their responses in advance. Often, even after being shown how to solve a problem, the institutionalized children were unable (or unwilling) to reach a solution. What solutions they did try were quite concrete, showing an inability to develop concepts, make hypotheses, and using inductive reasoning.

Goldfarb (1943) also tested these same subjects using the Rorschach inkblot test. Children in foster homes showed considerably more sophisticated and well-thought-out responses to the Rorschach cards, with 51% of foster children (as compared to 25% of institutionalized children) providing balanced responses. Thirteen of the 15 institutionalized children (as compared to 3 of 15 foster children) had an absence of balanced responses. Goldfarb concluded that institutionalized children were more irrational, primitive, and egocentric in their responses, lacking the ability to make considered, socially acceptable responses. It is difficult to interpret these results today, as the scoring system used by Goldfarb is no longer in use. However, his finding that institutionalized children made different types of responses to the Rorschach cards than did children placed in foster homes added to the mounting evidence gained in the 1930's, 1940's, and 1950's that children need to be raised in a family setting in order to develop normal social skills, control their aggressive impulses, and avoid delinquent behaviors.

At about the same time, Barbara Tizard of the United Kingdom was conducting a longitudinal study of a group of British children who had been placed in institutions since birth while awaiting either adoption or return to the birth mother. The children were first tested at age two (Tizard & Joseph, 1970), with an emphasis on intellectual and speech development. A group of 30 institutionalized children was compared with a group of 30 same-age peers from London whose fathers were in the skilled and unskilled working classes. Children living at home were found to be significantly more friendly with strangers, were more willing to climb up in the stranger's lap, and were less fussy and cried less than institutionalized children. The institutionalized children scored on average two months lower on an intelligence test than the London children, a significant finding for children this age. This difference was true for both verbal and non-verbal tasks. None of the London children had delayed speech, while 63% of the institutionalized children did.

As a result of these findings, the authors recommended that authorities make significant changes in the organization of institutions and the care that children received there. These same children were then re-evaluated two years later, after the suggested changes had been made. A greater effort had been made to expose the institutionalized children to intellectually stimulating activities, they were read to on a daily basis, and they were taken on "field trips" to expose them to activities similar to those experienced by children living in families (Tizard & Rees, 1974). The results showed that children living at home continued to be significantly more friendly with strangers than institutionalized children. Most notably, however, there were no significant differences between groups on measures of intelligence and speech. Some of the children in the first study had either been adopted (24 children), or returned to their birth mothers (15 children), with the result that only 25 children remained in the institution. Adopted and returned children were noted to be more friendly and cooperative than the institutionalized and London groups. Institutionalized children were significantly more restless than children in the other three groups. The authors concluded that expanding the life experiences and levels of stimulation of institutionalized children had significantly improved their intelligence test performance and speech.

In another report on these same four-year-olds, Tizard and Rees (1974) found institutionalized children to engage in significantly more attention seeking behaviors, (42%), than did children who had previously been institutionalized, but were now adopted (29%) or returned to their birth mothers (39%), or London children (29%). London children had more frequent problems with eating, overactivity, and disobedience. Institutionalized children had more frequent problems with concentration, peer relationships, tantrums, and clinginess. It is interesting to note that, while these children were very clingy, their caretakers noted that their affections were very shallow. Both institutionalized and London children had more problems settling down at bedtime. Adopted children had the fewest number of behavior problems, and institutionalized children had the highest. Because the children who had previously been institutionalized, but had now been adopted or returned to their mothers showed such significant improvements in many areas, the authors concluded that institutionalization per se was not responsible for the problems these children had. It was the poor quality of care often provided in institutions that was more likely to be responsible. However, since the authors failed to note the percentages of adopted and returned children still having problems (they only reported mean scores of these groups), it was difficult to determine whether some children adjusted well, while others did not. Such prevalence data would be highly useful in understanding why some children with early deprivation experience more problems than do others.

By the time these same groups of children were followed-up at age eight (Tizard & Hodges, 1978), only eight of the original group of 65 children remained in the institution. Twenty children had been adopted between ages two and four, nine were returned to their mothers between ages two and four, five were adopted after age four, four were returned to their mothers after age four, three were placed in foster homes after age four, three had been in multiple placements, and 29 remained in the London comparison group (originally 30). Children who left the institution at age two (29) were compared with those who left after age four (12), those still in the institution (7), and the London children (29). The IQ scores of children still in the institution and those placed in foster homes after age four showed the greatest drops. IQ scores of children returned to their mothers at age two were the only ones that increased. IQ scores of adopted children remained fairly constant, regardless of the age at which they were adopted. There was a significant relationship between a child's reported level of attachment to adults and IQ scores, with more attached children in the adopted, returned, and institutionalized groups having significantly higher IQ scores. In addition, there was a significant relationship between IQ scores and frequency of behavior problems, with children in all groups who had higher IQs having fewer behavior problems both at school and at home.

Children were also compared on frequency of behavior problems by being divided into groups of adopted (25), returned (13), and institutionalized (7) groups. Returned children had significantly more nervous habits, poor sibling relationships, were less cuddly, and were rated as being overly friendly than children in the other groups. Adopted children were rated as being not very sensible in making decisions. Institutionalized children were lower than the other groups on all these behaviors. Three of the five children adopted after age four had significant behavior problems, as did three of the four children returned to their mothers after age four. Similar results for children still institutionalized and those adopted or returned at age two were not reported. Nearly two-thirds of the returned children (and 12% of adopted children) were subsequently taken to a therapist for help with behavior problems. Thus, the subsequent development of children with histories of early institutionalization depended mostly on the environment to which the child was moved. The later the child was returned to the mother, the more problems there were, but this was not true for adopted children. Both adopted and returned children had more behavior problems than institutionalized children, who had become passive and detached, only rarely causing problems for their caretakers, but showing lower intelligence (but not retardation) and school performance. Twenty of the 25 adopted children had adjusted well in their adoptive homes, but about half of them had problems at school and with peers. Thus, returned children fared worse on all measures than adopted and institutionalized children.

Following the results of these studies, efforts were made in both the U.S. and the U.K. to move children out of institutions and into foster or adoptive homes as soon as possible. As a result, few children now reside in institutions for more than a few months at a time, so comparable research to these early studies can no longer be done. Child development experts seemed to assume that placement in a loving foster or adoptive home would be sufficient to allow previously abused, neglected, or separated children to recoup any losses they had experienced during their early years. As a result, research interest thus turned to other areas, in particular the attachment behavior of normal, middle-class infants.

Mary Ainsworth became interested in the budding field of infant attachment in the early 1950's when she joined in Bowlby's studies of the effects of institutional care on children's behavior. These studies revealed that, "persistent insecurity of child-mother attachment endured for some years after long, institutional separation, with very few (children) having regained a secure attachment-- but indeed few having continued in a condition of affectionless detachment" (Ainsworth, 1991; p. 335). After leaving this research project, Ainsworth traveled to Kampala, Uganda to observe babies and their mothers using an anthropological approach. She found that babies naturally sought out their mothers when they were alarmed or hurt, used their mothers as a secure base from which to explore and operate in the world, and were distressed and tried to follow their mothers when they were separated from them. She divided the babies into three groups in terms of types of attachment; secure, insecure, and nonattached. Insecurely attached babies cried a lot even when the mother was present, while securely attached babies cried only when separated from their mothers or if the mother was about to leave. Nonattached babies were left alone for long periods of time by unresponsive mothers, and eventually did not cry or protest being left (Ainsworth, 1967).

After returning to the U.S., Ainsworth began a longitudinal study of mother-infant interactions in normal, middle-class children. She observed mothers interacting with their infant for several hours at a time every three weeks during the first year of the infant's life, much in the same way as she had observed Ugandan mother-infant dyads.

She then developed a technique to measure attachment called "the strange situation" (1970). In the strange situation, the mother and infant (usually close to one year of age) are taken to a playroom by an observer, who then leaves them to play. The mother then puts the infant in a designated play area and sits on a chair to watch for three minutes. A stranger enters the room and sits quietly for one minute, converses with the mother for one minute, and then approaches the infant while showing him a toy. After one minute of this interaction between the infant and the stranger, the mother quietly leaves the room without telling the infant she is doing so. The stranger then plays with the child for three minutes before the mother re-enters the room, standing in the doorway to allow the infant to respond to her return. The stranger then leaves quietly, and the mother and infant interact with each other for as long as it takes for the infant to settle into playing alone. Then the mother leaves again for three minutes after saying "bye-bye" to the infant. The stranger then re-enters the room and tries to engage the infant in play for three minutes. Finally, the mother returns, the stranger leaves, and the reunion of mother and infant is observed. During any of the periods that the infant may show distress, the length of these timed sequences may be shortened so that infants are not overly distressed.

Ainsworth and her co-workers found that the attachment behavior of children could be divided into three major categories: 1) secure attachment, in which children actively seek out contact or interaction with the mother upon her return to the room, and when contact with the mother leads to an end of the infant's distress and a return to play (67% of infants studied); 2) insecure-avoidant attachment, in which children avoid or ignore the mother upon her return, and generally show minimal emotion throughout the strange situation (23% of infants); and 3) insecure-ambivalent, in which children refuse to be comforted by their mother when mothers return to the room, and may mix contact-seeking with the mother with turning away from her or pushing her away (10% of infants). Later researchers sometimes refer to insecure infants as being anxiously attached, and the term anxious-resistant is used in place of Ainsworth's terms even if these were not used by the authors of the studies being discussed.

Ainsworth, Blehar, Waters, and Wall (1978) also reported differences in mothering behaviors that seemed to lead to different styles of attachment in infants. They found few differences between American and Ugandan children, with American children kissing their mothers more and Ugandan children clapping more. Otherwise, both maternal and infant behaviors were quite consistent across the two cultures. Mothers of secure infants were noted to be better at picking up on signals from their infant as to what the infant needed, and to change their behavior to meet the needs of their infant. They were quicker to pick their infant up when the infant cried, to hold the infant for longer periods of time, and to be more pleased about caring for their infant. They were rated by observers as being significantly higher in sensitivity, acceptance, cooperation, and emotional availability. Mothers of ambivalent infants were noted to be highly inconsistent in their treatment of their infant, responding appropriately to the infant's cues at times, and then being incredibly obtuse as to the infant's needs at other times. Mothers of avoidant infants were noted to avoid contact with their infant, to reject approaches to be picked up, to seem uncomfortable with close physical contact, and to have limited ability to express their emotions. Many were well-meaning mothers who simply could not seem to adjust their timing and pace to that of their infant. About half of them were noted to handle their infant roughly, as compared to 8% of mothers of secure infants. Mothers in both insecure groups were more easily overwhelmed by fussy and demanding behavior by their infant. The authors concluded that there were clear relationships between certain maternal behaviors and the attachment style demonstrated by one-year-old infants of these mothers.

The work of Ainsworth and her colleagues spurred a virtual snowstorm of research on various aspects of attachment in infants and young children. Much of this research was conducted as part of a longitudinal study by Everett Waters, Brian Vaughn, and Byron Egeland in Minnesota. Closely on the heels of these studies was a longitudinal study undertaken by Alan Sroufe and various colleagues, in which attachment behaviors in lower-class and high-risk infants and young children were studied. In addition, Jay Belsky and Susan Crockenberg investigated how an infant's temperament affects his handling by his mother and its relationship to later attachment.

And Mary Main and Byron Egeland (with various co-workers) investigated attachment styles of abused/neglected children. In the remainder of this chapter, we shall discuss research with children in each of these categories with the goal of defining differences in attachment behaviors and attachment styles in normal middle-class, normal lower-class, high-risk lower-class, and abused/neglected children. Obviously, it will not be possible to discuss any of this research in detail in this forum. Therefore, we will summarize the most important findings of each study.

ATTACHMENT IN MIDDLE-CLASS CHILDREN

Ainsworth was involved in several studies about attachment behaviors in early infancy that were thought to lead to later attachment style. Tracy, Lamb, and Ainsworth (1976) found that an infant's ability to approach the mother was a key early step to later attachment security. Blehar, Lieberman, and Ainsworth (1977) found that early face-to-face interactions were also crucial attachment behaviors. Mothers of securely attached infants initiated more frequent face-to-face interactions than mothers of insecure infants, and responded more frequently to their infant's initiation of interactions. Maternal behaviors were quite consistent over the 3-month course of the study, indicating that interaction patterns are set early in the mother-infant relationship and are not subject to much change throughout the first year of the infant's life. Tracy and Ainsworth (1981) found that mothers of secure infants hugged and cuddled their infants more than did mothers of insecure infants, while mothers of avoidant infants kissed them more often and seldom picked them up to cuddle them. The authors noted, "It was not so much that rejecting mothers lacked loving, affectionate feelings toward their babies, as that these feelings were more frequently submerged by irritation, resentment, and sometimes outright anger" (p. 1343). The results of all three of the studies, as well as Ainsworth's original research, indicated that there were clear differences in maternal behaviors of mothers or secure versus insecure infants. Similar results were found by Main, Tomasini, and Tolan (1979). Mothers of securely attached infants were significantly more sensitive to their infant's needs, more emotionally expressive, and more accepting of the changing demands of their infant. Mothers of insecure infants had more frequent angry facial expressions, and were more easily frustrated by their infant's behavior.

Alan Sroufe became interested in Ainsworth's attachment research in the mid-1970's, spawning a tremendous amount of research using families in the Minneapolis area. While much of his later research involved low-income families, in his early work he conducted a longitudinal study with middle-class families. Matas, Arend, and Sroufe (1978) found that 62% of children were securely attached at 18 months of age, but only 29% of children had the same attachment classification at 24 months of age, showing little consistency of attachment status. Securely attached children were found to engage in more imaginative play, were more enthusiastic, cried less, and were less negative and aggressive than insecure children. Mothers of securely attached children were better able to match their interventions to the needs of their child, to intervene in more helpful and less critical ways, and to be more competent and sure of themselves.

Waters, Wippman, and Sroufe (1979) found that securely attached children smiled at their mothers more than insecure children, and that only secure children smiled and vocalized while showing their mothers a toy. Secure children showed more emotions and shared those emotions more than insecure children. Arend, Gove, and Sroufe (1979) followed-up on the children from the 1978 study, who were now four years old. Securely attached children were rated as being more ego-resilient and curious, and to have better problem-solving skills than insecure children.

However, because this study did not report on percentages of secure and insecure children who were either doing well or poorly, its results should be interpreted cautiously. Thus, Sroufe's early studies showed little consistency of attachment style across time, and that secure children functioned better on several variables than insecure children.

A variety of researchers conducted studies on various aspects of attachment. Several researchers were interested in the stability of attachment styles over time. Waters (1978) was among the first to investigate this, finding that 48 out of 50 infants had the same attachment style at both 12 and 18 months of age. Thompson, Lamb, and Estes (1982) found that only 53% of children had stable attachment at ages 12 and 20 months, although the percentages of children in each category were about the same (secure- 70% at 12 months and 76% at 20 months; avoidant- 16% at 12 months and 14% at 20 months; and ambivalent- 14% at 12 months and 19% at 20 months). Seven avoidant and four ambivalent children had become securely attached. Five secure children had become avoidant, and five had become ambivalent. Pipp, Easterbrooks, and Harmon (1992) found a higher level of stability of attachment in the 122 children they studied. Seventy-nine percent of children had the same attachment status at 12 and 24 months of age.

No one knows why there were such differences in stability rates between these three studies, other than that the group that Waters studied was a more stable group in terms of living and work situations than the groups in the other studies. One would certainly expect that more stable living circumstances would lead to stability of attachment style. This issue will be discussed further below in the section on research with unstable families.

Several studies examined maternal and infant behaviors during the first year of life that would predict attachment style at age one. Antonucci and

Levitt (1984) found that avoidant infants were less likely to cry when their mothers were absent than were secure infants. Mothers of avoidant infants were less likely to vocalize to, look at, smile at, touch, and play with their infants than mothers of secure infants. Levitt, Antonucci, and Clark (1984) reported that insecure infants were more likely to show object-permanence (the knowledge that an unseen object continues to exist even if the infant cannot see it) than person-permanence, indicating that these infants were more interested in objects than they were in people. Fonagy, Steele, and Steele (1991) found that insecure-avoidant infants were more likely to have mothers with dismissive attachment styles (73%), insecure-ambivalent infants were more likely to have mothers with preoccupied attachment styles (73%), and secure infants were more likely to have mothers with autonomous attachment styles (75%). This study showed a relationship between maternal and infant attachment styles, suggesting that attachment style may be passed on from generation to generation in the majority of families.

Several studies have examined behavior in children at various ages as related to their attachment status at age one. Fagot (1984) studied behavior problems in 300 children at 27 months of age and found no relationship between attachment style and the presence of behavior problems. Fagot and Kavanagh (1990) re-assessed these same children at age four and again found no relationship between attachment status and behavior problems as rated by parents. Teacher ratings, however, showed that avoidant girls (but not boys) were more difficult to manage in the classroom and had more peer difficulties than secure girls. Jacobsen and Wille (1986) found that insecurely attached three-year-olds spent more time in solitary play and were less creative in their play than secure children.

However, there were only negligible differences in peer interactions between secure and insecure children at this age. Turner (1991) assessed attachment behaviors in four-year-olds and their relationship to peer interactions, rather than relying upon one-year-old attachment styles and assuming that they would be unchanged between ages one and four. She found that insecure girls had more positive interactions with peers than secure girls, but that insecure girls were less assertive and more compliant with peers. Insecure boys showed fewer positive behaviors toward peers, more assertiveness, more indirect attention seeking, and were more aggressive and controlling with peers than were secure boys.

Lewis, Feiring, McGuffog, and Jaskir (1984) studied levels of psychological problems in six-year-olds according to their attachment style at age one. Seventeen out of 113 children showed diagnosable psychiatric disorders at age six. Seven of these children were insecurely attached (19% of the insecure group), and ten were secure (13% of the secure group). Thus, attachment status was not related to whether or not psychiatric problems were likely to develop by age six, although the number of stressful life events, whether the child was an unplanned pregnancy, and a low number of friends at age six were all related to insecure attachment styles. Cohn (1990) found that insecurely attached boys were less well-liked by both their peers and teachers at age six than secure boys, but no similar differences were found for girls.

Thus, studies of attachment in normal, middle-class children show that there is only marginal stability between attachment behaviors at age one and age four, with the result that attachment behaviors at age one fail to consistently predict behavior and peer problems at ages four through six. When attachment behaviors are assessed at age four, insecure children are noted to have more peer difficulties and are rated by their teachers (but not parents) as having more behavior problems than secure children. Therefore, while Ainsworth's research on attachment styles and the maternal behaviors that produces them was an exciting finding in the early 1970's, later research failed to provide much support for the importance of attachment behaviors at age one and the later development of problems by age six, at least in the normal, middle-class population. These findings support Bowlby's theory that attachment behaviors were a reflection of the internal working model, which would change over time as later experiences modified the beliefs that were developed during infancy. However, some researchers (most notably Jay Belsky and Jerome Kagan) hypothesized that the lack of relationship between attachment style in infancy and later behavior problems was likely to be due to the fact that a child's temperament style plays a major role in whether or not behavior problems are developed. In the next section, I shall discuss some of the research on temperament and attachment styles to determine if this hypothesis is true.

TEMPERAMENT AND ATTACHMENT

Crockenberg (1981) was among the earliest researchers to investigate the relationship between temperament and attachment. She found that irritable infants with difficult temperaments were more likely to be second born, and to have greater difficulty responding to comfort from their mothers. However, infant irritability was not related to attachment style. Mothers with lower amounts of social support available were more likely to have insecurely attached infants (11 of 14 insecure infants had mothers with low social support), and unresponsive mothers were more likely to have insecure infants (10 of 11 insecure infants had unresponsive mothers). Infants low on irritability seemed impervious to having unresponsive mothers with poor social support. Thus, maternal behaviors and lack of social support were more highly related to an infant's attachment style than were any infant temperament factors, but an easy-going temperament made an infant more impervious to maternal behavior and lack of social support. Bates, Maslin, and Frankel (1986) found that no temperament variables assessed at ages six or 24 months was related to attachment style, nor was attachment style related to the later development of behavior problems. The best predictor of later behavior problems was the mother's rating of the infant's hostility and difficultness (but not as observed by the researchers) at age one. Thus, while observers may not rate an infant as having a difficult temperament, if the mother perceives her infant as having a difficult temperament, the child is more likely to develop behavior problems by age three. These findings were consistent with those of Chess and Thomas (1982), who found that how well an infant's temperament matched with the parents' expectations, as well as how well parents were able to adapt to handling the infant's temperament, were more related to the later development of behavior problems than was the infant's temperament per se. Some very difficult infants had no behavior problems at age six, while some easy-going infants developed behavior problems. Belsky, Rovine, and Taylor (1984) similarly found that no infant behaviors measured at one, three, and nine months of age were related to attachment style at age one. Maternal responsiveness was related to attachment style, with less responsive mothers being more likely to have insecurely attached infants. Belsky, Fish, and Isabella (1991) studied changes in temperament styles in infants from three to nine months of age and its relationship to attachment styles at age one. Sixty-three percent of infants had stable temperaments at both ages, while 17% changed from an easy temperament at three months to a difficult one at nine months, and 20% changed from a difficult temperament at three months to an easy one at nine months. While the authors had expected that temperament would be independent of parental factors, they found that easy-going infants had parents who were more psychologically healthy, and more complementary relationships between the marital partners. Infants with an easy temperament could become difficult if parents had enough limitations. Finally, Calkins and Fox (1992) assessed temperament at two days, and five, 14, and 24 months to determine its relationship to attachment style at 14 and 24 months. No relationships were found between temperament at two days and five months and later attachment style. However, some relationships were found between mothers' ratings of their infant's temperament and attachment style.

Avoidant infants were more active at five months. At later ages, the findings for the relationship between temperament and attachment were quite mixed and confusing, so they will not be reported here. Suffice it to say that the results failed to show any support for the hypothesis that attachment is more related to an infant's in-born temperament style than it is to any maternal behaviors. The studies of infant temperament provided further support for Bowlby's and Aisnworth's hypotheses that attachment is primarily caused by mother-infant interaction patterns. This finding is even more clear in studies with high-risk and abused/neglected children, which is where we will now turn our attention.

ATTACHMENT IN LOW-INCOME AND HIGH-RISK FAMILIES

In studies with middle-class families, about 60%-70% of infants were rated as securely attached at age one, 13%-25% were rated as insecure-avoidant, and 7%-23% were rated as insecure-ambivalent. A major question in the longitudinal studies with low-income families was whether or not these families would produce a higher frequency of insecurely attached children, and whether children of low-income families would have higher incidence of behavior problems. The major longitudinal study to investigate these issues was conducted by Alan Sroufe and Byron Egeland (with various colleagues at different times). Vaughn, Egeland, Sroufe, and Waters (1979) found that, at age one, 55% of low-income infants were securely attached, 23% were avoidant, and 22% were ambivalent. At 18 months, 66% were secure, 23% were avoidant, and 11% were ambivalent. Sixty-two percent of children had the same attachment style at 12 and 18 months (compared to between 53% and 79% in middle-class children). Mothers of children who changed from secure to insecure attachment styles reported higher levels of stress in their lives, while no factors were related to a change from insecure to secure attachment.

In a later report on these same families, Egeland and Farber (1984) found mothers of avoidant infants were less interested in their infants and were more lenient or controlling of their infant's behavior at three months of age, but this relationship disappeared by the time infants were a year old. At three and six months of age, mothers of insecure infants had more difficulty matching their responses to the needs of their infants (a similar finding to Ainsworth's with middle-class families), were less competent in handling their infants, and vocalized less often to their infant. When the authors re-examined the data on maternal variables and attachment, they found that, in almost every case when an infant's attachment status changed from secure it insecure, mothers lacked interest in their infant, were more angry and dissatisfied with their lives, and had experienced major disruptions in relationships with their boyfriend/husband.

Very few, if any, infant factors were related to changes in attachment style. In 1985 Erickson, Sroufe, and Egeland reported on these same children at age three, comparing only those children whose attachment style had remained unchanged. Avoidant children were rated as being more dependent on their teachers, and as having poorer social skills.

Ambivalent children were rated as being less confident and assertive, and as having poorer social skills. Avoidant children were also noted to be less compliant, to express more negative emotions, to be more whiny and angry in the classroom, as giving up more easily, being more impulsive and exhibitionistic, and more hostile and aggressive than securely attached children. Six of the 16 (38%) insecure children had significant behavior problems, as compared to eight of the 22 secure children (36%). Both secure and insecure children with behavior problems came from homes where mothers provided less stimulation and were less involved with their children.

Insecure children with problems had mothers who were less supportive, provided less structure and less clear instructions, and lacked confidence in their abilities to help their children solve problems. LaFreneiere and Sroufe (1985) re-assessed attachment styles in these children at ages four and five. They found that 40% of children were securely attached, 23% were avoidant, and 23% were ambivalent.

Secure children had better social competence, social dominance, and social participation, and less negative emotions than insecure children. Troy and Sroufe (1987) reported on other aspects of these same children at four to five years of age. They found that any interactions between an avoidant child and a secure or ambivalent child involved victimization, with the avoidant child always being the victimizer.

All ambivalent children were either victims or victimizers, and none of the secure children were victimizers (but some were victims). This study clearly showed the peer difficulties of insecurely attached children that had been less evident in other studies. Renken, Egeland, Marvinney, Mangelsdorf, and Sroufe (1989) reported on aggressive and passive behaviors in these same children during the primary grades.

They found that the presence of aggressive behavior problems was related to avoidant attachment style, the experience and expression of more negative emotions, a history of physical abuse by the mother, maternal hostility, stressful life events for the mother, and a lack of emotional support from the mother. Passive behavior problems were related to avoidant attachment style and a history of physical abuse by the mother. Thus, children who had experienced physical abuse were more likely to have avoidant attachment styles and to have either aggressive or passive behavior problems. Sroufe, Egeland, and Kreutzer (1990) reported on adaptation in these same children during the primary grades. They compared those children who had done well during the first two years of life and then poorly thereafter (N=11) with those who had always done poorly (N=16). They found that children who had functioned well the first two years had a better ability to recover from difficulties than children who had always had difficulties.

Attachment styles were about as consistent in low-income children as they were in middle-class children. Shaw and Vondra (1993) reported on the relationship between attachment style and chronic family difficulties. Nine of ten severely stressed mothers had insecurely attached children. Single parenthood was highly associated with behavior problems in children.

These studies showed no increase in the percentage of insecurely attached infants in low-income families, and no increase in the percentage of insecurely attached children who had significant behavior problems. The findings with low-income families were also consistent with Ainsworth's findings with middle-class families in that mothers of insecurely attached children had greater difficulty matching the timing and pace of their interactions to the needs of their infant, were rougher in handling their infant, were less involved in the needs of their infant (and laer their child), and were more angry and dissatisfied with their child.

As was found in middle-class children, few infant behaviors were related to later attachment status. However, insecurely attached low-income children were noted to have greater peer difficulties and to be more angry and aggressive in interactions with peers, a finding that was not consistently shown in middle-class children. However, as was seen in middle-class children, no more insecurely attached low-income children had diagnosable psychiatric disorders than did secure children.

Thus, again we see that attachment styles in infancy and early childhood are not related to the development of behavior problems in middle-class and low-income preschool and school-age children. Although insecure children show difficulties with peer relationships, these are not serious enough to cause psychiaric disorders. The question that next arose was whether or not these same feelings would be true for children who experienced abuse, neglect, or a combination of abuse and neglect. We will address these issues in the next section.

ATTACHMENT IN ABUSED/NEGLECTED CHILDREN

Early research on abuse/neglect and attachment focused primarily on identifying characteristics that distinguished abusing from nonabusing mothers. Egeland and Brunquell (1979) found that only 30% of abusing mothers had completed high school (100% of nonabusers), 74% were single parents (32% of nonabusers), 42% had outside social support (83% of nonabusers), 17% of children were planned pregnancies (46% of nonabusers), 30% attended childbirth preparation classes (100% of nonabusers), 29% had made preparations for bringing the baby home after birth (88% of nonabusers), 18% had realistic expectations about infant needs and behavior (90% of nonabusers), and 27% planned to breast feed (73% of nonabusers). Mothers in both groups experienced about the same amount of life stress, so this was not a factor in predicting abuse, nor was low-income.

Egeland, Breitenbucher, and Rosenberg (1980) found that abusing mothers were more likely to have high levels of stressful events during the first year of the child's life (38% of abusing and 13% of nonabusing mothers had very high levels of stress). Highly stressed nonabusing mothers were less suspicious, aggressive, and defensive than highly stressed abusing mothers. Abusing mothers were much more disoriented and anxious about handling stress. Nonabusing mothers were more sensitive to their infant's needs, were more appropriate in the timing and pacing of interactions with their infant, and responded more appropriately to their infant's cues. Thus, amount of stress, in and of itself, was not a sufficient predictor of abuse. The mother's ability to cope with stress and to avoid blaming her infant as a source of stress were crucial factors in separating abusing from nonabusing mothers.

Crittenden (1981) observed mother's interactions with their infant and divided mothers into four groups; abusive, neglecting, inept, and sensitive. Abusive mothers more often had infants with a difficult temperament, neglectful mothers more often had passive infants, and cooperative infants were split equally between sensitive and inept mothers. The primary difference found between sensitive and inept/abusive mothers was that, while both used similar parenting tactics with their children, inept/abusive mothers tried very hard to control the child's behavior and were unable to adapt their interventions to the timing and pacing needs of the child. When the child failed to respond to these interventions, the inept/abusive mothers became frustrated and even more controlling.

Thus, as other researchers have found, when there is a poor match between the infant's needs and the mother's ability to adapt to the changing demands of the infant (as well as to life stress), there is more likely to be abusive and/or neglectful mothering, which may lead to a higher frequency of insecure attachment in these children.

As in other areas of attachment research, Egeland and Sroufe (1981) were among the first to investigate the relationship between abuse/neglect and attachment styles. At 12 months of age, 37% of abuse/neglected infants were securely attached (60%-70% in normals), 24% were avoidant (17%-30% in normals), and 37% were ambivalent (7%-15% in normals). Thus, the greatest increase was in ambivalent attachment. Half of the ambivalent infants had neglectful mothers. At 18 months, 56% of abused/ neglected infants were securely attached, 33% were avoidant, and 11% were ambivalent, which is consistent with findings in nonabused infants. Again, the difference is seen primarily in ambivalent attachment, although 52% of abused/neglected infants had changes in their attachment styles (25% in normals). Many of the ambivalent infants became avoidantly attached, and many avoidant infants became securely attached. Thus, early abuse and neglect are highly associated with unstable and insecure attachments, but may stabilize during the second year of life when infants are less needy and demanding of the mother's time.

Dante Cicchetti is another psychologist who has explored the relationship between abuse and attachment using a longitudinal approach. Schneider-Rosen and Cicchetti (1984) found that 33% of abused/neglected infants were securely attached, 39% were avoidant, and 28% were ambivalent at 12 months of age. In a later report in these same children, Schneider-Rosen, Braunwald, Carlson, and Cicchetti (1985) found that 23% of abused/neglected infants were securely attached at 18 months, 46% were avoidant, and 31% were ambivalent. At 24 months, 32% were securely attached, 47% were avoidant, and 22% were ambivalent.

Only 42% of abused/neglected children had the same attachment style at all three ages (compared to 76% of nonabused children). In addition, the incidence of insecure attachment increased as children grew old, with the greatest increase seen in avoidant attachment. When these researchers re-evaluated their data a few years later (Carlson, Cicchetti, Barnet, & Braunwald, 1989), they came to the conclusion that the secure-avoidant-ambivalent attachment classification system developed by Ainsworth was not appropriate for use with abused and neglected children because too many children were being incorrectly classified as securely attached whose behavior in the strange situation was quite disorganized and almost frenetic. As a result, they described a fourth category of attachment behavior, called disorganized or disoriented. Using this category, they found that 82% of abused/neglected children had disorganized attachment, compared to 19% of nonabused children. They then re-evaluated attachment styles of abused/neglected children in several other studies that had not had the disorganized category available to them at the time they were done.

They found that 64%-85% of abused/neglected children in these studies showed the disorganized attachment style. This research was very important in establishing that a significant majority of abused/neglected children show marked differences in strange situation attachment behavior that had not been seen in any of the many middle-class or low-income children in other studies.

Lamb, Gaensbauer, Malkin, and Schultz (1985) found that 34% of abused/neglected infants were securely attached, 53% were avoidant, and 13% were ambivalent (they did not use the disorganized category, as it had yet to be defined). Lyons-Ruth, Connell, Zoll, and Stohl (1987) found that 90% of abused/neglected infants had insecure attachment, with 50% of the infants being classified as disorganized. Abusing mothers differed from nonabusing mothers in that they had significantly more hostility toward their infant, and jerked the infant's body around when moving her. Patricia Crittenden has also conducted several studies on the effects of abuse/neglect on attachment.

In a 1981 study she found that 88% of abusive mothers were observed to behave abusively toward their infant while being observed by a researcher. In addition, 88% of neglectful mothers were observed to be neglectful toward their infant. Abusive mothers most often had infants with a difficult temperament, while neglectful mothers most often had passive infants. Thus, the way the mother treated the infant was strongly related to the temperament style the infant demonstrated at age one. In 1984 Crittenden reported that she had also found that there was a fourth category of attachment behavior seen in abused/neglected infants, which she called mixed insecure (but whose criteria are the same as those developed by Carlson et al., 1989). No nonabused infants fell into the mixed category, while all of the severely abused/neglected infants (N=10) were classified as having mixed insecure attachment. Infants who were abused but not neglected had primarily avoidant or angry ambivalent attachment. Infants who had been neglected but not abused had primarily avoidant or passive ambivalent attachment. Infants who were both neglected and abused had mixed insecure attachment.

Finally, several researchers have investigated the influence of abuse/neglect on the social interactions of young children. George and Main (1979) found that abused children approached adults and other children less often, and often approached others from the side or by walking sideways or backwards toward the person they were approaching. All of the abused children assaulted other children twice as often as did nonabused children, and half of the abused children assaulted adult caregivers. The authors concluded that abused children were significantly more aggressive, assaultive, and avoidant than nonabused children. Dean, Malik, Richards, and Stringer (1986) studied abuse/neglect victims between ages six and 14 and found that abused/neglected children told significantly fewer stories that involved reciprocal interactions between a child and an adult, or a child and another child, than nonabused children. Abused/neglected children perceived parents as being justified in mistreating their children, believing that the child deserved whatever punishment the parent saw fit to dish out. Children between nine and 14 saw themselves as worthless, and their parents as perfect. Physical aggressiveness toward peers was common in the abused/neglected children, although this decreased as children grew older.

The results of these studies consistently show that abused/neglected children are more likely to have insecure types of attachment than middle-class or low-income children. Most notably, abused/neglected children show a distinctly different type of insecure attachment than was seen in any of the studies with middle-class or low-income children.

Unfortunately, no research as yet has shown whether or not there is a higher incidence of behavior problems in abused/neglected children, although several studies showed impairments in peer interactions, as well as a much higher incidence of aggressive and assaultive behavior.

It is my hope that future researchers will have a greater interest in exploring the incidence of behavior problems in abused/neglected children as they have done with low-income children. Such information would be invaluable to those of us who treat severely abused and neglected children and who believe that these children do have a much higher incidence of aggressive, assaultive, oppositional, dangerous, and self-defeating behavior than nonabused children, or children whose abuse/neglect was less extreme. Perhaps some of you who are reading this chapter will conduct such research. Failing further research, we are left with the anecdotal reports of therapists as our only research.

REFERENCES:

Ainsworth, M.D.S. (1969). Object relations, dependency and attachment. A theoretical review of the infant-mother relationship. Child Development, 40, 969-1025.

Ainsworth, M.D.S. and Bell, S.M. (1970). Attachment, exploration and separation illustrated by the behavior of one-year-olds in a strange situation. Child Development, 41, 49-67.

Ainsworth, M.D.S. and Bowlby, J. (1991). An ethological approach to personality development. American Psychologist, 46, 333-341.

Antonucci, T.C. and Levitt, M.J. (1984). Early prediction of attachment security: A multivariate approach. Infant Behavior and Development, 7, 1-18.

Arend, R., Gove, P.L., and Sroufe, L.A. (1979). Continuity of individual adaptation from infancy to kindergarten: A predictive study of ego-resiliency and curiosity in preschoolers. Child Development, 50, 950-959.

Bates, J.E., Maslin, C.A., and Frankel, K.A. (1985). Attachment security, mother-child interaction and temperament as predictors of behavior-problem ratings at age three years. Monographs of the Society for Research in Child Development, 50, 167-193.

Bell, S.M. and Ainsworth, M.D.S. (1972). Infant crying and maternal responsiveness. Child Development,43, 1171-1190.

Belsky, J., Fish, M. and Isabella, R. (1991). Continuity and discontinuity in infant negative and positive emotionality: Family antecedents and attachment consequences. Developmental Psychology, 27, 421-431.

Belsky, J. and Rovine, M. (1987). Temperament and attachment security in the strange situation: An empirical approchement. Child Development, 58, 787-795.

Belsky, J., Rovine, M., and Taylor, D.C. (1984). The Pennsylvania infant and family development project, III. The origins of individual differences in infant-mother attachment: Maternal and infant contributions. Child Development, 55, 718-728.

Blehar, M.C., Lieberman, A.F., and Ainsworth, M.D.S. (1977). Early face-to-face interactions and its relation to later infant-mother attachment. Child Development, 48, 182-194.

Bowlby, J. (1944). Forty-four juvenile thieves: Their characters and home-life, I. International Journal of Psychoanalysis, 21, 19-53.

Bowlby, J. (1944). Forty-four juvenile thieves: Their characters and home-life, II. International Journal of Psychoanalysis, 21, 107-127.

Bowlby, J. (1982). Attachment and loss: Retrospect and prospect. American Journal of Orthopsychiatry, 52, 644-678.

Calkins, S.D. and Fox, N.A. (1992). The relations among infant temperament, security of attachment, and behavioral inhibition at 24 months. Child Development, 63, 1456-1472.

Carlson, V., Barnett, D., Cicchetti, D., and Braunwald, K. (1989). Disorganized/disoriented attachment relationships in maltreated infants. Developmental Psychology, 25, 525-531.

Cassidy, J. (1988). Child-mother attachment and the self in six-year-olds. Child Development, 59, 121-134.

Chess, S. and Thomas, A. (1981). Infant bonding: Mystique and reality. American Journal of Orthopsychiatry, 52, 213-222.

Cicchetti, D. (1987). Developmental psychopathology in infancy: Illustration from the study of maltreated youngsters. Journal of Consulting and Clinical Psychology, 55, 837-845.

Cline, F. (1972). Understanding and Treating the Severely Disturbed Child. Evergreen, CO: EC Publications.

Cohn, D.A. (1990). Child-mother attachment of six-year-olds and social competence at school. Child Development, 61, 152-612.

Crittenden, P.M. (1981). Abusing, neglecting, problematic, and adequate dyads: Differentiating by parents of interaction. Merrill-Palmer Quarterly, 27, 201-218.

Crittenden, P.M. (1985). Maltreated infants: Vulnerability and resilience. Journal of Child Psychology and Psychiatry, 26, 85-96.

Crittenden, P.M. (1991). Children's strategies for coping with adverse home environments: An interpretation using attachment history. Child Abuse and Neglect, 16, 329-343.

Crockenberg, S.B. (1981). Infant irritability, mother responsiveness, and social support influences on the security of infant-mother attachment. Child Development, 52, 857-865.

Egeland, B., Breitenbucher, M., and Rosenberg, D. (19880). Prospective study of the significance of life stress in the etiology of child abuse. Journal of Consulting and Clinical Psychology, 48, 195-205.

Egeland, B. and Brunquell, D. (1979). An at-risk approach to the study of child abuse. Journal of the American Academy of Child Psychiatry, 18, 219-235.

Egeland, B. and Farber, E.A. (1984). Infant-mother attachment: Factors related to its development and changes over time. Child Development, 55, 753-771.

Egeland, B. and Sroufe, L.A. (1981). Attachment and early maltreatment. Child Development, 52, 44-52.

Erickson, M.F., Sroufe, L.A., and Egeland, B. (1985). The relationship between quality of attachment and behavior problems in preschool in a high-risk sample. Monographs of the Society for Research in Child Development, 50, 147-165.

Fagot, B.I. (1984). The consequents of problem behavior in toddler children. Journal of Abnromal Child Psychology, 12, 385-396.

Fagot, B.I. and Kavanagh, K. (1990). The prediction of antisocial behavior from avoidant attachment classifications. Child Development, 61, 864-873.

Fonagy, R., Steele, H., and Steele, M. (1991). Maternal representations of attachment during pregnancy predict the organization of infant-mother attachment at one year of age. Child Development, 62, 891-905.

George, C. and Main, M. (1979). Social interactions of young abused children: Approach, avoidance, and aggression. Child Development, 50, 306-318.

Goldfarb, W. (1942). Infant rearing and problem behavior. American Journal of Orthopsychiatry, 249-265.

Goldfarb, W. (1943). The effects of early institutional care on adolescent personality. Journal of Experimental Education, 12, 106-129.

Jacobsen, J.L. and Wille, D.E. (1986). The influence of attachment pattern on developmental changes in peer interaction from the toddler to the preschool period. Child Development, 57, 338-347.

Karen, R. (1994). Becoming Attached. New York: Warner Books.

LaFreniere, P.J. and Sroufe, L.A. (1985). Profiles of peer competence in the preschool: Interrelations between measures, influence of social ecology, and relation to attachment history. Developmental Psychology, 21, 56-69.

Lamb, M.E., Gaensbauer, T.J., Malkin, C.M., and Schultz, L.A. (1985). The effects of child maltreatment in security of infant-adult attachment. Infant Behavior and Development, 8, 35-45.

Levitt, M.J., Antonucci, T.C., and Clark, M.C. (1984). Object-person permanence and attachment: Another look. Merrill-Palmer Quarterly, 30, 1-10.

Lewis, M., Feiring, C., McGuffog, C., and Jaskir, J. (1984). Predicting psychopathology in six-year-olds from early social relations. Child Development, 55, 123-136.

Londerville, S. and Main, M. (1981). Security of attachment, compliance, and maternal training methods in the second year of life. Developmental Psychology, 17, 289-299.

Lyons-Ruth, K., Connell, D.B., Zoll, D., and Stahl, J. (1987). Infants at social risk: Relations among infant maltreatment, maternal behavior, and infant attachment behavior. Developmental Psychology, 23, 223-232.

Main, M. (1983). Exploration, play, and cognitive functioning related to infant-mother attachment. Infant Behavior and Development, 6, 167-174.

Main, M. and Cassidy, J. (1988). Categories of response to reunion with the parent at age six: Predictable from infant attachment classification and stable over a one-month period. Developmental Psychology, 24, 415-426.

Main, M. and Stadtman, J. (1981). Infant response to rejection of physical contact by the mother. Journal of the American Academy of Child Psychiatry, 20, 292-307.

Main, M., Tomasini, L., and Tolan, W. (1979). Differences among mothers of infants to differ in security. Developmental Psychology, 15, 472-473.

Matos, L., Arend, R.A., and Sroufe, L.A. (1978). Continuity of adaptation in the second year: The relationship between quality of attachment and later competence. Child Development, 49, 547-556.

Pipp, S., Easterbrooks, M.A., and Harmon, R.J. (1992). The relation between attachment and knowledge of self and mother in one- to three-year-old infants. Child Development, 63, 738-750.

Renken, B., Egeland, B., Marvinney, D., Mangelsdorf, S., and Sroufe, L.A. (1989). Early childhood antecedents of aggression and passive-withdrawal in early elementary school. Journal of Personality, 57, 257-281.

Schneider-Rosen, K., Braunwald, K.G., Carlson, V., and Cicchetti, D. (1985). Current perspectives in attachment theory: Illustration from the study of maltreated infants. Monographs of the Society for Research in Child Development, 50, 194-210.

Schneider-Rosen, K. and Cicchetti, D. (1984). The relationship between affects and cognition in maltreated infants: Quality of attachment and the development of visual self-recognition. Child Development, 55, 648-658.

Shaw, D.S. and Emery, R.E. (1988). Chronic family adversity and school-age children's adjustment. Journal of the American Academy of Child Psychiatry, 27, 200-206.

Shaaw, D.S. and Vondra, J.I. (1993). Chronic family adversity and infant attachment security. Journal of Child Psychology and Psychiatry, 34, 1205-1215.

Thompson, R.A., Lamb, M.E., and Estes, D. (1982). Stability of infant-mother attachment and its relationship to changing life circumstances in an unselected middle-class sample. Child Development, 53, 144-148.

Tizard, B. and Hodges, J. (1978). The effect of early institutional rearing on the development of eight-year-old children. Journal of Child Psychology and Psychiatry, 19, 99-118.

Tizard, B, and Joseph, A. (1970). Cognitive development of young children in residential care: A study of children aged 24 months. Journal of Child Psychology and Psychiatry, 11, 177-186.

Tizard, B. and Rees, J. (1974). A comparison of the effect of adoption, restoration to the natural mother, and continued institutionalization on the cognitive development of four-year-old children. Child Development, 45, 92-99.

Tizard, B. and Rees, J. (1975). The effect of early institutional rearing on the behavior problems and affectional relationships of four-year-old children. Journal of Child Psychology and Psychiatry, 16, 61-73.

Tracy, M. and Sroufe, L.A. (1987). Victimization among preschoolers: Role of attachment relationship history. Journal of the American Academy of Child and Adolescent Psychiatry, 26, 166-172.

Tracy, R. L. and Ainsworth, M.D.S. (1981). Maternal affectionate behavior and infant-mother attachment patterns. Child Development, 52, 1341-1343.

Turner, B.J. (1991). Relations between attachment, gender, and behavior with peers in preschool. Child Development, 62, 1475-1488.

Waughn, B., Egeland, B., Sroufe, L.A., and Waters, E. (1979). Individual differences in infant-mother attachment at 12 and 18 months: Stability and change in families under stress. Child Development, 50, 971-975.

Waters, E. (1978). The reliability and stability of individual differences in infant-mother attachment. Child Development, 49, 483-494.

Waters, E., Vaughn, B.E., and Egeland, B. (1980). Individual differences in infant-mother attachment relationships at age one: Antecedents in neonatal behavior in an urban, economically disadvantaged sample. Child Development, 51, 208-216.

Appendix II

Children's Behavior Questionnaire Items

1. My child uses his/her "cuteness" or charm to get others to do what he/she wants.
2. My child has difficulty making eye contact with others while talking to them.
3. My child goes up to strangers and becomes overly affectionate with them or asks to go home with them.
4. My child refuses affection and pushes me away unless he/she is in control of how and when that affection is received.
5. My child responds with prolonged arguing, when asked to do something.
6. My child needs to be in control of events in his/her life, tending to boss others.
7. My child responds to my complaints about his/her behavior by acting innocent or by making light of that behavior.
8. My child seems to enjoy the thrill of doing dangerous things, ignoring how he/she may be hurt in the process.
9. My child deliberately breaks or ruins things.
10. My child seems to lack a conscience or does not seem to experience appropriate guilt for his/her actions.
11. My child seems to enjoy hurting others.
12. My child becomes overly upset if he/she is asked to wait before someone responds to his/her needs or wishes.
13. My child steals.
14. My child tries to get my attention by demanding things instead of asking for them.
15. My child becomes clingy or affectionate only when he/she wants something.
16. My child plays alone because others don't want to play with him/her.
17. My child "shakes off" hurt from events that would hurt most people.
18. My child seems to enjoy being sneaky.

19. My child lies, for no apparent reason, or when it would have been just as easy to tell the truth.
20. My child is bossy in his/her play with others.
21. My child hoards or sneaks food, or has other unusual eating habits (eats paper, glue, paint, flour, etc.)
22. My child has difficulty making friends, or keeping friends for more than a week.
23. My child is less interested in the needs of others than most children his/her age.
24. My child chatters non-stop, or asks repeated nonsensical questions.
25. My child is surprised when others are upset by his/her actions.
26. My child is cruel to animals or other people.
27. My child is fascinated with or preoccupied by fire, blood, or morbid activities.
28. My child underachieves in school.
29. My child was physically or sexually abused, or was neglected during the first year of his/her life.
30. My child lived with, or was cared for by, various people during the first year of his/her life.

Appendix III

RESOURCES/READING LIST:
A listing of persons/organizations familiar with attachment theory, assessment and/or treatment of attachment disorder:

ALABAMA

Linda S. Jowers
11 W. 23rd St., #B4
Panama City, FL. 32405
(904) 785-0280
(800)249-2975

ARIZONA

Association of Family
  Attachment Therapists:
Mary Alexander, MSW, ACSW
2700 E. Fry Blvd. #B8
Sierra Vista, AZ 85282
(602) 459-3928

Elene Cregut, MC, BA
2019 S. Sierra Vista Dr.
Tempe, AZ. 85282-2243
(602) 967-7033

Pricilla Misner, MSW, ACSW
525 West Wetmore
Tucson, AZ. 85705
(602) 888-6116

Kenneth E. Miller, CISW
Esperero Family Center
1840 N. Craycroft
Tucson, AZ 85712
(602) 888-6116

ARKANSAS

Virginia E. Bolan, ACSW, LCSW
Carl Wilson, MS, CSAC
Family Guidance Center
11825 Hiinson Rd., Ste 101
Little Rock, AR 72212
(501) 228-7500

CALIFORNIA

Harvey & Nancy Ng
F.A.I.R.
P.O. Box 51436
Palo Alto, CA 94301
(415) 494-3057

Tom Young
11941 Peach Court
Nevada City, CA 95959
(916) 265-3307

Wes Adams
San Diego D.S.S.
5454 Ruffin Road
San Diego, CA 92123
(619) 495-5246

Center for Attachment Therapy
Training and Education (CATTE)
101 Hawk Point Ct.
Folsom, CA 95630
(916) 988-6233

Dorothy Luce-Kostiriken, MFCC
739 Tenth Street
Arcata, CA 95521
(707) 822-2324

Liz Randolph, Ph.D.
8655 Water Road
Cotati, CA. 94931
(707) 795-4878

COLORADO

John Alston, MD
P.O. Box 3490
Evergreen, CO 80439
(303) 670-0926

Paula L. Pickle, LCSW
Paula Cyd Seigel, MA
Margaret Meinike, MA
Forrest Lein, ACSW
The Attachment Center
    at Evergreen, Inc.
P.O. Box 2764
Evergreen, CO. 80439
(303) 674-1910

Terry M. Levy, Ph.d.
Michael Orlans, MA
Connie Dawson
Walter Buenning, Ph.D.
Christopher Waldmann, MA, NCC
Evergreen Consultants
P.O. Box 2380
Evergreen, CO. 80439

Randolph Stanko, LMFT
Mountain Family Living
P.O. Box 4329
Evergreen, CO 80439
(303) 674-5810

Conrad Boeding, MA
John Welch, MA
Human Passages Institute
Bldg, 1, Suite 105
777 S. Wadsworth
Lakewood, CO. 80226
(303) 914-9729

Lloyd Boggs, LCSW
109 W. Olive Street
Fort Collins, CO 80524
(303) 484-7762

Neil Feinberg, MSW, LCSW
P.O. Box 1684
Evergreen, CO. 80439
(303) 674-9851

Martha Hipp, Ph.D.
P.O. Box 3490
Evergreen, CO. 80439
(303) 670-1658

Carole A. McKelvey, MA
3901 E. Orchard Road
Littleton, CO. 80121
(303) 694-4192

Peggy Waldmann, MA, LPC
1818 Woodside Dr.
Pine, CO. 80470

Joe Metz, Ph.D.
23606 Lone Park Trail
Evergreen, CO, 80439
(303) 674-0142

Marcia Murphy, Ph.D.
4211 S. Yarrow Court
Lakewood, CO. 80235
(303) 987-2401

Lani Tolman
Family Attachment Institute
27972 Meadow Drive
Evergreen, CO. 80439
(303) 674-0547

Connell Watkins, ACSW
Connell Watkins & Associates
28753 Meadow Drive
Evergreen, CO. 80439
(303) 674-6860

Beverly B. White, MA, LPC
7061 S. University Blvd, #207
Littleton, CO. 80122
(303) 730-7633

Richard J. Delaney, Ph.D.
375 E. Horsetooth Rd.
Shores Office Park, Bldg. 2
Suite 203
Fort Collins, CO. 80525
(303) 233-9669

CONNECTICUT

Michael B. Pines, Ph.D.
Ilene Gruenberg, Ph.D.
200 A. Oak Street
Glastonbury, CT 06033
(203) 659-0579

FLORIDA

Linda S. Jowers
11 W. 23rd St., #B4
Panama City, FL 32405
(904) 785-0280
(800) 249-2975

GEORGIA

Elizabeth Moye, Ph.D.
836 Sycamore St.
Decatur, GA. 30030
(404) 377-1509

HAWAII

Keith A. Kuboyama, ACSW
The Casey Family Program
1848 Nuuanu Ave.
Honolulu, HI 96817
(808) 521-9531

Jesse Hernandez
The Casey Family Program
32 Kinoole St., Ste. 103
Hilo, HI 96720
(808) 935-2876

IDAHO

Kurt Lyles, MSW
P.O. Box 190721
Boise, ID 83710-1721

ILLINOIS

Barbara L. Mackey-Bruzetti,
  LCSW, ACSW
1128 S. Fifth St.
Springfield, IL. 62703
(217) 544-0388

INDIANA

Carolyn Doss
Marion County D.P.W.
145 S. Meridian St.
Indianapolis, IN 46225
(317) 232-0966

KANSAS

Paula Vink
P.O. Box 1569
Great Bend, KS 67530
(316) 792-7067

Lawrence P. Lehman,
  ACSW, LSCSW
AAMFT
10709 Barkley, Suite #2
Overland Park, KS 66221
(913) 381-3315

MAINE

Dan A. Hughes, Ph.D
67 Silver Street
Waterville, ME 04901
(207) 872-2121

MASSACHUSETTS

John Meicklejohn, MSW
Broad St. Pychotherapy Assn.
45 Broad Street
Westfield, MA 01085
(413) 568-9858

MICHIGAN

Wanda Vilet, MSW
Bonding & Attachment
Center of Michigan
2511 Monroe
Blanchard, MI 49310
(517) 561-2899

Michael M. Katz, Ph.D.
7600 Grand River, Ste 290
Brightton, MI 48116
(313) 531-9659
Blanchard, MI 49310

MINNESOTA

CeCe Keeling
Winona County D.S.S.
202 W. 3rd St.
Winona, MN 55987

Stephen Nesser, MCAT
821 Raymond Ave., Ste 100
St. Paul, MN 55114
(612) 645-1923

Marlene Marks
180 S. Grotto
St. Paul, MN 55104
(612) 224-1395

Barbara Yelle, MSW
10822 Cty Rd. 40 NE
Spicer, MN 56288
(612) 354-5192

Robert Hinman, M.ED LP
P.O. Box 652
Bemidji, MN 56601
(218) 751-3280

MONTANA

Jerry Norstrom, MSW
Spectrum Counseling &
　Resource Center
3203 3rd Ave, N. Ste. 208
Billings, MT 59101
(406) 252-4270

Revel R. Miller, Ph.d.
414 N. Benton
Helena, MT 59601
(406) 443-4211

NEBRASKA

Debra Combs, MSW
Therapy Resource Asso.
10855 W. Dodge Rd., Ste. 180
Omaha, NE 68154
(402) 330-6060

NEW YORK

Dr. Martha Welch, MD
952 5th Ave.
New York, NY 10021
(212) 879-6505

NORTH CAROLINA

Bill Goble
The Resource Center
P.O. Box 128
Newland, NC 28657
(704) 733-0202

OHIO

Kathleen G. Moss, LISW, ACSW
Beach Brook
3737 Lander Road
Cleveland, OH 44124
(216) 831-2255

Gregory C. Keck, Ph.D.
Parma Psychological & Counseling
Asso.
7441 W. Ridgewood Dr. #259
Parma, OH 44129
(216) 843-7600

OKLAHOMA

Michael Debriwny, MD
Shadow Mountain Institute
6262 S. Shridan
Tulsa, OK 74133
(918) 492-8200

Mark S. Sadker. Ph.D.
Michael Locke, Psy.D.
4520 S. Harvard, Ste. 200
Tulsa, OK 74135
(918) 743-2221

OREGON

Myrth Ogilivie
P.O. Box 25160
Portland, OR 97225

Kathie Bishop, MA
Family Attachment Counseling
461 W. Azalea
P.O. Box 40803
Eugene, OR 97404
(503) 688-2353

SOUTH DAKOTA

Melita Rank
South Dakota D.S.S.
P.O. Box 430
Chamberlain, SD 57325-0430
(605) 734-6581

Ron Goldsmith, ACSW, CSW-PIP
Goldsmith Counseling Svs.
P.O. Box 625
Brookings, SD 57006
(605) 697-5650

TENNESSEE

Dave W. Amonette, MSW
Tennessee Children's Home
P.O. Box 10
Spring Hill, TV 37174
(615) 486-2274

Sharon Gary, MS
Psychological Svs. of Memphis
5500 Poplar Ave., Ste. D-1
Memphis, TN 38119
(901) 682-4238

TEXAS

Kathryn Backzynski
750 8th Ave. Place, Ste. 530
Fort Worth, TX 76104
(817) 332-7199

Psychiatric Inst. of Fort Worth
Ann Bassinger
P.O. Box 693
Fort Worth, TX 76101
(817) 335-4040

Nancy Hernandez
400 Tranvestine Lane
San Antonio, TX 78123
(512) 525-9843

Joe B. Adams, Ph.D.
Peggy Busby, M.ED., LPC
Loretto Clarkson, MA
Child & Family Resources
2775 Villa Creek, #240
Dallas, TX 75234-7400115
(214) 243-5817

Sherry Odenthal, MSW
4737 Rosinante Rd.
El Paso, TX 79922
(915) 833-9285

Barbara Rila, Ph.D.
2775 Villa Creek, Ste. 240
Dallas, TX 75234-7400
(214) 243-5817

Brenda Tompkins
Annetta Vaughn, MA, LPC, CCDC
M. Elaine Litsey, ACSW, LMSW-
ACP, LMFT
SW Attachment Center
2012 Colquitt
Houston, TX 77098
(713) 764-3471

Cheryl Jordan, MSSW, CSW
Therapeutic Foster Care
2701 Burchill Road
Forth Worth, TX 76015
(817) 534-0814

Sherri J. Chapell Pratt,
   LMSW-ACP
1174 Country Club Lane
Forth Worth, TX 76112
(817) 496-9796

Mark J. Wernick, Ph.D.
4532 Pine St.
Bellair, TX 77401
(713) 586-6545

UTAH

Carol Stenger
Utah Div. Family Services
2835 S. Main
Salt Lake City, UT 84115
(801) 468-5477

VIRGINIA

Fairfax Cty, DHD
Marilyn Durbin, LCSW
12011 Gov't Ctr. Pkwy. #200
Fairfax, VA. 22035-1102
(703) 324-7588

WASHINGTON

Tom A. Bill, MSW, ACSW
Beverly Cuevas, MSW, ACSW
13128 Totem Lake Blvd. NE ste
Kirkland, WA 98034
(206 823-5732

WEST VIRGINIA

Marilyn Holschuch, ACSW
Family Center for Indiv. & Family
Counseling
100 Murdock Ave.
Parkersburg, WV 26101
(608) 251-0738

WISCONSIN

Nancy Schiro
1 South Park
Madison, WI 53711
(608) 257-9700

NOTE: The Attachment Center at Evergreen holds no responsibility for the actions of individuals on this list and claims no direct knowledge of their clinical skills. This information is provided as a network function only.

APPENDIX IV

READING LIST

BOOKS

Bascom, BB & McKelvey, CA (1996) forthcoming, Through The Golden Door: A Guide to International Adoption, Pocket Books, New York

Bowlby, J. The Making and Breaking of Affectional Bonds, 1984, London: Tavistock Publications.

Cline, F. M.D., Hope for High Risk and Rage Filled Children, Evergreen, CO., EC Publications.

Cline, F. M.D., Conscienceless Acts Societal Mayhem, 1995, Golden, CO. Love & Logic Press.

Delaney, Richard, Ph.d. & Kunstal, FR (1993) Troubled Transplants, University of Southern Maine, Portland, ME.

Dunn, L. ed. Adopting Children with Special Needs: A Sequel, 1993, Washington, DC: North American Council on Adoptable Children.

Jewett, C. Helping Children Cope with Separation and Loss, 1982, Harvard Common Press.

Kreck, Greg & Kupecky, Regina Adopting the Hurt Child: Hope for Families with Special Needs Kids., 1994, Pinon Press, Colorado Springs, CO.

Magid, K & McKelvey, C.A. (1988) High Risk Children Without a Conscience, Bantam Books, New York.

Mansfield, LG & Waldmann, CH, 1994, Don't Touch My Heart, Colorado Springs: Pinon Press.

Melina, L. Making Sense of Adoption: A Parent's Guide, 1989, New York: Harper & Row.

McKelvey, CA, Stevens, JE Adoption Crisis: The Truth Behind Adoption and Foster Care, 1994, Fulcrum Publishers, Golden CO.

Randolph, Elizabeth, (1994) <u>Children Who Shock and Surprise: A Guide to Attachment Disorders</u> RFR Publications, 8655 Water Rd., Catati, CA 94931

Welch, Martha, M.D. <u>Holding Time</u>, 1988, New York: Simon & Schuster

Appendix IV

Finding A Therapist

When your child needs special help.
by Tim Bandy

Not uncommonly, parents who adopt older children find their joy less-ening with the emergence and persistence of significant emotional or behavioral problems. Although many of these parents have been told before the adoption that their child has emotional problems caused by a history of early trauma, they may not entirely connect what they have been told with the types of behavior they should expect. These parents find themselves limited in their capacity to effectively parent and manage their child or to provide adequate help to resolve his or her problems. They may become demoralized when they learn that love and life with a functional family are not enough to change patterns of feelings and behav-ior based in stressful earlier lives.

INEFFECTIVE TREATMENT

Many parents who seek professional help for their troubled children are disappointed with the service they receive or the results. Conventional therapies that focus on the child's misbehavior, talk therapy, or family functioning are often not sufficient for a number of reasons. Although parents may find themselves believing or fearing their child's behavioral problems are genetic, many times they stem from early trauma. Generally, the most severely disturbed patterns seem to occur in children who have experienced the loss of a parent (especially the mother) before age 5 through state termination of parental rights, death, divorce, or abandon-ment. They may have been abused, rejected, neglected, and damaged from experiencing such losses and from multiple foster home placements. Some also have serious medical problems, attention deficit disorder, or

other significant learning disorders. Treatments that focus only on changing misbehavior are ineffective because they do not heal the child who
has residual effects from his or her experiences.

Talk therapy alone may be ineffective with troubled children who have
histories of early trauma. Very young children think in concrete terms and
experience and express personal feelings in concrete, active ways. They
may have difficulty both understanding abstract information and interpreting complex social situations. The more deeply troubled a child is, the
more his or her behavior is likely to parallel the social and cognitive
development of a much younger child. Therefore, even older children
may have difficulty talking about complex issues.

Many therapists who treat children are trained primarily to identify and
treat family dysfunction. Therapists from such backgrounds--and school
staff, family physicians, and social workers--may focus on treating the
parents, holding them responsible for their children's problems. In some
cases, these professionals mistake parents' emotional reaction to months
of highly disruptive and frustrating behavior as the cause rather than the
result of the children's persistent problems. In other cases, children who
have trouble with mother figures behave much differently when adult men
are present than when they are alone with their adoptive moms. Their
dichotomous behavior may prompt spouses to question and interfere with
their partner's parenting, leading therapists to focus on the marriage
relationship and family dysfunction rather than on the child. Some severely
troubled children have made false reports of physical or sexual abuse,
putting the child professional into the difficult position of assessing the
parents' trustworthiness.

The tendency of therapists to refer troubled children to hospital or
residential treatment facilities without clear goals in mind may also lead
to disappointment with treatment. Placement in such facilities is more
likely to be successful if it is based on clear and positive answers to four
important questions: 1. What exactly is the problem? 2. What evidence
suggests that the proposed treatment can or will solve the problem? 3.
How logical is the supporting argument (e.g., how reasonable is it to
expect the treatment to resolve the problem)? 4. If the treatment doesn't
work, could it be harmful?

HELPING YOUR CHILD

Getting effective help for a troubled child requires finding a therapist
who has knowledge of adoption issues and experience assessing and
treating children who have experienced early trauma and loss. However,
finding such a therapist is no easy task. The information about mental
health services that is available to consumers may not be sufficiently clear
or specific to guide the selection of a specialized therapy provider. To

find help for their children, parents may need to work on becoming informed consumers of mental health services. Many parents find this process difficult or uncomfortable because the medical and health professions have a tradition of expecting patients/clients to be passive and grateful beneficiaries of "expert" knowledge and services. However, the person most qualified to look after your child's interests is you.

In the field of medicine, there is a long-standing tradition of effort to base care on science and on clear, established practice standards and ethics. Child mental health service specialists do not have such a uniform minimum level of practice competency. In many states, anybody can call him- or herself a therapist, and paraprofessionals (aides trained to assist professionals) are allowed to provide therapy. Many states also allow pastoral counselors, guidance counselors, and social workers with master's degrees to perform psychotherapy whether or not they have training in psychotherapy. A look through university catalogues to compare requirements for degree programs will reveal a wide range of training and qualifications among professionals allowed to call themselves therapists. Parents need to know not only where to look for help but also what to look for.

The best advice parents should heed is to shop around. Interview a number of therapists. Remember, you are a consumer looking to hire the services of a child professional who expects to be paid. You are entitled to be treated like a paying customer. Don't let yourself be blinded or humbled by titles, and do not be afraid to ask persons who have titles to explain their credentials, qualifications, and level of training.

A therapist who is properly trained will have had as a part of the degree program an extended period of supervised therapy internship experience. Avoid therapists who have not been required to do an extensive internship. Although you may want to consider a therapist who is highly recommended by special education school personnel, your local department of social services adoptions supervisor, or members of an adoptive family organization, there is no substitute for thinking for yourself.

No task is more important than that of trying to parent and nurture a child into a happy, healthy adult, and no task is more important than finding a qualified therapist when your child needs help. Trust your instincts. Help is available.

QUESTIONS TO ASK A PROSPECTIVE THERAPIST

Screening candidates through brief phone contact or consultation visits will help you find the right therapist. Here's a list of questions to ask. Remember, trust your gut feelings.

1. What specialized training, supervision, or continuing education have you had to prepare for work with adoptive families, and how much experience do you have?

2. Have you ever worked with children who were adopted (especially children who were not infants at the time of their adoption) or with children in foster care? How do you think these situations differ from children living in their birthparents' home? What are some of the important but different issues for children adopted as newborns and those placed later?

3. Are you willing to learn about the issues unique to adoption and foster care that you are unfamiliar with? (A response of no to this question is a major red flag.)

4. What do you see as key issues involving adopted children? (Key issues for children in placement may involve loss, attachment disorders, fear of abandonment, anger, identity problems, and acting out. Histories of physical or sexual abuse may add to other care issues for children adopted at older ages.)

5. Have you had training or done work with children who have post-traumatic stress disorder? (If your child has a history of abuse and neglect, have the therapist describe the disorder and relate it to experiences of abuse and neglect.)

6. Do you see the needs of adopted/foster children and families as unique? Or, do you believe "just plain old family therapy" will be sufficient? (The needs of adopted children and their caregivers are unique. You will feel most comfortable with a therapist who recognizes this.)

7. Will you work with the entire family or just with the child? (Look for therapists who will combine approaches. Those who work only with the child may label him or her as the problem. Those who work only with the entire family may neglect special needs of the individual child.)

8. Do you work as part of a network with other agencies or professionals or use other resources in addition to therapy services in the office or clinic?

9. What particular type of therapy or theory guides your approach? (Consider how well this will match your needs and the needs of your child. Will the approach be compatible with other services you might be using?)

Reprinted with permission by "Adoptive Families" July/August 1995.

Tim Bandy is a child and family therapist at the Therapy Center for Adoptive, Divorced, and Step Families, Box 15078, Ann Arbor, MI 48106.

Bibliography/Resources

Ainsworth, M.D.S. (1969). Object relations, dependency and attachment: A theoretical review of the infant-mother relationship. Child Development, 40, 969-1025 .

Ainsworth, M.D.S. & Wittig, B.A. (1969). Attachment and exploratory behavior of one-year-olds in a strange situation. In B.M. Foss (Ed.), Determinants of Infant Behavior (Vol. 4) London: Methuen; New York: Barnes and Noble.

Ainsworth, M.D.S. and Bell, S.M. (1970). Attachment, exploration and separation illustrated by the behavior of one-year-olds in a strange situation. Child Development 41,49-67.

Ainsworth, M.D., Blehar, M.C., Waters, E., and Wall, S. (1978). Patterns of Attachment: A Psychological Study of the Strange Situation. Hillsdale, N.J.: Erlbaum.

Ainsworth, M.D.S. and Bowlby, J. (1991). An ethological approach to personality development. American Psychologist, 46, 333-341.

Antonucci, T.C. and Levitt, M.J. (1984). Early prediction of attachment security: A multivariate approach. Infant Behavior and Development, 7, 1-18.

Arend, R., Gove, P.L., and Sroufe, L.A. (1979). Continuity of individual adaptation from infancy to kindergarten: A predictive study of ego-resiliency and curiosity in preschoolers. Child Development, 50, 950-959.

American Psychiatric Association (1994). Diagnostic and Statistical Manual (4th ed.). Washington, D.C.: Authors.

Bates, J.E., Maslin, C.A., and Frankel, K.A. (1985). Attachment security, mother-child interaction and temperament as predictors of behavior-problem ratings at age three years. Monographs of the Society for Research in Child Development, 50, 167-193.

Bath, H. (1994). The physical restraint of children: Is it therapeutic. American Journal of Orthopsychiatry, 64, 40-49.

Bell, S.M. and Ainsworth, M.D.S. (1972). Infant crying and maternal responsiveness. Child Development, 43, 1171-1190.

Belsky, J., Fish, M. and Isabella, R. (1991). Continuity and discontinuity in infant negative and positive emotionality: Family antecedents and attachment consequences. Developmental Psychology, 27,421-431.

Belsky, J. and Rovine, M. (1987). Temperament and attachment security in the strange situation: An empirical rapprochement. Child Development, 58, 787-795.

Belsky, J., Rovine, M., and Taylor, D.C. (1984). The Pennsylvania infant and family development project, III. The origins of individual differences in infant-mother attachment: Maternal and infant contributions. Child Development, 55, 718-728.

Biringen, A. (1994). Attachment theory and research: Application to clinical practice, American Journal of Orthopsychiatry, 64, 404-420.

Blehar, M.C., Lieberman, A.F., and Ainsworth, M.D.S. (1977). Early face-to-face interactions and its relation to later infant-mother attachment. Child Development, 48, 182-194.

Bowlby, J. (1944). Forty-four juvenile thieves: Their characters and home-life, I. International Journal of Psychoanalysis, 21, 19-53.

Bowlby, J. (1944). Forty-four juvenile thieves: Their characters and home-life, 11. International Journal of Psychoanalysis, 21, 107-127.

Bowlby, J. (1951) Maternal Care and Mental Health. Geneva: World Health Organization; London: Her Majesty's Stationary Office; New York: Colu]mbia University Press. Abridged version: Child Care and the Growth of Love (2nd edition, 1965) Harmondsworth: Penguin.

Bowlby, J. (1958). The nature of the child's tie to his mother, International Journal of Psycho-Analysis, 39, 350-373.

Bowlby, J. (1958). Attachment and Loss: Vol. 1 Attachment. New York: Basic Books.

Bowlby, J. (1973) Attachment and Loss: VOL. 2. Separation Anxiety and Anger. New York: Basic Books.

Bowlby, J. (1977a). The making and breaking of affectional bonds: I. Aetiology and psychopathology in the light of attachment theory. British Journal of Psychiatry, 130, 201-210.

Bowlby, J. (1980). <u>Attachment and Loss: Vol. 3. Loss, Sadness, and Depression</u>. New York: Basic Books.

Bowlby, J. (1982). Attachment and loss: Retrospect and prospect. <u>American Journal of Orthopsychiatry</u>, 52, 644-678.

Bowlby, J. (1988) <u>A Secure Base</u>. New York: Basic Books.

Cadoret, R. J., & Cain, C. (1980) Sex differences in predictors of anti-social behavior in adoptees. <u>Archives of General Psychiatry</u>, 37, 1171-1175.

Calkins, S.D. and Fox, N.A. (1992). The relations among infant temperament, security of attachment, and behavioral inhibition at 24 months. <u>Child Development</u>, 63, 1456-1472.

Carlson, V., Barnett, D., Cicchetti, D., and Braunwald, K. (1989). Disorganized/disoriented attachment relationships in maltreated infants. <u>Developmental Psychology</u>, 25, 525-531.

Cassidy, J. (1988). Child-mother attachment and the self in six-year-olds. <u>Child Development</u>, 59, 121-134.

Chess, S. and Thomas, A. (1981). Infant bonding: Mystique and reality. <u>American Journal of Orthopsychiatry</u>, 52, 213-222.

Children's Defense Fund, (1994). <u>The State of America's Children</u>. Washington, D.C: Author.

Cicchetti, D. (1987). Developmental psychopathology in infancy: Illustration from the study of maltreated youngsters. <u>Journal of Consulting and Clinical Psychology</u>, 55, 837-845.

Cicchetti, D. & Carlson, V. (1989). <u>Handbook of Child Maltreatment: Clinical and Theoretical Perspectives</u> (pp. 432-463), New York: Cambridge University Press.

Cline, F. (1972). <u>Understanding and Treating the Severely Disturbed Child</u>. Evergreen, CO: EC Publications.

Cline, F. W. (1979). <u>Understanding and Treating the Severely Disturbed Child</u>. Evergreen, CO: EC Publications.

Cline, F.W. (1992). <u>Hope For High-Risk and Rage-Filled Children: Reactive Attachment Disorder Theory and Intrusive Therapy</u>. Evergreen, CO: EC Publications.

Cline, F.W. (1995) Conscienceless Acts: Societal Mayhem. Golden, CO: Love and Logic Press.

Cohn, D.A. (1990). Child-mother attachment of six-year-olds and social competence at school. Child Development, 61, 152-162.

Cohn, D.A., Silver, D.H., Cowan, C.P., Cowan, P.A., & Pearson, J. (1992). Working models of childhood attachment and couple relationships. Journal of Family Issues, 13 432-449.

Crittenden, P.M. (1981). Abusing, neglecting, problematic, and adequate dyads: Differentiating by patterns of interaction. Merrill-Palmer Quarterly, 27, 201-218.

Crittenden, P.M. (1985). "Maltreated infants: Vulnerability and resilience." Journal of Child Psychology and Psychiatry, 26(1), 85-96.

Crittenden, P.M. (1992). Children's strategies for coping with adverse home environments: An interpretation using attachment history. Child Abuse and Neglect, 16, 329-343.

Crockenberg, S.B. (1981). Infant irritability, mother responsiveness, and social support influences on the security of infant-mother attachment. Child Development, 52, 857-865.

De-Jong, M.L. (1992). Attachment, individuation, and risk of suicide in late adolescence. Journal of Youth and Adolescence 21, 357-373.

Delaney, R.J. and Kunstal, F.R. (1993). Troubled Transplants: Unconventional Strategies for Helping Disturbed Foster and Adoptive Children. US: National Child Welfare enter, University of Southern Maine.

Egelund, B., & Sroufe, L.A. (1981 a). Attachment and early maltreatment. Child Development, 52, 44-52.

Egelund, B., & Sroufe, L.A. (1981b). Developmental sequelae of maltreatment in infancy. In R. Rizley & D. Cicchetti (Eds) Developmental Perspectives on Child Maltreatment (pp. 77-92). San Francisco: Jossey-Bass.

Egeland, B., Breitenbucher, M., and Rosenberg, D. (1980). Prospective study of the significance of life stress in the etiology of child abuse. Journal of Consulting and Clinical Psychology, 48, 195-205.

Egeland, B. and Brunquell, D. (1979). An at-risk approach to the study of child abuse. Journal of the American Academy of Child Psychiatry, 18, 219-235.

Egeland, B. and Farber, E.A. (1984). Infant-mother attachment: Factors related to its development and changes over time. Child Development, 55, 753-77 1 .

Erickson, M.F., Sroufe, L.A., and Egeland, B. (1985). The relationship between quality of attachment and behavior problems in preschool in a high-risk sample. Monographs of the Society for Research in Child Development, 50, 147-165.

Exner, J. E. (1990). The Rorschach: A Comprehensive System (Vol. 2, 3rd ed.). New York: John Wiley & Sons.

Fagot, B.I. (1984). The consequent of problem behavior in toddler children. Journal of Abnormal Child Psychology, 12, 385-396.

Fagot, B.I. and Kavanagh, K. (1990). The prediction of antisocial behavior from avoidant attachment classifications. Child Development, 61, 864-873.

Feeney, J.A., & Noller, P. (1990). Attachment styles as a predictor of adult romantic relationships. Journal of Personality and Social Psychology. 58, 281-291 .

Fonagy, R., Steele, H., and Steele, M. (1991). Maternal representations of attachment during pregnancy predict the organization of infant-mother attachment at one year of age. Child Development, 62, 891-905.

George, C. and Main, M. (1979). Social interactions of young abused children: Approach, avoidance, and aggression. Child Development, 50, 306-3 18.

Goldfarb, W. (1942). Infant rearing and problem behavior. American Journal of Orthopsychiatry, 249-265.

Goldfarb, W. (1943). The effects of early institutional care on adolescent personality. Journal of Experimental Education, 12, 106-129.

Greco, C. M. and Cornell, D. G. (1992). Rorschach object relations of adolescents who committed homicide. Journal of Personality Assessment, 59(3), 574-583.

Grossman, K.E., & Grossman, K. (1990). The wider concept of attachment in cross-cultural research. Human Development. 21, 31-47.

Harlow, H.F. (1958). The nature of love. American Psychologist. 13, 673-685.

Harrington, A. (1972). Psychopaths. New York: Simon & Schuster.

Hendrick, C., & Hendrick, S. (1989). Research on love: Does it measure up? Journal of Clinical Psychology. 40 (1).

Hinde, R.A., & Stevenson-Hinde, J. (1990) Attachment: Biological, cultural and individual desiderata. Human Development. 33. 62-72.

Jacobsen, J.L. and Wille, D.E. (1986). The influence of attachment pattern on developmental changes in peer interaction from the toddler to the preschool period. Child Development, 57, 338-347.

Karen, R. (1994). Becoming Attached. New York: Warner Books.

LaFreniere, P.J. and Sroufe, L.A. (1985). Profiles of peer competence in the preschool: Interrelations between measures, influence of social ecology, and relation to attachment history. Developmental Psychology, 21, 56-69.

Levy, T. (1983). Practical issues and applications in family therapy. In P. Keller and L. Ritt (Eds.) Innovations in Clinical Practice: A Source Book, (Vol.2). Sarasota, FL: Professional Resource Exchange.

Levy, T. (1984). Understanding family therapy. In P. Keller and L. Ritt (Eds.) Innovations in Clinical Practice: A Source Book, (Vol.3). Sarasota, FL: Professional Resource Exchange.

Levy, T. (1987). Brief family therapy: clinical assumptions and techniques. In P. Keller and L. Ritt (Eds.) Innovations in Clinical Practice: A Source Book, (Vol.6). Sarasota, FL: Professional Resource Exchange.

Levy, T. & Orlans, M. (1995). Intensive short-term therapy with attachment-disordered children, Innovations in Clinical Practice: A Source Book (Vol. 14) by L. VandeCreek, S. Knapp, & T.L. Jackson (Eds) Sarasota, FL: Professional Resource Press, Professional Resource Exchange, Inc., P.O. Box 15560, Sarasota, FL. 34277-1560. (Reproduced in part with permission)

Lamb, M.E., Gaensbauer, T.J., Malkin, C.M., and Schultz, L.A. (1985). The effects of child maltreatment in security of infant-adult attachment. Infant Behavior and Development, 8, 35-45.

Lamb, M.E. (1987). Predictive implications of individual differences in attachment. Journal of Consulting and Clinical Psychology, 55(6), 817-824.

Lewis, M., Feiring, C., McGuffog, C., and Jaskir, J. (1984). Predicting psychopathology in six-year-olds from early social relations. Child Development, 55, 123-136.

Levitt, M.J., Antonucci, T.C., and Clark, M.C. (1984). Object-person permanence and attachment: Another look. Merrill-Palmer Quarterly, 30, 1-10.

Londerville, S . and Main, M. (1981). Security of attachment, compliance, and maternal training methods in the second year of life. Developmental Psychology. 17, 289-299.

Lorenz, K. (1965). The Evaluation and Modification of Behavior. Chicago: University of Chicago Press.

Lyddon, W.J., Bradford, E. & Nelson, J.P. (1993) Assessing adolescent and adult attachment: A review of current self-report measures. Journal of Counseling and Development, 71, 390-395.

Lyons-Ruth, K., Connell, D.B., Zoll, D., and Stahl, J. (1987). Infants at social risk: Relations among infant maltreatment, maternal behavior, and infant attachment behavior. Developmental Psychology 23, 223-232.

MacDonald, K. (1985). Early experience, relative plasticity and social development. Developmental Review, 5, 99-121.

Main, M. (1983). Exploration, play, and cognitive functioning related to infant-mother attachment. infant Behavior and Development, 6, 167-174.

Main, M. and Cassidy, J. (1978). Categories of response to reunion with the parents at age 6: Predictable from infant attachment classifications and stable over a l-month period. Developmental Psychology, 24(3), 415-426.

Main, M. and Cassidy, J. (1988). Categories of response to reunion with the parent at age six: Predictable from infant attachment classification and stable over a one-month period. Developmental Psychology, 24, 415-426.

Main, M. & Hesse, E. (1990). Lack of resolution of mourning in adulthood and its relationship to infant disorganization: Some speculations regarding causal mechanisms. In M. Greenberg, D. Cicchetti, & M. Cummings (Eds.) Attachment in the preschool years: Theory, research and intervention (pp. 161-182). Chicago: University of Chicago Press.

Main, M. & Stadtman, J. (1981). Infant response to rejection of physical contact by the mother. Journal of the American Academy of Child Psychiatry, 20, 292-307.

Main, M., Tomasini, L., and Tolan, W. (1979). Differences among mothers of infants judged to differ in security. Developmental Psychology, 15, 472-473.

Main, M. & Solomon, J. (1990). Procedures for identifying infants as disorganized/disoriented during the Ainsworth Strange Situation. In M. Greenberg, D. Cicchetti, & N. Cummings (Eds), Attachment in the Preschool Years: Theory, Research and Intervention. (pp. 121-160) Chicago: University of Chicago Press.

Marshall, W.L., Seidman, B., & Check, J.V. (1991). Intimacy and loneliness in sex offenders and non-offender males. Unpublished data.

Marshall, W.L., Hudson, S.M., & Hodkinson, S. (1993). The importance of attachment bonds in the development of juvenile sex offending. In H.E. Barbaree, W.L. Marshall, & S.M. Hudson (Eds.) The Juvenile Sex Offender (pp 164-181). New York: Guilford Press.

Matos, L., Arend, R.A., and Sroufe, L.A. (1978). Continuity of adaptation in the second year: The relationship between quality of attachment and later competence. Child Development, 49, 547-556.

McKelvey, C.A. & Magid, K. (1988) High Risk: Children Without A Conscience, Bantam Books, New York, NY.

McKelvey, C.A., & Stevens, J.E. (1994) Adoption Crisis: The Truth Behind Adoption and Foster Care, Fulcrum Publishers, Golden, CO.

McKelvey, C.A. & Bascom, B.B. (upcoming, 1996) Through the Golden Door:A Guide to International Adoption, Pocket Books, New York, NY.

Minuchin, S. (1974). Families and Family Therapy. Cambridge: Harvard University Press.

Minuchin, S.& Fishman, C.H. (1981). Family Therapy Techniques. Cambridge: Harvard University Press.

Paterson, R.J., & Moran, G. (1988). Attachment theory, personality development and psychotherapy. Clinical Psychology Review. 8, 611-636.

Pipp, S., Easterbrooks, M.A., and Harmon, R.J. (1992). The relation between attachment and knowledge of self and mother in one- to three-year-old infants. Child Development, 63. 738-750.

Radke-Yarrow, M., Cummings, E.M., Kuczynski, L. & Chapman, M. (1985). Patterns of attachment in two- and three-year-olds in normal families and families with parental depression, Child Development 56, 884-893.

Randolph,E.M.(1995). Does attachment disorder really exist? Unpublished manuscript.

Randolph, E.M. (1983). Children Who Shock and Surprise. RFR Publications, Cotati, CA. 94931.

Renken, B., Egeland, B., Marvinney, D., Mangelsdorf, S., and Sroufe, L.A. (1989). Early childhood antecedents of aggression and passive-withdrawal in early elementary school. Journal of Personality, 57, 257-281.

Schneider-Rosen, K., Braunwald, K.G., Carlson, V., and Cicchetti, D. (1985). Current perspectives in attachment theory: Illustration from the study of maltreated infants. Monographs of the Society for Research in Child Development, 50, 194-210.

Schneider-Rosen, K. and Cicchetti, D. (1984). The relationship between affect and cognition in maltreated infants: Quality of attachment and the development of visual self-recognition. Child Development,55, 648-658.

Shaw, D.S. and Emery, R.E. (1987). Chronic family adversity and school-age children's adjustment. Journal of the American Academy of Child and Adolescent Psychiatry, 27, 200-206.

Shaw, D.S. and Emery, R.E. (1988). Chronic family adversity and school-age children's adjustment. Journal of the American Academy of Child Psychiatry, 27, 200-206.

Shaw, D.S. and Vondra, J.l. (1993). Chronic family adversity and infant attachment security. Journal of Child Psychology and Psychiatry,34, 1205-1215.

Sroufe, L.A. (1983). Infant-caregiver attachment and patterns of adaptation in preschool: The roots of maladaptation and competence. in M. Perlmutter (Ed.), Minnesota Symposium on Child Psychology. (Vol. 16) (pp. 41-83) Hillsdale, NJ: Erlbaum.

Sroufe, L.A., Schork, E., Frosso, M., Lawroski, N., & LaFrenier, P. (1984). The role of affect in social competence. in C.E. Izard, J. Kagan, & R.B. Zajonc (Eds.) Emotions, Cognitions and Behavior (pp. 289-319). Cambridge, England: Cambridge University Press.

Thompson, R.A., Lamb, M.E., and Estes, D. (1982). Stability of infant-mother attachment and its relationship to changing life circumstances in an unselected middle-class sample. Child Development, 53, 144-148.

Tizard, B. and Hodges, J. (1978). The effect of early institutional rearing on the development of eight-year-old children. Journal of Child Psychology and Psychiatry, 19, 99-118.

Tizard, B. and Joseph, A. (1970). Cognitive development of young children in residential care: A study of children aged 24 months. Journal of Child Psychology and Psychiatry, 11, 177-186.

Tizard, B. and Rees, J. (1974). A comparison of the effects of adoption, restoration to the natural mother, and continued institutionalization on the cognitive development of four-year-old children. Child Development, 45, 92-99.

Tizard, B. and Rees, J. (1975). The effect of early institutional rearing on the behavior problems and affectional relationships of four-year-old children. Journal of Child Psychology and Psychiatry, 16, 61-73.

Tracy, M. and Sroufe, L.A. (1987). Victimization among preschoolers: Role of attachment relationship history. Journal of the American Academy of Child and Adolescent Psychiatry, 26, 166-172.

Tracy, R.L. and Ainsworth, M.D.S. (1981). Maternal affectionate behavior and infant-mother attachment patterns. Child Development, 52, 1341-1343 .

Turner, B.J. (1991). Relations between attachment, gender, and behavior with peers in preschool. Child Development, 62, 1475-1488.

Verny, T., & Kelly, J. (1981). Secret Life of the Unborn Child. New York: Dell.

Verrier, N., (1993). Primal Wound. Baltimore, MD: Gateway Press, Inc.

Wartner, U.G. (1986). Attachment in Infancy and At Age Six, and Children's Self-Concept: A Follow-up of a German Longitudinal Study, Doctoral Dissertation. University of Virginia.

Waters, E. (1978). The reliability and stability of individual differences in infant-mother attachment. Child Development, 49, 4830494.

Waters, E., Vaughn, B.E., and Egeland, B. (1980). Individual differences in infant-mother attachment relationships at age one: Antecedents in neonatal behavior in an urban, economically disadvantaged sample. Child Development, 51, 208-216.

Waughn, B., Egeland, B., Sroufe, L.A., and Waters, E. (1979). Individual differences in infant-mother attachment at 12 and 18 months: Stability and change in families under stress. Child Development, 50, 971-975.

Weber, C.A., Meloy, J.R., and Gacono, C.B. (1992). A Rorschach study of attachment and anxiety in inpatient conduct-disordered and dysthymic adolescents. Journal of Personality Assessment, 58(1), 16-26.

To order additional copies of **Give Them Roots, Then Let Them Fly: Understanding Attachment Therapy**, complete the information below.

Ship to: (please print)

Name _____

Address _____

City, State, Zip _____

Day phone _____

_____ copies of *Give Them Roots...* @ $15.65 each $ _____

Postage and handling @ $5.00 per book $ _____

Total amount enclosed $ _____

Make checks payable to: *Attachment Center at Evergreen,Inc.*

Send to: *The Attachment Center at Evergreen, Inc.*
P.O. Box 2764 • Evergreen, CO 80439

To order additional copies of **Give Them Roots, Then Let Them Fly: Understanding Attachment Therapy**, complete the information below.

Ship to: (please print)

Name _____

Address _____

City, State, Zip _____

Day phone _____

_____ copies of ***Give Them Roots...*** @ $15.65 each $ _____

Postage and handling @ $5.00 per book $ _____

Total amount enclosed $ _____

Make checks payable to: *Attachment Center at Evergreen,Inc.*

Send to: *The Attachment Center at Evergreen, Inc.*
P.O. Box 2764 • Evergreen, CO 80439